ONE SIGNAL
PUBLISHERS

ATRIA

VIGILANTE NATION

NATION

HOW STATE-SPONSORED TERROR
THREATENS OUR DEMOCRACY

JON D. MICHAELS AND DAVID L. NOLL

ONE SIGNAL
PUBLISHERS

ATRIA

New York London Toronto Sydney New Delhi

ONE SIGNAL
PUBLISHERS

ATRIA

An Imprint of Simon & Schuster, LLC
1230 Avenue of the Americas
New York, NY 10020

First One Signal Publishers/Atria Books hardcover edition October 2024

ONE SIGNAL PUBLISHERS / ATRIA BOOKS and colophon
are trademarks of Simon & Schuster, LLC

Simon & Schuster: Celebrating 100 Years of Publishing in 2024

For information about special discounts for bulk purchases, please contact Simon
& Schuster Special Sales at 1-866-506-1949 or business@simonandschuster.com.

The Simon & Schuster Speakers Bureau can bring authors to your live event.
For more information or to book an event, contact the Simon & Schuster Speakers
Bureau at 1-866-248-3049 or visit our website at www.simonspeakers.com.

Interior design by Silverglass

Manufactured in the United States of America

1 3 5 7 9 10 8 6 4 2

Library of Congress Cataloging-in-Publication Data

Names: Michaels, Jon D. author. | Noll, David L., author.
Title: Vigilante nation : how state-sponsored terror threatens our democracy /
Jon Michaels and David Noll.
Description: New York, N.Y. : Simon & Schuster, 2024. | Includes
bibliographical references and index.
Identifiers: LCCN 2024017937 | ISBN 9781668023235 (hardcover) |
ISBN 9781668023242 (paperback) | ISBN 9781668023259 (ebook)
Subjects: LCSH: Right-wing extremists—United States—History. |
Vigilantes—United States—History. | Vigilantism—United States—History. | Militia
movements—United States—History. | Violence—Political aspects—United States.
Classification: LCC HN90.R3 M426 2024 | DDC 303.48/40973—dc23/eng/20240625
LC record available at https://lccn.loc.gov/2024017937

ISBN 978-1-6680-2323-5
ISBN 978-1-6680-2325-9 (ebook)

To Blaine and Toni, my heroes
JDM

To my kids, in the hope that vigilantes will lose once again
DLN

CONTENTS

"You Just Have to Impose Your Will"
The Right Resurrects Vigilantism

Harry Dunn finally had a moment to catch his breath. It was the afternoon of January 6, 2021, and the veteran Capitol Police officer had spent hours battling the rioters who stormed the Capitol. With the insurrection suppressed, Dunn collapsed onto a bench in the Rotunda. Until that day, he had never once been assaulted while in uniform. Nor had he been called the N-word on the job.

Reliving everything he just witnessed—the violence, the righteous rage, the murderous fury—Dunn turned to a colleague slumped alongside him and asked: "Is this America?"[1]

Millions of Americans shared Dunn's bewilderment, but Steve Bannon wasn't one of them. A driving intellectual force behind MAGA Republicanism, Bannon hosted a podcast, *The War Room*, whose listeners were as loyal as they were frenzied. For weeks, Bannon had been hammering away at the need to overturn the 2020 presidential election. His relentless trumpeting of the Big Lie culminated on January 5.[2]

Bannon claimed that the Democrats in Congress were going to "steal" the election. They'd do so by "illegally put[ting] forward electors from the state legislatures" and then certifying the bogus results.

Still, President Trump was "on the cusp of victory." The reason, Bannon added, was Trump's legions of loyal supporters: "You all turned out for the landslide, everything that was asked of you, knocking on doors, going to rallies, going to caravans, you did it all. You got people out . . . you did everything."

Now the make-or-break moment was nigh. The following morning, Trump supporters would rally at the Ellipse. Like the "mass of heathens" following the "rising of a star in the east" to Bethlehem, the "army of Trump" was "following that star" and about to experience "the big reveal." *"You are,"* he underscored, *"an active part of this."* Bombarding his listeners with metaphors ranging from Jesus to the military to home makeover shows, Bannon closed with yet another: football—the MAGA faithful were "on the eve of a great victory for America if we just run the play."

"Remember," Bannon implored his listeners, "we control the state legislatures. We control these executives. You just have to *impose your will.*"

IMPOSE

Let's pause to consider exactly what Bannon meant. We can start with the obvious. Bannon wasn't calling for his listeners to assemble at the Ellipse for a peaceful vigil. Nor would this be a conventional persuasion campaign. They'd tried persuasion—on Election Day and in lawsuit after lawsuit challenging vote counts—and failed. This was a campaign of force, of coercion, pressure, and perhaps violence—tools the desperate MAGA Republicans needed to use and use immediately.

YOUR

"There's not a liberal America and a conservative America—there's the United States of America."[3] Barack Obama's message of inclusiveness and unity befitted a man whose 2008 election and 2012 reelection gave hope to those audacious enough to believe that the nation might finally exorcise the ghosts of Jim Crow.

Donald Trump's victory shattered that hope. Trump made clear that he represented the MAGA faithful and the MAGA faithful alone. Other Americans were not mere political rivals who differed over, say, tax or labor policies. They were threats—a danger to the United States and to the *real* Americans who built it.

Bannon had served as Trump's 2016 campaign strategist and then as his senior counselor in the White House. Now out of government, but still fiercely committed to the MAGA movement, Bannon didn't specify during his January 5 podcast which members of American society got to do the imposing—and on whom. And he didn't need to. Everyone knew. The "us" in the Trump/Bannon coalition define themselves by their place atop traditional hierarchies of race, religion, and gender. They're primarily white. They're overwhelmingly evangelical Protestants and Catholic traditionalists. And, though they skew male, all of those in the coalition embrace patriarchal understandings of sex, gender, and the family.

WILL

Political equals resolve conflict through majority voting rules—precisely what the nation's voters had done just sixty-three days prior to Bannon's cri de coeur. If voting fails to provide an acceptable outcome, those equals might litigate their dispute in court—just as Trump's lawyers did in November and December. Bannon's emphasis on "will" implies a fundamental rejection of democracy and democratic governance. "Will" is an intense, likely personal preference or conviction. It's the furthest thing from a collective judgment arrived at through the rigors of democratic voting, lawmaking, or adjudication. And those who insist on exerting their "will" do not yield to the majority.

Bannon's directive to his listeners to "impose your will" implies something else, too: desperation.

Bannon droned on and on about the opioid epidemic, economic backsliding, and bailouts of the big financial companies. But the two political parties weren't that far apart on those issues—certainly not far enough to motivate folks to storm the Capitol. What made this a "storm the Capitol" election was the fact that it was a referendum on white Christian control over the levers of government.

Some years earlier (not coincidentally during the Obama presidency), Bannon had argued to an audience at the Vatican that Western civilization had gone "off track." He exhorted "the people in the church" to "bind together" to create "the church militant, to really be able to not just stand with our beliefs, but to fight for our beliefs against this new barbarity."[4] Trump was the MAGA corrective. Now, with Joe Biden and Kamala Harris poised to take the reins of federal power—and nominate record numbers of Black, Latino, and LGBTQ+ people to key government posts—the new barbarity was about to be realized. Storming the Capitol and thwarting Congress's attempt to certify the election would preserve and further entrench Bannon's brand of Christian nationalism.

Of course, the January 6 insurrection failed. After hours spent roaming the Capitol, brandishing clubs and Confederate flags, hunting members of Congress and the vice president, and livestreaming their exploits, the rioters were directed by Trump to go home in peace. The D.C. National Guard arrived. Order was restored.

But all was not well. Shortly after Harry Dunn, the embattled Capitol Police officer, had his moment of rest, the two houses of Congress reconvened. And clues to the question Dunn posed—"Is this America?"—started to appear. One hundred and forty-seven Republican members of Congress held firm to the lie that the election had been stolen, and voted against certification. In time, 197 House Republicans would vote against impeaching Donald Trump for "incitement to insurrection," and 43 of their colleagues in the Senate would vote to acquit. Though Fortune 500 firms swore up and down that they'd cut off donations to insurrection-supporting politicians, most quickly reopened the cash spigots. Right-wing politicians and media personalities labeled an enraged rioter, whom a besieged Capitol policeman had to shoot, a martyr. And they classified those convicted of January 6–related offenses as political prisoners.

Other, more damning clues were kept further from the public's gaze.

While workers were still cleaning up the wreckage from January 6, MAGA strategists were busy devising new, improved ways to impose their will. This cadre of lawyers, politicians, judges, and clerics had the kind of training, credentials, and public credibility that Bannon and Trump—not to mention discredited lawyers like Rudy Giuliani and Sidney Powell—could only dream of. While they seemingly shared Bannon's commitment to the forceful imposition of Christian nationalist rule, these strategists were mindful of the need to win over figures like Utah senator Mike Lee.

The son of a highly regarded Justice Department official, former clerk to Justice Samuel Alito, and darling of the Federalist Society, Lee was, and is, a master at straddling the line between old-school Republican conservatism and right-wing MAGA populism. Before the 2020 election, Lee proclaimed that the United States was "not a democracy" and that "democracy isn't the objective." Pressed to clarify, or withdraw, his claims, Lee doubled down, deriding what he termed "rank democracy."[5]

Lee also backed Trump's effort to overturn the election. In a series of text messages with White House chief of staff Mark Meadows and others in and around the Trump administration, Lee never objected to Trump's plan to impose his will after the voters rejected him. But he differed with Bannon on a crucial question of strategy: Where Bannon urged force, Lee counseled Trump to stay within the bounds of the law and employ legal arguments and reasoning to remain in office. Republican state legislatures inclined to disregard their voters' preference for Biden and nominate a slate of Trump electors should do so "pursuant to state law," Lee advised. He warned, "This will end badly for the President unless we have the Constitution on our side." His proposal: "We need something from state legislatures to make this legitimate."[6]

We need something from state legislatures.

We need to make this legitimate.

As the MAGA faithful took stock of the failed insurrection, they came around to Lee's way of thinking. What Lee, and no doubt others, found anathema was the brash lawlessness and sheer chaos of the January 6 insurrection. (Lee voted to certify the results.) Going forward, for the Right to impose its will on the rest of the nation, it would have to take Bannon's project and make it legitimate. The MAGA strategists, in other words, would have to *institutionalize* antidemocratic assertions of political control.

VIGILANTE NATION

CHAPTER 1

"We Need Something from State Legislatures to Make This Legitimate":
The January 7 Project

This book tells the story of those not chastened but rather energized by January 6—the story of their breathless rhetoric, their authoritarian ambitions, their brazen recruitment strategies, the radical initiatives they've launched, and the canny ways these operatives have managed to secure legal cover for their campaigns of political domination and terror. We shine a light on a new, or rather renewed, vision of terroristic governance, one that's as paradoxical as it is devastatingly effective. We call it **Vigilante Democracy**.

Vigilante Democracy is not the brainchild of any one politician, philosopher, activist, or lawyer. It was not hatched all at once by an assembly of right-wing culture warriors. Bits and pieces of the project were crafted and refined over time, across dozens of states, counties, and municipalities, and—at least at first—with little awareness of how (or whether) the pieces would come together.

But come together they have. Across huge swaths of the United States, Vigilante Democracy is transforming how Americans work, have fun, study, love, and participate in the civic and political life of their communities and their country. Relying on legions of citizen culture warriors—everyone from PTA moms to abortion snitches to heavily armed white nationalist militiamen—Vigilante Democracy is resurrecting and enforcing (at times with violence) traditional status hierarchies, and punishing women, racial and religious minorities, and LGBTQ+ people who make dignity and equality demands that threaten white Christian political and cultural power.

The media have hardly been asleep at the wheel. Dogged reporters have documented the physical, economic, and psychic toll imposed on transgender children in public schools, on pregnant women having to be medevaced across state lines to receive emergency abortions before sepsis kicks in, and on teachers who dare delve into the racist causes of the Civil War. They've recounted harrowing tales of violence against Black Lives Matter protesters and cataloged campaigns of intimidation and harassment against election officials in key districts in swing states.

But in-the-trenches reporting of specific vigilante practices doesn't capture how discrete spasms of Christian nationalist rage do systemic damage to the body politic. Vigilantes force the targets of these campaigns of control and terror to conceal their true identities, censor their words and activities, refrain from political and civic engagement, or flee vigilante-friendly jurisdictions for good.

Some see vigilantes as waging and winning a "culture war." As we'll explain, this is not MAGA's ultimate objective. Its prosecution of a culture war is in service of a broader, downstream electoral strategy, one that aims to forestall, if not altogether subvert, true democratic equality in America. Whereas someone like the *Atlantic*'s Adam Serwer might say that *the cruelty is the point* of the MAGA movement, we believe that the cruelty is a means to an end. And that end is to further subordinate already vulnerable and marginalized individuals and communities. If successful, the American Right will prevent the targets of their campaigns from making what would otherwise be powerful and effective political demands at precisely the moment when white Christians fear the loss of their dominant position in society.

As we see it, *suffocating democracy is the point.*

The January 6 insurrection was lawless and undemocratic, a last-minute, last-ditch attempt. The architects of Vigilante Democracy nonetheless saw tremendous potential in the phalanxes of culture warriors who descended on the Capitol, risking life, limb, and livelihood in pursuit of an ill-defined and near-impossible goal.

Future assertions of private power (and impositions of "your" will) would, these architects realized, have to be lawful. So if MAGA officials wanted to harness partisans who act like a bunch of thugs—and win over the likes of Mike Lee—they would need to first *legalize* thuggery. And all across red states, from Indiana to Idaho and Texas to Tennessee, state legislatures got busy doing precisely that.

LEGAL VIGILANTISM?

We're all familiar with *extralegal* vigilantes—individuals or groups of citizens who take it upon themselves to enforce their understanding of the social order, especially when they think government officials aren't able or willing to do so. In old Westerns, vengeful posses chase down suspected horse thieves and cattle rustlers. Eager to lynch these presumptive outlaws, the posses would clash with the no-nonsense sheriff who insists the accused receive a full and fair trial.

Vigilantism of that sort is hardly limited to life on the frontier. There's a gritty, urban counterpart. Take Charles Bronson's character in the seventies classic *Death Wish*—a film sufficiently popular to garner four sequels and a 2018 Bruce Willis remake. In the original, furious over the NYPD's inability to keep New Yorkers safe, Bronson takes matters into his own hands, breaking every law on the books along the way. Then there's *24*'s Jack Bauer, the ruthlessly zealous federal agent who exits what he sees as an overly sclerotic, timid bureaucracy so he can operate *outside the law*, employing unconstitutional methods to grill suspects and protect the homeland.

So long as we're thinking of vigilantes in pop culture, the modifier *extralegal* in front of vigilantism seems redundant. But

Hollywood depictions aside, vigilantism needn't be unlawful, and vigilantes needn't be at odds with government officials.[1] The state may well encourage vigilantism. Through statutes and regulations, judicial decrees, executive directives, winks from high-ranked government officials, and assurances by police and prosecutors that they'll "look the other way," the state emboldens individuals and groups to surveil their communities and enforce existing laws or desired social norms. The state can go even further, providing financial incentives for those eager to prosecute some partisan or cultural agenda through vigilantism. Thus, just as the term extralegal vigilantism is no redundancy, legal vigilantism is far from an oxymoron.

This latter style of vigilantism is less familiar today, but throughout most of our nation's history, legal vigilantism was not only commonplace but also a foundational feature of American life. This was certainly true in antebellum times, when state and federal laws authorized plantation owners, bounty hunters, and other agents to uphold and ruthlessly enforce the slavocracy. And it was just as true during the long decades of Jim Crow, when lawmakers, judges, sheriffs, mayors, and governors devised vicious legal strategies relying on private actors to expand and intensify state efforts to reinstall and then perpetuate white supremacy.

January 6 was extralegal, for sure. There was no authority for MAGA diehards to impede the business of Congress, to hang Vice President Mike Pence, to get "the big Jew" (a reference to Senator Chuck Schumer), or "shoot" House Speaker Nancy Pelosi.[2] Harry Dunn and his fellow Capitol Police officers were hardly looking the other way. And the Justice Department has prosecuted hundreds of trespassers, rioters, and insurrectionists.

The plan for January 7—and beyond—was to legalize attacks on democracy.

DEMOCRATIC VIGILANTISM?

Just because Mike Lee self-identifies as a critic of "rank democracy"—and Steve Bannon is comfortable sounding downright thuggish when imploring his listeners to impose their will on the rest of the American public—doesn't mean that others (including others in the MAGA inner sanctum) are similarly brazen. Certainly not after January 6.

It looks bad to lay siege to county board of election offices while votes are being tallied. It looks bad to follow election officials home and harass them and torment their families. It looks bad to threaten to hang a vice president on the day Congress is charged with certifying a presidential election. And it looks bad to storm the Capitol. The key to the January 7 Project was, and is, to do enough before the ballots are counted to ensure the "real Americans" win without breaking a sweat.

This would be no small feat given the cultural, economic, and demographic tides lifting the prospects of Black and brown Americans, non-Christians, LGBTQ+ persons, and women who consider themselves the equals of men.

To that end, menacing campaigns of harassment and violence couldn't be limited to big political events—rallies, voter registration drives, and election days. Those would be swept in, for the sake of completeness, but they'd hardly be enough. Private enforcement of the ancien régime would instead have to be an "everyday crusade."[3] And it would have to operate across different domains, using different tools, and targeting different constituencies who threaten white Christian political and cultural hegemony.

The innumerable triggers for right-wing outrage made mobilizing the everyday crusade straightforward. There'd still be a role for brute force. But, going forward, what the *New York Times'* Charles Blow called an "army of the aggrieved"[4] would be expanded. They would recruit from among the ranks of persnickety K–12 parents, gun-wielding teens, petty athletic coaches, road-raging commuters, nosy neighbors, prying colleagues, and buck-chasing lawyers. Once these armies were assembled, they could monitor school libraries and ball fields, sniff around their communities and workplaces, and mount counterprotests at rallies for reproductive autonomy, racial justice, and LGBTQ+ rights.

To describe this as a mere culture war would be misleading in another respect: It trivializes the stakes. This is, again, a war on American democracy. Here's why: The targets of the culture war may be compelled to conceal their identities, keep their political opinions to themselves, censor what they say and teach their children, forgo life opportunities, incur physical and emotional abuse, and refrain from full participation in the civic community. Some—perhaps many—will leave the jurisdictions where these armies of the aggrieved are permitted, even encouraged, to operate.

Put more bluntly, the targets are targets because they threaten not only white Christian sensibilities but also white Christian political power. The nation is at an inflection point. Are we going to march onward in the quest for a true democracy (and a multiracial one at that)? Or are we going to halt, even reverse, that march, allowing the old guard to hold on longer, perhaps forever?

WHY *PRIVATE* ACTORS?

We've already said the plan going forward would be to legalize vigilantism. But if the governors, legislators, sheriffs, prosecutors, county supervisors, and local school boards were willing to authorize the waging of these culture wars—thus entrenching white Christian social and political power—why not use the instruments of the states themselves? Wouldn't private partisans just be duplicating what the government can (and is willing to) do?

Far from it. Vigilantes make sense in solidly red communities as a force multiplier; there simply are more private, would-be culture warriors than there are government officials. Just as importantly, private partisans can be more effective actors, both because they blend into social, educational, and workplace settings more effortlessly than government officials and, as we will explain, because they operate with fewer constitutional constraints.

Legal vigilantes also lock in community norms beyond those explicitly codified in law. Deputized and mobilized neighbors and colleagues are likely to deter a broader array of political, civic, and personal expressions than those the state has specifically proscribed. And their mere presence may motivate liberals or demographically diverse families to move away from jurisdictions that embrace vigilantism (and dissuade others from moving into those jurisdictions), further boosting the political power of right-wing community members.

Legal vigilantes are socialized, subsumed, and at times subsidized by the MAGA governing regime. Deputized in these ways, vigilantes are likely going to be even more reliably enthusiastic right-wing voters and, further, may feel emboldened to run for state or local offices.

Legal vigilantes also provide useful cover to so-called respectable Republicans in office. If and when administrators and politicians are called to task for absurdities such as banning Art Spiegelman's *Maus* or a Jackie Robinson picture book, those officials can distance themselves from overly zealous community members' actions and play up their sobriety and moderation by chiding or reining in the private partisans.[5]

Last but hardly least, legal vigilantes are especially useful in urban, progressive pockets within solidly red states. Locally elected prosecutors in Democratic strongholds such as Houston and Memphis may well refuse to enforce state abortion bans. With a vigilante law like Texas's S.B. 8, the local prosecutors are no longer the final word. Now, even a handful or two of right-wing partisans can do powerful work upholding that statewide ban, ensuring comprehensive compliance notwithstanding the clear democratic preferences of local communities.

THE PLAYBOOK

Vigilante Democracy is a sprawling, suffocating, and ever morphing and metastasizing approach to law, politics, and governance. We've been tracking it since shortly after the insurrection, when lawmakers in Florida, Texas, and Tennessee began to revive legal vigilantism and supercharge it to meet the MAGA moment. From our study of those states and a dozen or so more, we have gleaned four distinct strategies and pathways. Both individually and collectively, these four approaches reflect the resourcefulness, resilience, and ruthlessness of a MAGA regime that learned from the mistakes it made in 2020 and early 2021 and is determined not to repeat them.

Dissenter Vigilantism

In a well-functioning, modern democracy, the majority gets to decide most questions of public policy. When there are concerns that those decisions might impose particular hardships on those who are conscientious objectors of one sort or another, legislatures or regulatory bodies may authorize opt-outs. Historically, these opt-outs acted like a *shield* against overreaching state power. If you or your family had especially strong objections to, say, sex-ed classes or vaccine requirements, the state wouldn't force you to participate. But you couldn't impose your will on everyone else. The sex-ed class would go on. Dissenters would have to sit in study hall until the lesson ended. And the vaccine requirement would stay in effect, protecting public school kids from the ravaging effects of measles and polio. Dissenters would have to be privately educated.

Post–January 6, Vigilante Democracy is flipping the script and giving dissenters offensive power—*swords*—over those in the majority. It's doing so, notably, at a moment when white Christian political power is no longer democratically assured. Equipped now with swords instead of shields, students of dissenting families can ignore public health regulatory requirements, continue attending public schools, and endanger the entire student body. And whereas students of dissenting families once were excused from not only sex-ed lessons but also certain history, literary, or science assignments, they now have the right in some jurisdictions to insist those lessons and assignments never be taught in the first place, to any of their peers. Their dissents effectively override the will of the locally elected members of a city council or school board.

Courthouse Vigilantism

Next is what we call courthouse vigilantism: Private individuals are deputized and financially rewarded for bringing proceedings against individuals or institutions that offend their sensibilities. Laws such as Texas's S.B. 8, Florida's infamous "Don't Say Gay" law, and a slew of far less publicized statutes authorize right-wing partisans to initiate lawsuits and disciplinary proceedings to punish teachers, librarians, medical providers, and school administrators.

Using private actors to shape and police community norms is, once again, devastatingly powerful. The state can't be everywhere, all the time. But regular people certainly are. And it takes just a few of them to stamp out reproductive healthcare, kick transgender children off sports teams and out of restrooms, strip school libraries of books during annual celebrations of Black History Month, and deter teachers from putting Pride stickers on their corkboards. Because you never know who might be sufficiently outraged, sufficiently greedy (to collect a cash bounty), or sufficiently petty to use these laws to settle long-standing personal grudges, everyone needs to be on guard, and on edge, all the time—a terrifying way to live even if no suit is ever filed.

Street Vigilantism

Harnessing and further legalizing a project that started gaining momentum before January 6, all three branches of state governments are creating conditions favoring those who would deter and disrupt legitimate political rallies or protests. Look no further than the acquittal and subsequent far-right beatification of Kyle Rittenhouse.

The then-seventeen-year-old Rittenhouse traveled from his Illinois home to Kenosha, Wisconsin, ostensibly to protect Kenosha business owners from property damage. Armed with an AR-15, Rittenhouse ended up shooting three BLM protesters, killing two of them. Even though he intentionally sought out conflict, and traveled miles to engage in it, Rittenhouse insisted he was acting in "self-defense." Acquitted in a trial in which the judge admonished prosecutors for referring to those Rittenhouse killed as "victims," Rittenhouse left the courthouse and went straight to Fox News. And, ever since, right-wing media, politicians, and the restive Republican base have treated the high school dropout like a cross between a MAGA rock star and cuddly mascot.

The extremely permissive state of gun regulation in this country, the broadening of self-defense laws from a duty to retreat to stand your ground, and a political culture that privileges force over reason helped ensure that Rittenhouse would walk out of the courtroom a free man. Now, thanks to new rounds of "anti-riot" legislation (and courts' continued attacks on long-standing gun control laws), those enraged by racial justice, LGBTQ+ rights, or reproductive rights demonstrations can roll up armed to the teeth in a show of menacing force and, in some states, ram their cars into the protesters (provided the motorists feel "threatened"). The message these laws send is unmistakable: Continue to protest at your peril. Semiautomatic weapons and accelerating trucks speak louder than words and land more devastating blows.

Electoral Vigilantism

Last is the direct assault on elections themselves, with states deputizing or condoning right-wing culture warriors' efforts to surveil, unilaterally challenge, and harass voters, candidates, voter registrants, and election officials. Since 2020, harrowing attacks on election officials have threatened to upend election results. Though they've operated at the local level (where almost all election administration happens in the United States), these campaigns have national, and even global, effects. After all, successfully cowing even tiny percentages of voters or election administrators in heavily Democratic cities and counties in Nevada, Arizona, and Georgia could easily swing a presidential election or change which party controls the U.S. Senate.

THE VIGILANTE STATES OF AMERICA

These four pillars of Vigilante Democracy undergird a regime of terror and subordination. In red states across America, citizens are encouraged and empowered to Make America Great Again by re-creating or reinforcing traditional hierarchies of race, gender, religion, and wealth. Their efforts result in the demoralization and deprivation of LGBTQ+ children seeking to play sports or use public restrooms; of women exercising their reproductive rights; of teachers and students examining questions of race, sex, and gender; and of all those taking to the streets and to the polls in support of greater democratic equality. Their efforts result, too, in the incapacitation of would-be allies, who are threatened with financial ruin, the loss of professional status, and quite possibly bodily harm if they lend too much support to those targeted for subordination.

Vigilante Democracy isn't about shackling society writ large. The partisans who structure it and those who enforce it have no intention of closing the streets to *all* political activism; of shuttering entire hospitals; or of banning basketball. They're aiming to deny or restrict access to those deemed inauthentic Americans. So far, their success has been nothing short of staggering.

Reporting suggests that, for the first time since the end of Jim Crow, substantial numbers of Americans are considering fleeing jurisdictions where legal vigilantism imperils or diminishes their lives or livelihoods. And then there is the even larger number who can't or won't contemplate leaving—because of family ties or financial constraints. Those Americans are increasingly resigning themselves to life as second-class citizens.[6]

Meanwhile, red states are competing with one another to ratchet up the pressure they apply on their citizens; threatening to prosecute those who leave the state to seek abortions; and even going after blue state individuals and organizations for providing financial or medical assistance. And those at the forefront of the legal vigilante movement—everyone from members of the ethnonationalist Proud Boys militia to book banners to religious fundamentalists—are beginning to run for, and win, local offices.

The net effect is the enforcement of Christian nationalist values in nearly half the states in the Union, the entrenchment of MAGA political power (including at the national level), and the enervating and dispersing of left-of-center political challengers who otherwise would be on the precipice of unseating right-wing incumbents in free and fair elections.

As we look ahead to the next few rounds of critical elections, we remain haunted—less by the feverish rioters of January 6 than by the cool, calculating strategists who spent the subsequent days, months, and years devising and legitimating a vigilante-based regime that aims to ensure Christian nationalism never comes up short again.

For the same reason, we consider Mike Lee an even more central figure than Steve Bannon. On January 6, Mike Lee played the part of the respectable Republican. He flagged for all involved the importance of legal authority; but if there had been a basis in law to negate the election results, Lee seemingly would have counseled the few remaining old-school conservatives in Congress and the White House to *go right ahead*. So, rather than treat Lee as one of the proverbial adults in the room outraged at the prospect of anyone conspiring to overturn a presidential election, we should look to him as putting a lawyerly spin on one of Donald Trump's most revealing of aphorisms.

"When you're a star," Trump grotesquely boasted, "they let you do

it. You can do anything. Grab 'em by the p★ssy. You can do anything."
Lee may not share anything like Trump's penchant for fetishizing
fame and denigrating women. But he does fetishize legalisms and
denigrate (real) democracy. For him, *once you pass a law, they let you
do it. You can do anything.* Even subvert democracy.

PART I

Who We've Always Been

CHAPTER 2

"Absconded"
The Confederate Roots of Legal Vigilantism

art of George Washington's mystique turns on the fact that he was a reluctant president. Having vanquished the British and resigned his military commission, Washington returned to Mount Vernon, where he planned to enjoy life as a planter aristocrat. Yet Washington's sojourn was short-lived. The fledgling nation needed a strong leader. So Washington put away his plowshare and hustled up to Philadelphia, where he presided over the Constitutional Convention and, soon afterward, the American republic.

Though taxing in its own right, the presidency called for none of the sacrifices that Washington endured when wintering with his troops at Valley Forge, let alone when battling dysentery or fighting the French and their Indian allies during the Seven Years' War. Washington had a warm, inviting home in the nation's then-capital of Philadelphia, the company of his wife, Martha, and a contingent of eight slaves whom he brought with him from Virginia.

Among them was Ona Judge.[1] One night in the waning months of Washington's second term, Judge seized upon what may have been her last chance for freedom before the household headed "home" to Virginia. Aided by free Black abolitionists, she climbed aboard a ship bound for New Hampshire, never to return.

The Washingtons were livid. Judge, said Martha, "was brought up and treated more like a child than a Servant."[2] Martha's characterization notwithstanding, Judge was legally considered the Washingtons' property. And the Washingtons wanted their property back. Within days, advertisements were placed in the *Philadelphia Gazette* and the *Daily Advertiser* offering a $10 bounty for Judge's return and "a reasonable additional sum" for travel expenses.

Ten Dollars Reward.

ABSCONDED from the houfehold of the Prefident of the United States, on Saturday afternoon, ONEY JUDGE, a light Mulatto girl, much freckled, with very black eyes, and bufhy black hair—She is of middle ftature, but flender and delicately made, about 20 years of age. She has many changes of very good clothes of all forts, but they are not fufficiently recollected to defcribe.

As there was no fufpicion of her going off, and it happened without the leaft provocation, it is not eafy to conjecture whither fhe is gone—or fully, what her defign is ; but as fhe may attempt to efcape by water, all mafters of veffels and others are cautioned againft receiving her on board , altho' fhe may, and probably will endeavour to pafs for a free woman, and it is faid has, wherewithal to pay her paffage.

Ten dollars will be paid to any perfon, (white or black) who will bring her home, if taken in the city, or on board any veffel in the harbour ; and a further reafonable fum if apprehended and brought home, from a greater diftance, and in proportion to the diftance. FRED. KITT, Steward.
May 24   ‖3

Claypoole's American Daily Advertiser, *May 26, 1796.*

Some years later, Washington learned that Judge was living in Portsmouth, New Hampshire, where she had married a Black sailor and given birth to a child. Still incensed at her insolence, Washington summoned a nephew, Burwell Bassett, Jr., to head north and find Judge, who, having taken her husband's name, was now known as Ona Staines. His directions: "Take her by force, and carry her back."[3]

Bassett was a fellow member of Virginia's planter elite and would go on to serve in Congress and see battle as a lieutenant colonel in the War of 1812. Upon arriving at Ona Staines's Portsmouth home, he first attempted to coax her to return to Mount Vernon. To Bassett's astonishment (but we imagine no one else's), Staines "utterly refused to go."[4] Offended and eager to avoid disappointing Uncle George, Bassett devised plans to kidnap her, which he shared with John Langdon, with whom he was staying.

Little did Bassett know, his host—a U.S. senator who also served multiple terms as New Hampshire's governor—had manumitted his family's slaves and had no intention of abetting the kidnapping. Langdon quietly sent word to Staines that she needed to flee. She left Portsmouth in the middle of the night and reestablished herself in a town some eight miles away.

It's hard to describe a woman who spent decades in bondage, lived decades more as a runaway, and remained—officially—the property of one of America's most powerful families as "fortunate." But compared to many who attempted to flee slavery, Staines was lucky. A senator happened to be looking out for her, and the Washingtons gave up the fight. The bumbling Bassett moved on to Congress, and Staines and her husband welcomed two more children into their life.

But Staines's relative good fortune is precisely the point of the story. Even the luckiest of those formerly enslaved were subject to abject terror and the specter of violence. There's a broader lesson, too: Leading figures of the founding generation were all deeply, integrally invested not just in the physical and psychological cruelty of slavery but also in the political brutality of state-sponsored vigilantism.

THE ROOTS OF STATE-SANCTIONED VIGILANTISM

When Ona Judge fled Philadelphia and the Washingtons plotted to recapture her, there were few local constabularies, let alone anything like today's thick network of law enforcement agencies to help them recover their "property." Government law enforcement was even patch-ier on the frontier—and remained that way into the twentieth century. When the nearest sheriff might have been days, maybe weeks away, it became necessary to rely on the private dispensation of "justice." This partially explains the prevalence of deputized or self-appointed posses; private parties sometimes had little choice but to serve as judge, jury, and executioner.[5]

Given that there's no longer any need for improvised law enforce-ment, why today's resurgence? Why has it become acceptable (and lawful) for militiamen to bring semiautomatic weapons into public spaces, including ones where lawmakers convene and ballots are counted; for angry motorists to ram their cars into Black Lives Mat-ter protesters; and for bitter townspeople and their bounty-hunting attorneys to menace those providing reproductive healthcare, sup-porting LGBTQ+ schoolchildren, and teaching all kids hard lessons in history and really basic ones in biology?

To answer those questions, we need to turn to a different, more sinister explanation for vigilantism. It's one that animated the Jan-uary 6 insurrectionists: deep distrust of government, of the motives and capabilities of government actors, and of a democratic system in which people from another "political tribe" can win elections and legislate accordingly. The issue for today's vigilantes is not that government is too small or far-flung to enforce the law. It's that government is run by the *wrong people* with the *wrong priorities*.

Consider Daniel Penny, the former Marine who in 2023 killed a Black, thirty-year-old, mentally ill street performer who Penny claimed was menacing subway straphangers. Penny had to have known that New York City has nearly forty thousand officers on patrol, including a dedicated transit police force. And we hazard to guess George Washington didn't think New Hampshire, even sleepy, eighteenth-century New Hampshire, was incapable of keep-ing law and order in one of the busiest and most developed coastal cities of our new nation. The problem, in both contexts, was that governmental officials were insufficiently committed to enforcing a particular social order.

It's when distrust is so high, when the political "tribes" are so polarized, and when the old social order is so acutely (and, by its lights, unjustly) threatened, that legal vigilantism comes back with, well, a vengeance.[6]

ENFORCING AND EXTENDING THE SLAVOCRACY

To appreciate the audacity and dangerousness of today's state-supported policies of private terror, we need to see how legal vigilantism has operated in the past—and how and when it was disabled. In this chapter and the next, we'll trace how legal vigilantism surged in the decades before the Civil War, how it surged again in the ashes of the war, and how it was vanquished in the post–World War II era.

We begin at the founding. When the second Congress convened in 1791, the white men who had been elected to represent the thirteen newly united states faced a problem. Four years earlier, the delegates to the Constitutional Convention had adopted the Fugitive Slave Clause. Anticipating that Black slaves escaping north—and finding safe haven there—would lead to protracted battles between northern and southern states, the framers crafted Article IV, Section 2, Clause 3:

> No Person held to Service or Labour in one State . . . escaping into another, shall . . . be discharged from such Service or Labour.

The Fugitive Slave Clause established clear legal rights for some, namely slave owners. It withheld rights from others, principally slaves— but also the rights of free states themselves, whose legislatures would otherwise have the authority to enact laws and regulations protecting all people, fugitives included, within their borders.[7] But like so many other provisions of the Constitution, the specific contours of those rights—not to mention the practicalities of enforcement—were left to be worked out by future generations.

The newly arriving representatives and senators weren't especially keen to do that work. Slavery threatened to derail the Continental Congress, bedeviled the signatories of the short-lived Articles of Confederation, and dogged the delegates at the Constitutional Convention. But ongoing interstate disputes over fugitive slaves cried out for clearer federal regulation.

Participants in state ratifying conventions barely had time to return home when Pennsylvania indicted a trio of Virginia-based slave hunters who'd crossed into Pennsylvania to recapture a fugitive whom abolitionists had earlier helped escape. The indictment set off a legal and political firestorm over free states' authority to punish bounty catchers operating in the North. In the South, plantation slavery was maintained through a vast network of overseers, slave catchers, traders, sheriffs, constables, judges and justices of the peace, and lawyers.[8] The slavers knew that those they held in bondage would continue to attempt to flee north. To safeguard slavers' "property" rights, the South's network of interlocking public and private enforcers had to be extended nationwide.

But there was a hitch. Leaving aside any moral duty to protect fugitives, free states could not be expected to devote their tax dollars and limited administrative resources to the retrieval of human chattel on behalf of the South. Moreover, officials in northern states would want to defend their territorial integrity from out-of-state bandits.[9] So, as often was the case, the South used its power in Congress to ensure that white supremacists would have the run of the entire nation.

In this instance, the South had an ally in the president as well. For it was George Washington who leaned on the reluctant Congress to give effect to the Constitution's Fugitive Slave Clause. A new federal law would authorize slavers to operate within free states and retrieve runaways, by force if necessary. And, yes, it was this very law that, several years later, Washington relied on *as a private citizen* when he dispatched Burwell Bassett to New Hampshire to kidnap Ona Staines and return her to Mount Vernon.

THE FUGITIVE SLAVE ACT OF 1793

The law recognized the right of any slaver and "his agent or attorney" to roam the North in search of fugitives and bring them before a local judge or magistrate.[10] This official was obligated to determine whether the fugitive "owe[d] service or labor to the person claiming him or her." Though proceedings under the act were covered in a veneer of legality, they made a mockery of due process. The law gave alleged fugitives no right to counsel or a jury trial. Fugitives weren't authorized to testify in their own defense. The law didn't permit courts to issue writs of habeas corpus, a legal device recognized in both the Magna Carta and the Constitution and used to free individuals who are wrongfully detained. There was no statute of limitations, meaning that not even decades of living in free states protected fugitives from the prospect of sudden, violent rendition back to the South.

If the judge's examination supported a slaver's claim, he was obligated to issue a "certificate" that functioned as a license to traffic Black Americans. Armed with such a certificate, slavers had every right to complete their mission without interference. Through measures that are uncannily similar to vigilante laws being passed in red states today, would-be good Samaritans inclined to help a runaway slave evade capture faced penalties of $500 (about $15,000 in present-day dollars). Appreciating that northern officials wouldn't prosecute those abolitionists, Congress authorized the slavers to bring their own lawsuits, suing anyone who obstructed their efforts and keeping for themselves whatever fines courts levied.[11] Yes, that means Senator Langdon, Burwell Bassett's host and confidant, could well have been forced to stand trial for helping Ona Staines escape.

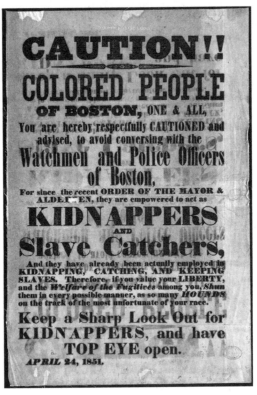

Broadside warning Black Boston residents of bounty hunters
operating under an amended version of the Fugitive Slave Act that took effect in 1850.
(National Park Service) (Library of Congress)

So, within a decade of the nation's founding, federal authorities overrode the prerogatives of northern states to legislate and enforce key components of criminal and civil law within their boundaries. The Fugitive Slave Act dragooned judges and other officials and made them complicit in the intensification and perpetuation of America's original sin. It effectively outlawed northern compassion, holding would-be allies liable for financial penalties, and, needless to say, further terrorized fugitives and made life even more harrowing for free Black citizens. The latter easily could have gotten swept up by overzealous slavers and, thanks to the one-sided judicial proceedings, found themselves dragged south. In short, no Black American, anywhere in the United States, was ever truly safe from the South's vigilantes. And no ally, whether a scratch farmer or sitting senator, could *legally* do anything about it.

CHAPTER **3**

"We Are the Oppressed"
From Jim Crow to the Border Militias

he Civil War was supposed to put an end to the terroristic power that the states in rebellion had been exercising over Black Americans. And Reconstruction was supposed to ensure that both state and private regimes of racial terror were gone for good. The radical Republicans in Congress passed, and the states ratified, the Thirteenth, Fourteenth, and Fifteenth Amendments. Respectively, these measures prohibited slavery; granted citizenship, due process, and equal protection of the law to all persons (including those formerly enslaved); and forbade states from denying citizens the right to vote on account of race.

But old habits die hard. And old prejudices die harder still. Rather than accept the prospect of sharing political, economic, and cultural power with their former "property," the unreconstructed Confederates contrived plans to create a system of institutionalized white supremacy that closely approximated the antebellum order.

VIGILANTES AGAINST RECONSTRUCTION

Notable among any number of efforts was one launched by six veterans of the Confederacy on Christmas Eve 1865, just eight months after Robert E. Lee's surrender at Appomattox. Led in its infancy by

Confederate general Nathan Bedford Forrest, that particular assembly would soon grow into the Ku Klux Klan. The Klan attracted what one historian calls

> a chaotic multitude of anti-black vigilante groups, disgruntled poor white farmers, wartime guerrilla bands, displaced Democratic politicians, illegal whiskey distillers, coercive moral reformers, bored young men, sadists, rapists, white workmen fearful of black competition, employers trying to enforce labor discipline, common thieves, neighbors with decades-old grudges, and even a few freedmen and white Republicans who allied with Democratic whites or had criminal agendas of their own.[1]

Still, members drawn to the Klan and allied white militias had more than enough in common. Most significantly, they shared a hatred of Black Americans, particularly as new cohorts of freedmen began making equality and dignity demands. Klansmen responded with violence and vandalism. They torched homes, whipped and murdered Republican officeholders, and menaced freedmen attempting to vote. Lest their campaigns of terror be overlooked, the Klan would often leave mutilated bodies scattered along roadsides and hanging from trees.

Again, organized, violent resistance of this sort started up right after the war's end—that is, during the still-vibrant days of Reconstruction, when proponents of Black equality dominated southern state governments, and Union soldiers were still deployed throughout the South. And because it was in those still-vibrant days, the Republicans in Congress had the passion and votes to outlaw vigilantism. Between 1870 and 1871, Congress enacted three "enforcement" acts granting federal officials the necessary authority to make good on the rights guaranteed by the Thirteenth, Fourteenth, and Fifteenth Amendments.[2] The third of these enforcement acts, referred to as the Ku Klux Klan Act, outlaws conspiracies to deprive any person of the equal protection of the law or to violently prevent any person from voting in federal elections.

Federal prosecutions under the enforcement acts succeeded for a time in safeguarding Reconstruction governments and suppressing Klan violence. But northern political leaders soon tired of propping up Reconstruction governments, which they viewed as corrupt and incompetent. They tired of financing the protracted military occupation of the South, especially when westward expansion requiring federal money and troops beckoned. And most of all, they tired of spending political capital to protect Black Americans' political and civil rights.[3]

The Supreme Court didn't make things any easier. The Fourteenth Amendment's Privileges and Immunities Clause barred states from "mak[ing] or enforc[ing] any law which shall abridge the privileges or immunities of citizens of the United States."[4] But in the *Slaughter-House Cases*, the Court eviscerated the clause, insisting it protected against federal, not state, deprivations of rights.[5] One of the dissenting justices—well aware it was the southern states that were hell-bent on suppressing the rights of Black citizens—lashed out at the majority, accusing his colleagues of gutting the new and hard-fought amendment and reducing it to little more than "a vain and idle enactment."[6]

Two years later, the Court continued the work it started in the *Slaughter-House Cases*. In *United States v. Cruikshank*, decided in 1875, the Court reversed the only three convictions the Justice Department had secured against perpetrators of the Colfax Massacre, wherein Klansmen and other white terrorists killed dozens of Black men in Grant Parish, Louisiana. The Court ruled that the Fourteenth Amendment's due process and equal protection clauses reached actions undertaken by state officials, not private individuals. To punish *private* violence, "the people must look to the States"—the same states that were falling quickly back into the hands of unreconstructed Confederates.[7] As Eric Foner, perhaps the preeminent authority on Reconstruction, remarks, the *Cruikshank* "decision rendered national prosecution of crimes committed against [Black Americans] virtually impossible and gave a green light to acts of terror where local officials either could not or would not enforce the law."[8]

In effect, between Congress signaling it would end Reconstruction and the Court in the *Slaughter-House Cases* and *Cruikshank* announcing that federal courts could neither vindicate civil rights deprivations perpetrated by state governments (the *Slaughter-House Cases*) nor be used to punish instances of private violence (*Cruikshank*), the federal government allowed white supremacists to seize and maintain power once again throughout the South. This time around, "redemption" southern governments and their private deputies could effectively strip Black people of their civil rights and property and shut them and their white allies out of the political process. This punishing project of publicly designed and privately prosecuted racial terrorism, caste subordination, and antidemocratic politics—known as Jim Crow—would last nearly a century.

Publicly designed and privately prosecuted racial terrorism is, of course, American legal vigilantism—nothing more, nothing less. That the redemption governments led by old Confederates regained control of state and local offices throughout the South didn't mean that government officials could enforce Jim Crow on their own.

The war-torn southern states could invest only modestly in public infrastructure, so they needed private help on many fronts. But economics was only part of the story. Especially in the early years of Jim Crow, when the feds still were keeping close tabs on things, southern states couldn't overtly and aggressively discriminate, subordinate, or otherwise terrorize their Black citizens. Thanks to *Cruikshank*, however, private actors could do the dirty work—and do it with impunity. Mobs and militias were populated by angry white citizens, many of whom were relatives, business associates, or old army buddies of high-ranking state and local officials. They could and would take cues from their pals in government to persecute southern Black farmers and business owners, and would-be voters.[9]

Surely, the Supreme Court justices would have caught wind of this brazen circumvention. They'd have recognized that the militias were private in name only. They'd have decided that southern states were exploiting the state actor/private actor distinction to evade federal law and make a mockery out of Supreme Court jurisprudence. And, once an opportunity presented itself, the justices would put an end to this nonsense once and for all.

But when that opportunity arose in 1883, in the enticingly captioned (but ultimately disappointing) *Civil Rights Cases*,[10] the Court reaffirmed the public/private distinction, essentially telling state officials and their private cronies to carry on. And that's precisely what they did.

In the decades that followed, militias and ad hoc gangs enforced and expanded a political, economic, and social system of white supremacy. Beatings, lynchings, cross burnings, arson, wage theft, and myriad other forms of harassment and violence continued; the slightest, most careful gestures or assertions in the direction of racial equality (or even racial dignity) risked provoking murderous violence. One Mississippi Klansman explained the thinking this way: "Every little insolence, if left unnoticed, would be bragged about by its perpetrator. . . . The news would spread with great rapidity, and there was no telling where it would end."[11] As one historian observes, this thinking drove white men to "commit the most brutal forms of aggression, convinced all the while that they were acting defensively."[12]

In time, southern white militias expanded their list of enemies. The Klan reached its zenith in the 1920s, when waves of immigration to the United States and national and global efforts in the direction of democratic liberalism threatened the political and economic hegemony of white Christian traditionalists. Lashing out at Jews, Catholics, labor unionists, immigrants from southern Europe, and Bolsheviks, the Klan and affiliated groups helped insulate the South from liberalizing forces and extended Jim Crow through the New Deal, World War II, and for some years hence.[13]

Ultimately, Jim Crow succumbed. But its unnaturally long life is a testament to the power of the public-private partnerships southern states relied on to maintain white supremacy. We already emphasized the ways those partnerships were beneficial to the government actors who needed to maintain a semblance of clean hands and to the private actors who could continue hurting, humiliating, and profiting from the subordination of Black men and women.

But before moving on, we want to pause on how *efficient* these partnerships were and, as we'll see, still can be for groups alarmed at the prospect of America becoming a multiracial democracy. Though they looked, and in many respects were, wildly chaotic, they leveraged free manpower, as plenty of ordinary citizens were eager to surveil Black transgressions and join angry mobs.[14] As political scientist Adolph Reed, Jr., explains in his poignant memoir of life under Jim Crow, the specific contours of white supremacist practices varied from town to town and state to state. Expectations of segregation were not invariably rigid; the system could and did tolerate a good deal of informal interaction across the color line. Yet lurking everywhere was the threat that violence could be inflicted at a moment's notice against any Black person who was even suspected of threatening a white individual's dignity or social position.[15] Perhaps there was discretion as to *when, where, and how* to enforce Jim Crow. But the underlying, systemic commitment to enforcing white supremacy and subjugating Black Americans was never open to debate or dissent.[16]

A MATURING DEMOCRACY SWEARS OFF VIGILANTISM

The American South likes to do things its own way, forcing the rest of the nation to yield or fight. The rest of the nation yielded far too much in the antebellum period, fought during the Civil War and Reconstruction, and then yielded again during the long reign of Jim Crow. But just as in the buildup to the Civil War, there came a point when continuing to yield to Jim Crow became untenable.

After World War II, campaigns of white terror that previously attracted little attention were covered nationally, at times internationally. Newspapers, television, the new federal highway system, and soon, jet planes, made it impossible for elites in Washington, D.C., and on Wall Street to ignore the outcries for justice. Media attention also meant that London, Paris, Moscow, and Beijing—not to mention the capitals of newly independent nations in Africa and Asia—saw the firebombing of children in a Birmingham, Alabama, church, the debasement of Black college students seeking meals at Woolworth's lunch counters from Virginia to Texas, and the dead bodies of Black and white civil rights activists discarded like trash outside Philadelphia, Mississippi. Those far-flung audiences heard, read, and watched leaders like Dr. Martin Luther King, Jr., and were either won over to the cause or willing to exploit America's caste system to embarrass the United States.[17]

Activists, voters, business leaders, and diplomats and defense strategists (who worried about America's standing around the world) pushed the feds to intervene. President Dwight Eisenhower deployed the 101st Airborne Division to protect the Little Rock Nine, who sought to integrate Central High following the Supreme Court's *Brown v. Board of Education* decision. Congress enacted the sweeping Civil Rights Act of 1964, the Voting Rights Act of 1965, and the Fair Housing Act of 1968. The courts, for their part, moved from sabotaging federal civil rights protections to fortifying them.[18]

The new federal protections—backed by federal officials, organizations such as the NAACP and the ACLU, civil rights and celebrity activists with national, if not international, followings, and key union and business leaders—helped usher in a new era of democratic liberalism. Between 1960 and 1970, the percentage of Black children who attended integrated schools in states of the former Confederacy rose from 0.16 percent to 85.9 percent.[19] In 1961, there were three Black members of Congress; by 1991, there were twenty-six.[20] In 1965, there were essentially no Black state legislators in the South. In 1985, they constituted some 10 percent of lawmakers.[21] Between 1960 and 1990, the percentage of Black Americans aged twenty-five and older with a high school degree increased by roughly 35 percent. The percentage with college degrees increased from just under 5 percent to around 15 percent.[22]

THE LIBERAL DEMOCRATIC ORDER HOLDS . . . FOR NOW

In dismantling Jim Crow, the United States was, for the first time, beginning to truly live up to its democratic ideals. Not coincidentally, the post–Jim Crow era was also when state support for private political violence bottomed out and vigilantes found few sympathizers.

The growing consensus against vigilantism was all the more impressive given that the late 1960s and most of the 1970s were rife with cultural and social conflicts. Urban riots, the antiwar movement, and battles over school busing were, after all, testaments to persistent, perhaps permanent, fissures in America's social and political tectonic plates.[23] What's more, these years made clear that political violence was not an exclusively right-wing project, as evidenced by the marked uptick in leftist violence perpetrated by the likes of the Black Panthers, the American Indian Movement, and the Weather Underground. Perhaps political violence no longer being the near-exclusive domain of the Right represented progress of a perverse sort. But for us, the more important lesson is that violence—from either the left or the right—was anathema to the vast majority of U.S. citizens and found no sympathy, including among political elites.[24]

As we moved into the 1980s, this consensus against vigilantism continued to be tested. For the most part it held.

THE SUBWAY VIGILANTE

A couple of days before Christmas Day 1984, a slightly built electronics specialist named Bernhard Goetz boarded a downtown 2 train at the 14th Street station in Manhattan.[25] Four Black teenagers who were already on the train approached Goetz and "asked" him for $5.

Goetz had been mugged before and had twice attempted to protect women from being robbed or assaulted, so he counted himself among the New Yorkers who thought the NYPD had allowed the city to spin out of control. Though his application for a firearms permit had been denied, Goetz carried a loaded .38-caliber pistol. At 1:44 p.m. on December 22, he fired all five rounds, hitting the four teens he claimed were about to rob him.

When he turned himself in, Goetz explained that he feared being "maimed" by the teenagers, and that he wanted to "murder . . . them, to make them suffer as much as possible." If he'd had more bullets, he "would have shot them again, and again, and again."[26]

The subway shooting and ensuing trial captured the nation's attention. In this angry thirty-seven-year-old, folks longing for "law and order" (and maybe, just maybe, feeling a desire to make sure that Black kids didn't forget their place) saw an everyman. As a *Washington Post* essayist put it, "Goetz embodied the image of an abused white man who would not take it any longer."[27] Senator Alfonse D'Amato, whose base was made up of white voters from the outer boroughs and suburbs, wrote, "We are living in fear. We are the oppressed."[28] Implying pretty clearly who the "we" were, New York's junior senator suggested that perhaps the Black teens, not Bernhard Goetz, should be the ones standing trial. In national polls, a majority of Americans expressed sympathy for Goetz. Support ran especially high "among men, Republicans, suburbanites and those who carry guns themselves."[29]

But with the exception of D'Amato, who himself acknowledged that Goetz didn't do "the right thing," and some truly fringe right-wing activists, the political class disavowed Goetz and his actions. New York's governor, Mario Cuomo, insisted that vigilantes like Goetz were "dangerous and wrong."[30] NYPD commissioner Benjamin Ward, the city's first Black police chief, said: "I think that the same kind of person that comes out and applauds the lynching is the first that comes out and applauds someone that shoots four kids."[31] Pennsylvania's Arlen Specter, a longtime member of the Senate Judiciary Committee, convened congressional hearings. Refusing to let Goetz supporters frame the story, the Republican insisted that it was Goetz's reaction (rather than the teens' actions) that represented "the kind of thing that happens when law and order break down."[32] Even Rudy Giuliani, then U.S. attorney for Manhattan, took Goetz's transgressions seriously enough to consider indicting him on federal civil rights charges.

Perhaps most striking was the disdain that then-president Ronald Reagan showed for Goetz. At a press conference on U.S.-Soviet relations, the champion of movement conservatism warned Americans of a "breakdown of civilization if people start taking the law in their own hands." Reagan cautioned that "while we may feel understanding or sympathy for someone [like Goetz] who was tested beyond his control, his ability to control himself, at the same time, we have to abide by the law and stand for law and order."[33] Pushed by reporters to acknowledge that "there is no law and order, that the police . . . are unable . . . to do their job," Reagan refused to take the bait. He shot back that crime was going down in America, and that law enforcement officers merited credit for making headway on that front.

When Goetz stood trial, the "everyman" narrative's influence was unmistakable. Although a Manhattan grand jury indicted him for attempted murder, assault, reckless endangerment, and criminal possession of a weapon, Goetz was acquitted of all charges but the gun violation. He received a one-year sentence and served eight months in prison.

While Goetz avoided serious jail time, he nonetheless was widely viewed as reckless, a pariah. Media executives didn't reach out to offer him TV and movie deals. There were no job offers from members of Congress seeking to work alongside him on the Hill. Goetz never spoke at a major political party's national convention. Instead, he was bankrupted in civil proceedings brought by his victims. In brief, the American Establishment wasn't about to give up the hard-earned economic, diplomatic, and cultural gains it had won by eradicating Jim Crow for the benefit of a priggish gunman who claimed the right to bring back vigilante justice.

MINUTEMEN AT THE BORDER

In the decades that followed, crime rates continued to drop, and lax law enforcement receded from the list of concerns that kept Americans up at night. But new threats, real and perceived, quickly filled that psychological (and political) void.

When the September 11 terrorists crashed four planes in New York, Washington, D.C., and rural Pennsylvania, fears that Islamic extremists might engineer additional attacks drove local, county, state, and federal officials to reallocate resources, adjust priorities, secure broader legislative authorities, and increase spending.[34]

While most were confident that the United States had secured the nation's airports against terrorism, some worried that our physical borders—particularly the long, porous border with Mexico—were far less protected. Already the nation was taking a sharp turn against Latin American immigration, as evidenced by California's Proposition 187, which denied social services to undocumented residents. With the possibility that al-Qaeda terrorists might be passing themselves off as migrants from such countries as Guatemala and El Salvador, fearful Americans voiced concern that the U.S. government wasn't doing enough. Their fears became the impetus for a new wave of vigilantism.[35]

In 2004, an ad appeared on the Aryan Nation's website touting the "Minuteman Project." Jim Gilchrist, a Vietnam vet who had run for Congress under the banner of the far-right American Independent Party, was among those spearheading the initiative. In the ad, labeled "a call for action on [sic] part of ALL ARYAN SOLDIERS,"[36]

Gilchrist said: "I invite you to join me in Tombstone, Arizona, in early spring of 2005 to protect our country from a 40-year-long invasion across our southern border with Mexico."[37]

That next spring, some one hundred Americans took up positions along a stretch of the southern border near Naco, Arizona. Among the Minutemen and their allies was a group calling itself "Team 14," a reference to a fourteen-word neo-Nazi slogan.[38] One mobilized citizen told a local news crew, "It should be legal to kill illegals. Just shoot 'em on sight. That's my immigration policy recommendation. You break into my country, you die."[39]

Largely white, and skewing middle-aged or older, these Minutemen, along with their patrons in Congress, quickly became fixtures on cable news. Credulous reporters boosted the Minutemen's exaggerated (if not outright false) claims that the border was being overwhelmed by floods of migrants. By 2007, just two years after the first Minuteman deployment in Arizona, observers counted 144 offshoots of the project's founding chapter operating across thirty-nine states. By 2009, the number of chapters had more than doubled.[40]

For readers today, the image of ordinary Americans, heavily armed, attempting to police migrants fleeing desperate conditions in their home countries might seem unremarkable. But in 2005, Republican officials were still attempting to chart a middle course between the country club conservative Establishment, which appreciated the economic benefits of immigrants as a supply of cheap labor, and right-wing populists, who distrusted Establishment Republicans and prioritized nativist fears over economic considerations.

California's independently minded Republican governor, Arnold Schwarzenegger, expressed support for the Minutemen and their cause.[41] So did Robert Bonner, the then federal head of Customs and Border Protection. Bonner saluted the Minutemen's work, praising their attempts to "help us gain control of our borders."[42]

But others saw a menace. In March 2005, George W. Bush denounced the Minutemen as vigilantes.[43] New Mexico's Democratic governor, Bill Richardson, reminded his constituents that there's no role for such vigilantes in a modern, mature nation-state: "We've got the Border Patrol. We've got New Mexico law enforcement. We can enforce our laws."[44]

And indeed, whatever political support the Minutemen enjoyed when they first appeared quickly disappeared. Just a few short months after Bonner celebrated the Minutemen, the Border Patrol was already backpedaling. The office announced that the Minutemen provided "no benefit to the [Border] Patrol's operations."[45] Schwarzenegger also walked back his earlier support.[46]

The media was slower to pivot, but then came the evening of May 30, 2009, when three armed militia members barged into the Arizona home of Raul Flores, an American citizen and small-time drug runner. Wearing official-looking uniforms and falsely claiming to be members of the Border Patrol, the threesome searched the house for drugs. Finding no contraband, they nonetheless shot and killed Raul and his nine-year-old daughter, also a citizen. They also shot Raul's wife, likewise an American citizen. A jury convicted all three killers of murder. Two were sentenced to death, the third to life in prison.[47]

As the militia members were tried, one after the other, "the gut-wrenching horror of the sequence of events became clearer," forcing the media to acknowledge the bigotry and murderous xenophobia that had driven the Minutemen from the beginning.[48] Even Maricopa County's arch-nativist sheriff, Joe Arpaio, turned on the militia. After a Minuteman pointed a rifle at one of Arpaio's deputies, the infamously cruel sheriff warned the vigilantes to steer clear or they'd end up with "30 rounds fired into them."[49] Today, between public disgust, the loss of political backing, and factional fighting within the Minutemen organization, the once booming movement is little more than a collection of badly designed websites.[50]

The Minutemen may be gone. But the xenophobic hatred that animated them found a new home first in the Tea Party and now in organizations such as the Oath Keepers, the Cottonwood Militia, the Three Percenters, and the Proud Boys. Unlike the Minutemen, these new groups aren't relegated to the kids' table at Republican Party dinners. And they aren't principally focused on external threats. They are a central part of a new political regime that treats *fellow Americans* as enemies of the Republic.

CHAPTER **4**

"The Way Things Ought to Be"
The Road to Vigilante Democracy

During the nearly forty years between the passage of the 1964 Civil Rights Act and George W. Bush's denunciation of the Minutemen, there was considerable bipartisan support for civil rights, civil liberties, and a moderately sized welfare state. Mainstream Republicans and Democrats embraced the fundamental democratic principle of one person, one vote, and recognized the importance of representative institutions making informed, politically accountable decisions.

Don't get us wrong. America's march toward equality could have been quicker and more inclusive. Still, we recognize what this era of "democratic liberalism" got right. The corollary of the political Establishment's commitments to majoritarian democracy and civil rights was a reflexive aversion to anything smacking of neo-Confederate policies or rhetoric, including calls for vigilantism and political violence. What's more, because we now inhabit a world in which bedrock commitments to liberal democracy are under attack, we also recognize the imperative to remind ourselves of what we achieved in the latter decades of the twentieth century, and to work tirelessly to revive and reclaim democratic liberalism for our generation and for those that follow.

Today, the Republican half of the bipartisan consensus has fallen apart completely. Elite, country club conservatives have been kicked to the curb. Taking their place are right-wing activists, lawyers, thugs, grifters, and plutocrats who rally around a twice-impeached president and blame their problems—real and manufactured—on Democrats, minorities, foreigners, scientists, bureaucrats, and educators. Using the old Jim Crow playbook, this now-dominant faction is deputizing partisan foot soldiers and licensing them to deploy a full arsenal of vigilante weapons to undermine civil and political rights, thereby endangering and disempowering a diverse and numerically sizeable contingent of Americans opposed to the overlapping projects of white supremacy and Christian nationalism.

Given the ugly, violent history of legal vigilantism in the United States and given the successes of the era of democratic liberalism, how can it be that a quarter of the way into the twenty-first century, legal vigilantism has reemerged as a credible and powerful weapon? The glib answer is that too many of us forgot that history: We let our guard down. But both the question we just posed and the answer we proffered ascribe too much agency to those of us alarmed by vigilantism's resurrection—and not enough to the forces that willed it back to life.

Our goal in this chapter is to identify those forces and explain their role in ending the era of democratic liberalism and ushering in this new moment we call Vigilante Democracy. We focus on what we think are the three most powerful and influential forces:

1. The creation and supercharging of a right-wing media empire that stoked, validated, and exacerbated the frustration and anger of Christian traditionalists who, thanks to democratic liberalism, had to share political, economic, social, and legal space with those they deemed inferior or *not real* Americans;

2. A series of seemingly never-ending and increasingly militant right-wing challenges to the leadership and policy priorities of the modern Republican Party, most notably in the U.S. Congress; and

3. The striking confluence of events that married a restive, heavily armed right-wing base with an opportunistic political leader whose recklessness and dangerousness find few parallels in American history.

RISE OF THE RIGHT-WING MEDIA JUGGERNAUT

When *The Rush Limbaugh Show* premiered on New York's WABC radio station on August 1, 1988, expectations were low.[1] A college dropout who lived with his parents after being fired by radio stations across the country, Limbaugh was such a broadcasting dud that the future Republican kingmaker even gave up for a spell and accepted a job in the group sales department for the Kansas City Royals. What folks didn't yet know was that Limbaugh had been developing a new on-air persona, one that gave voice and strength to the latent fury of white Christian America. In the decades that followed, Limbaugh would make a fortune while helping transform the Republican Party into one that prized cruelty, celebrated crassness, and treated Democrats (and insufficiently hard-edged Republicans) with contempt.[2]

At the core of Limbaugh's program was resentment. *How dare these racial minorities, professional women, radical Muslims, gays and lesbians— not to mention their effeminate and shrill liberal allies—have the temerity to challenge us? We're the real Americans, the ones who built this free and prosperous nation.* Limbaugh mocked "Dumbocrats" and "Feminazis." He called critics "sluts," ridiculed disabled people, and after the election of Barack Obama, told his millions of credulous listeners that the first Black president "hates this country [and] is trying to dismantle, brick by brick, the American dream."[3] Only his audience of "Dittoheads," as Limbaugh's loyalists called themselves, had the power to stop the descent into madness. They just had to flex.

And flex they did. The Dittoheads voted. They canvassed. They wrote letters. They badgered representatives and flooded the congressional switchboard. And, as the years wore on and Limbaugh began to reach a third generation of listeners, some might resort to violence.

Surely, if his listeners were to act aggressively, their favorite radio jock would have their back. After all, he celebrated the Minutemen, (baselessly) claiming that they were an effective border patrol[4] while downplaying their violence and ties to white supremacists.[5] And he backed George Zimmerman, who gunned down an unarmed Black teenager in a gated community in Sanford, Florida. Limbaugh decried Zimmerman's prosecution. Even Zimmerman's subsequent acquittal—by an all-white jury—wasn't enough. Limbaugh was outraged that there wasn't a greater outpouring of "compassion" for the man who treated a kid walking home with a bag of Skittles as a menacing villain who needed to be put down.[6]

Later, amid the 2020 racial reckoning, Limbaugh falsely claimed that the Black Lives Matter movement aimed "to totally tear down and tear apart the country." Insisting that his listeners' way of life was under attack, Limbaugh lamented that "whenever anybody on my side decides to try to push back against the Democrats, against the left, against the media . . . they get assaulted and attacked." Limbaugh couldn't stand the protests or the protesters. And it was high time the Dittoheads did their part. "Average, ordinary citizens who are being affected by this stuff, are just letting it happen." Excoriating Christian pastors who preached racial reconciliation from their Sunday pulpits, he told his drive-time flock that they needed to stop "ceding territory." "Who's got all the guns in this country?" he asked. "We've got all the guns."[7]

In this respect, Limbaugh outflanked even Donald Trump. The radio legend thought the president—who waited hours before finally instructing the January 6 rioters to "go home, and go home in peace"[8]—folded too readily on the day of the insurrection. Broadcasting the next day, Limbaugh "was glad Sam Adams, Thomas Paine, the actual Tea Party guys, the men at Lexington and Concord" didn't cave like today's submissive Republicans.[9]

Given how crowded the field of right-wing propagandists is today—and how jaw-droppingly racist, nativist, sexist, homophobic, transphobic, and contemptuous of democracy they're showing themselves to be—it can be hard to appreciate just how transformative and transgressive Rush Limbaugh was when he first arrived at WABC. But the normalization of someone like Limbaugh is very much relevant to any account of how sharply the Republican Party has moved to the right. In the early 1990s, while torching Bill and Hillary Clinton on a daily basis, referring to their then-thirteen-year-old daughter as "the White House dog," and mocking the deaths of gay men who succumbed to AIDS, Limbaugh secured major endorsement deals with Florida Citrus growers and Pizza Hut. (Around that time, Donald Trump was also a pitchman for the national chain.) And in 2003, amid incessant on-air attacks on Muslim Americans and their religion, ESPN hired Limbaugh as a football commentator. Though that particular partnership proved short-lived, the mere invitation for him to cross over into the world of sports was a testament to his remarkable migration from the periphery of civic culture to its epicenter. These forays into the American mainstream suggested that there was plenty of space even to Limbaugh's right—space soon filled by the likes of Laura Ingraham, Steve Bannon, Alex Jones, and Dan Bongino.

One person who was paying extremely close attention was media mogul and tabloid tsar Rupert Murdoch. In January 1996, Murdoch announced he was launching the Fox News Channel to take on then-dominant CNN. To run his new operation, Murdoch tapped Republican media strategist Roger Ailes.[10]

Over the years, Ailes and his lieutenants pushed programming further and further to the right—so much so that the network's "fair and balanced" slogan became a running joke. Hosts like Sean Hannity, Bill O'Reilly, Glenn Beck, Lou Dobbs, Tucker Carlson, Maria Bartiromo, Jeanine Pirro, and Jesse Watters promoted absurdities such as reports that Latin American migrants were bringing leprosy into the United States. They gave platforms to the Minutemen, "birthers" who declared Barack Obama ineligible for the presidency, and election deniers. They mocked climate change. They demonized women, people of color, scientists, and educators. And they slurred mainstream journalists and Democratic politicians.

Unsurprisingly, the Fox News frathouse fell hard for Trump. Knowing that he watched their shows with the fervor of a preschooler hooked on *Paw Patrol*, the hosts highlighted causes that some suspected the leader of the free world would then champion.[11] They also promoted QAnon conspiracies, dabbled in white replacement theory and transphobia, and blamed, shamed, and slandered Black victims of police brutality. And as goes without saying, they laughed off countless corruption charges, celebrated Trump's strongman persona, and defended his honor across two impeachment proceedings.

The rise and utter dominance of a right-wing media ecosystem that keeps expanding and pushing further to the right have contributed to the resurgence of legalized vigilantism in at least two ways.

First, Limbaugh, the Fox News hosts, and those occupying more extremist space on such platforms as Infowars and Newsmax have popularized and validated the practice of commingling news, entertainment, and nonsense. Their loyal viewers and listeners, in turn, likewise start blending their views on (and anger over) the latest happenings in Washington with their views on (and frustrations over) what goes on at home, work, at their kids' schools, and at the supermarket. If right-wing media is conflating politics and culture, treating both as part of some hybrid blood sport, and blasting their messaging 24/7, it's only natural for audiences to do the same thing.

Second, consumers of right-wing media are becoming more radical than the media personalities who radicalized them, a dynamic that Fox News feels acutely. Audiences, including avid viewer Donald Trump, have demanded that Fox News push more far-right views. But it is hard for Fox to keep up with its more radical copycats like Newsmax, One America News, RT, and the *Daily Caller*. That gap was never more evident than on January 6. The stars of Fox News spent good chunks of that afternoon privately pleading with, seemingly begging, White House officials to get Trump to call off the insurrectionists. And while Laura Ingraham, Sean Hannity, and Brian Kilmeade were backchanneling to the Oval Office, one of the hosts on the Infowars network was on the Capitol grounds (and soon to be arrested and prosecuted for "disorderly and disruptive conduct"[12]); another was, bizarrely and inexplicably, "holding firearms for certain January 6th participants."[13] What's more, while Fox executives refused to let Trump on the air that day and ended up parting ways with Trump enabler Tucker Carlson, Spotify pays Joe Rogan $200 million notwithstanding the podcaster's insistence that the insurrection was "a false flag [operation] orchestrated by the federal government."[14]

GOP CIVIL WAR

The rise of the right-wing media juggernaut helped fuel another transformation in law, culture, and politics—the extremist turn, and concomitant coarsening, of the Republican Party. Throughout the era of democratic liberalism, insurgent campaigns sought to establish a toehold in the Republican Party from which they could bring their ideas into the political arena and maybe even gain control over the party itself. Ronald Reagan. Pat Buchanan. David Duke. Newt Gingrich. Sarah Palin. These self-styled outsiders challenged and sought to undermine the Establishment conservatism practiced by the likes of Gerald Ford, George H. W. Bush, and John McCain. They sought to rehabilitate and galvanize the nativists and white supremacists who'd been pushed to the margins of both party and polite society as part of the post–Jim Crow settlement.

Some of the insurgents' campaigns, like those of the hate-spewing

Buchanan and the ex-Klansman Duke, were dead on arrival. Others, like Reagan's and Gingrich's, were wildly successful. And then there was Alaska's Sarah Palin, the party's 2008 vice-presidential nominee. Inexperienced, ill-informed, scandal-ridden, and far to the right of the presidential nominee, McCain, Palin seemed destined for the Buchanan/Duke trash heap rather than the Reagan/Gingrich electoral gold mine.

But within a ten-year period, the distinguished statesman and war hero McCain would become persona non grata in GOP circles—as would other Republican members of Congress who shared McCain's politics and sense of decorum. Meanwhile, many if not most Republicans who rose to positions of power and influence bore a striking resemblance to Palin.

In retrospect, Palin was a test case for whether flat-earthism and flat-out racism could remake the party from the bottom up. Without doubt, every political party worth its salt has its share of cranks, insurgents, and extremists. We're not pretending otherwise. What matters for the long-term health of parties—indeed, of nations—is not the presence or absence of extremists but how the Establishment deals with them.[15] And, in 2008, the Republican power brokers rolled out the welcome mat for Palin rather than politely ignoring her. They convinced themselves, and their standard bearer, that Palin would supercharge the McCain campaign. McCain's acceptance of Palin (privately, he preferred running with Joe Lieberman, a conservative Democrat) was an early warning sign that the party's country club elites would all-too-readily yield to an angry and reckless populist Far Right.[16]

In 2008, the country wasn't quite ready for "stunt" candidates and outright lies. Obama beat McCain by a solid ten million votes, and the Democrats made big gains in both houses of Congress, even managing to pick up a Senate seat in Palin's home state. But rather than view the November trouncing as evidence that Republicans should tack to the center, the insurgent Right intensified their efforts. Within weeks of Obama's inauguration, right-wing, anti-government Tea Party chapters had sprung up across the nation. While the Tea Partiers railed against corporate bailouts and (bipartisan) efforts to stabilize the economy after the 2008 global financial crisis, their outrage struck many as intensely personal. The overwhelmingly white movement—only 1 percent of Tea Party members identified as Black—barely disguised their contempt for America's first nonwhite president. "The Tea Party Movement," Palin explained, "wouldn't exist without Barack Obama."[17] Members accused Obama of governing in the interests of Black America. They leaned on birther claims.[18] According to an NAACP report, Tea Party leaders unleashed a movement that "believe[s] their country, their nation, has been taken from them," recruits white nationalists, and regularly amplifies the voices of "anti-Semites, racists, and bigots."[19]

Ultimately, the Tea Party itself didn't take over the GOP. Plagued by infighting, a lack of political acumen and organizational skill, and the absence of any coherent governing agenda, its official congressional caucus lasted only a few years. But the movement marked a turning point in American politics.

For starters, the Tea Party served as a vehicle for shifting the Republican Party from its late twentieth-century focus on libertarian commitments such as slashing government spending to that which predominates today—namely, brazenly MAGA Christian nationalism.

Just as importantly, the Tea Party normalized full-fledged attacks on Establishment Republicans. Even though he ran aggressive primary campaigns first against the quite moderate incumbent president Gerald Ford in 1976 and then again four years later against a candidate right out of country-club Republican central casting (George H. W. Bush), Ronald Reagan had always preached what he called the Eleventh Commandment: "Thou shalt not speak ill of another Republican."[20] Once in office, Reagan quite consciously governed as a mainstream conservative and foreclosed pathways for subsequent right-wing challenges.

That was then. Now no Republican—no matter how fiscally

conservative, stridently anti-abortion, passionately pro-gun, or fervently hostile to bipartisan governing—is safe from a right-wing challenge.

In truth, there have been so many rounds of primaries and purges in the years since the emergence of the Tea Party that Republicans whom we now treat as stabilizing, Establishment figures were considered fringe radicals just an election cycle or two ago. And it isn't because they've become more moderate or recognized the gravity and importance of the offices they hold. No, it's because they're simply less extreme, and less feral, than their colleagues determined to punish political rivals, sabotage government, crash our economy, roll back democracy, and imperil our national security *all in the name of owning the libs.*[21]

We could give you countless examples, but for brevity's sake let's just consider what's befallen recent Republican House speakers. In 2015, right-wing House members pressured Ohio Republican John Boehner to resign from the speakership. Four years later, Wisconsin's Paul Ryan, whose speakership likewise proved too constructive and conciliatory to satisfy the rank and file (and Donald Trump), declined to run for reelection. And in 2023, Speaker Kevin McCarthy, a faithful Trump cheerleader who voted against certifying the results of the 2020 presidential election, served a mere 269 days before a group of eight hard-liners led a campaign to unseat him. McCarthy's unpardonable sin? Working with Democrats to pass a funding bill to avert a government shutdown. The hard-liners were so reflexively outraged that they acted without first identifying a successor (let alone one who could unite the unruly Republicans). For the next twenty-one days, the caucus shuffled through a handful of candidates before settling on Louisiana's Mike Johnson. Like McCarthy, Johnson had refused to vote to certify Biden's 2020 victory. Unlike McCarthy, Johnson is explicitly Christian nationalist in orientation. As Yale sociologist Philip Gorski explained, Johnson "says out loud what most others just feel: that America was founded as a Christian nation . . . and that it is every good Christian's duty to make America Christian again."[22]

"YOU'VE JUST GOT TO DO IT"

This takes us to our third and last legal, political, and cultural force enabling a resurgence in state-sponsored vigilantism—the promotion and legitimation of a particularly combative brand of do-it-yourself (DIY) justice. If the American Right holds the likes of Kevin Mc-Carthy in contempt, the rest of us don't stand a chance. And, to be clear, the rest of us is a giant slice of America: not just LGBTQ+ people, immigrants, and racial minorities, but anyone—from doctors and schoolteachers to army generals and corporate executives—who supports democratic equality. The MAGA movement's extreme insularity (which intensifies with each round of political purges) makes outreach to and compromise with this giant slice of America unthinkable. And that, in turn, makes it difficult for MAGA Republicans to attain *and even more difficult to retain* democratic power. No matter. If democratic majorities are unwilling to roll back the civil rights, women's rights, and sexual revolutions, they can be bulldozed or worked around. And just as occurred with the rightward lurch of the American media and the Republican Party, the embrace of DIY justice found a perfect avatar in Donald Trump.

When Trump entered the political fray, the lecherous reality TV star—who lived in a three-story penthouse on Fifth Avenue and long curried favor with the likes of Bill and Hillary Clinton—struck many as an unlikely figure to lead a deeply anti-elitist GOP. But Trump seethed with the same resentment of elites and elite institutions that animated those who would soon become his rabid supporters. Trump pronounced that Wall Street and the media were crooked. Scientists were greedy liars. Corporations were corrupt. American Jews were disloyal.[23] Regulatory agencies that insisted on compliance with health and safety laws were just like Nazi ministries. Law enforcement was siding with criminals and foreigners at the expense of God-fearing Americans. The military was full of losers. Public schools had abandoned teaching real subjects and were grooming kids to question capitalism and Christianity.

On the campaign trail, Trump enjoyed and encouraged rowdy, violent behavior by his supporters, promising at one stop to pay the legal fees of those who beat up hecklers who disrupted his rallies.[24]

Trump's anger defined his candidacy, and a sizeable cohort of Americans displeased with . . . you name it—5G cellular technology, medical advice to give up smoking or red meat, universities who rejected their kid (because of affirmative action), firms that outsourced their job to Mexico, courts that mandated same-sex marriage, agencies that fined businesses for not complying with the Americans with Disabilities Act—eagerly embraced Trump's hostile messaging. They loved his simple, uninformed solutions to problems big and small, real or imagined: Bomb ISIS. Drain the swamp. Rip up bad trade deals. Bring Christmas back. Make Mexico pay for a wall. Lock her up.

Upon assuming the presidency, Trump didn't walk back his campaign hysterics, nor did he endeavor to work with institutions vital to the American people, not to mention to global security and public health. Instead, he kept lashing out. He rejected the reliable veteran GOP aides and advisors whom party leaders recommended to him. He instead staffed his administration with cronies, ideologues, and amateurs. He even mused that he'd like to bring his own private security team into the White House, to crowd out the Secret Service.

Between 2017 and 2021, Trump pardoned right-wing confederates such as Sheriff Joe Arpaio, Dinesh D'Souza, Bernard Kerik, military officers implicated in war crimes in Iraq and Afghanistan (over the forceful objections voiced by the Pentagon), and campaign and White House aides Paul Manafort, Roger Stone, Michael Flynn, and Steve Bannon. More recently, Trump has indicated that he'd pardon those convicted of January 6–related crimes if he's returned to office.

We associate Trump's defiance of norms, laws, and expert advice with big, dramatic moments: his firing of FBI director James Comey; his frequent mishandling of classified documents; his extortionate phone call to Ukraine's president Volodymyr Zelensky; his reckless theories on Covid transmission and treatments; his cozying up to right-wing militia groups; and, of course, his efforts to interfere with the 2020 election and, seemingly, to incite the rioters to action on January 6.[25]

For us, though, there's an even better illustration of Donald Trump's comfort with DIY justice. We like this example precisely because Trump stood to gain nothing from recommending—*nay coaxing*—others to disregard the law. In June 2017, some tribal leaders met with the president in the White House. In the course of their discussion with Trump, they identified federal regulatory barriers that restricted what the tribes could do with their land. Trump encouraged them to do what he'd surely do in that situation: "Just do it," he urged. That is, they should just defy federal law and extract whatever they wanted from the land.

When the chiefs, no doubt surprised by the president's advice, pushed back, Trump doubled down with the assurance that his administration was playing by a new set of rules: "Now it's me. The government's different now. Obama's gone; and we're doing things differently here." Picking up on one tribal leader's lingering skepticism, Trump persisted: "Chief, chief, what are they going to do? Once you get it out of the ground are they going to make you put it back in there? I mean, once it's out of the ground it can't go back in there. You've just got to do it. I'm telling you, chief, you've just got to do it."[26]

Militia groups, conspiracy theorists, and assorted right-wing cranks wouldn't need as many of the prompts and promises that Trump gave to the wary tribal leaders. Soon, the MAGA base would be defying public health officials, threatening school board members, haranguing retail clerks, screaming at children wearing masks, and using guns as well as vehicles to attack Black Lives Matter protesters. By the fall of 2020, they were menacing election administrators and even elected officials. By January 2021, they were storming the Capitol.

The developments we've described—the rise of the right-wing media juggernaut, the GOP civil war, and the rise of DIY justice—created the space, perceived need, and purported authority for the resurrection of state-supported vigilantism that we'll describe in the next part of this book. A small but passionate and heavily armed cohort of Americans believe they're under siege by those who want to injure, bankrupt, oppress, or emasculate "real" Americans. The right-wing media creates, validates, and amplifies these lies—and makes money by pushing more and more sensationalist and grotesque storylines. The GOP's intraparty civil wars have turned off or pushed out all but the most extreme Republicans, meaning that lamentably few reasonable Republicans remain in positions of influence or power to challenge these narratives or object to the policies these narratives are engendering. And the emergence of Donald Trump and the subsequent deification of a man who champions a chaotic, violent, consequence-free approach to commerce and politics have emboldened tens of thousands of his restive enthusiasts to take it upon themselves to Make America Great Again (as they themselves understand that to mean).

Of course, chaos is not an effective political strategy. And, as many a Trump world lackey has learned the hard way, a promise from President Trump is worth about the same as a diploma from Trump University. Fortunately for the MAGA diehards, there are plenty of right-wing officials and activists more steady and savvy than Trump. And they're the ones giving shape, direction, and legal cover to what otherwise would be chaotic and legally risky initiatives. Their weapon of choice is vigilantism.

They just needed to legalize it.

PART II

Legal Vigilantism

CHAPTER **5**

"An Institutionalization of the Heckler's Veto"
Dissenter Vigilantism

Everything about Glenn Youngkin screams country club Republican. A graduate of Harvard Business School, he worked at Credit Suisse First Boston and McKinsey before moving to the Carlyle Group, the uber-elite private equity firm, where he rose to the position of CEO. When Youngkin and his wife acquired a thirty-acre horse farm on the outskirts of Washington, D.C., they cut their tax bill by 95 percent by designating a portion of their land "agricultural property."[1] Their town, Great Falls, Virginia—which the *Wall Street Journal* recently described as "Where Washington, D.C.'s Elites Sleep"—is home to a great number of high-ranking government officials, diplomats, spies, and several members of the Saudi royal family.[2]

Given his zip code, his fancy educational pedigree, his hard-earned reputation as a "nice guy," his life's work in international finance, his hobnobbing with global leaders in Davos, and his campaign contributions to MAGA-certified RINOs such as Jeb Bush, Susan Collins, and Mitt Romney, one might have predicted that when Youngkin decided to run for governor, he would have embraced old-school conservatism. That is, he would have championed business-friendly economic policies and disdained populist firebrands, extremist agitators, and culture warriors.[3]

And that's precisely what Youngkin did, at first. It's also precisely why his campaign quickly cratered. The man whom *Forbes* estimates to be worth $470 million didn't fit into the Republican Party of 2021.[4]

But despite terrible polling numbers, Youngkin didn't bow out. He pivoted. Hard. Replacing country club conservatism with right-wing populism, Youngkin clawed his way to the Republican nomination and then toppled Terry McAuliffe in the general election.

What Youngkin accomplished was nothing short of remarkable. He out-MAGA'd a slew of MAGA primary candidates and then edged out a popular, experienced Democrat in a state most classified as reliably blue. Democratic candidates had won four out of the previous five gubernatorial races in Virginia and locked up the state's Electoral College votes four presidential cycles in a row. It's easy to be a Trumpy politician in deep-red states. But in Virginia? That's special. The new governor succeeded by trumpeting traditional Republican concerns—principally over public education—and updating them to meet the present moment. Under the banner of *parents' rights*, PTA moms wouldn't just hold meetings and raise objections. They'd be vigilantes.

Youngkin's MAGA makeover holds important lessons, for what the plutocrat turned populist underwent in a matter of months approximates what the Republican Party experienced over a fifty-year period. To appreciate the story of the GOP's slow, methodical radicalization, let's flash back to another Virginian: Lewis Powell.

We recognize that Lewis Powell, the patrician attorney who served on the United States Supreme Court from 1972 to 1987, is nobody's idea of radical. But stay with us. Before he was appointed to the bench, Powell sat on the boards of major tobacco companies and banking concerns, served as president of the American Bar Association, and helped his home state navigate its reluctant and rocky transition away from segregated schooling. It was Powell's clubby congeniality, business connections, and careful pragmatism that helped convince Richard Nixon to nominate him to the Supreme Court. It was those same attributes that helped Powell secure near-unanimous support during his Senate confirmation hearing.

Once installed at One First Street, Powell regularly broke with the Court's conservatives. He joined his liberal colleagues in *Roe v. Wade*, elaborated the "diversity" rationale upholding affirmative action, and voted to strike down state programs that denied elementary and secondary schooling to undocumented immigrant children.[5]

None of what we just described presages Vigilante Democracy. Quite the opposite. MAGA judges have all but demolished the Powell model of pragmatic constitutional jurisprudence. Their colleagues in Congress have repudiated the Powell model of nonpartisan public service—and they're even calling corporate law firms dangerously "woke."

But don't go about feeling sad for poor old Justice Powell. For Powell was, quietly and undoubtedly unintentionally, instrumental in accelerating the Republican Party's embrace of Christian nationalism, not to mention its revival of legal vigilantism.

POWELL THE POLEMICIST

More enduring than anything Powell wrote during his years on the Supreme Court was a confidential strategy memo that he prepared in 1971 just months before he was tapped to join the federal judiciary.[6]

Attack on American Free Enterprise System, as Powell titled it, is a thirty-four-page exhortation addressed to a senior official at the U.S. Chamber of Commerce (evidently with the expectation that the memo would be shared with corporate executives and other business elites). In it, Powell implores his readers to focus intently on the unprecedented threat imperiling "our" political and economic system. Powell castigates corporate America for watching from the sidelines as influential "communists" and "New Leftists" demonize the rich and clamor for the redistribution of wealth and power. Now is the time, Powell insists, for the Establishment to mobilize, to protect *our* way of life. His pitch? Through investments of money and political capital, lawyers and business leaders can counter the radical viewpoints being expressed on college campuses, in K–12 education, on television, and in print media.

Powell urges readers not only to invest in the kind of counterprogramming that we today associate with outfits like Turning Point USA and the Federalist Society. He says that they should start investing in political advocacy, too. Elected officials and government regulators have, according to Powell, been in the thrall of consumer and environmental activists. Powell goes so far as to argue that "few elements of American society today have as little influence in government as the American businessman, the corporation, or even the millions of corporate stockholders."[7]

Last, businesses should take more aggressive stances when it comes to litigation; specifically, Powell advises businesses to fund third-party advocacy and litigation groups that will blanket the courts with "friend of the court" briefs that make clear what positions corporate America is endorsing, and why.

POWELL'S LEGACY

Both because of its authorship and its impact, the Powell Memo has earned a place in American political lore—and rightfully so: The business community heeded Powell's call and spent the next few decades mobilizing, strategizing, financing, and transforming American politics, law, and culture. Though they didn't know it at the time, each generation of strategists, activists, and donors pushed the Republican Party and, by extension, the entire nation closer and closer to today's Vigilante Democracy.

We stated that the Powell Memo was impactful but that invites the question: *Why?* And *why* would it resonate as much with today's populist culture warriors as it did back in the 1970s with that decade's captains of industry? For starters, Powell framed political, economic, and seemingly cultural divisions within American society as a zero-sum struggle of existential proportions. There was nothing in the memo approaching compromise, nothing suggestive of common ground. To him, the enemies of free enterprise were "guerrilla" fighters "seeking insidiously and constantly to sabotage" the American way of life.[8]

This was a striking departure from the then-prevailing approach to partisan politics, when none other than Richard Nixon signed the Clean Air Act, the Clean Water Act, the Endangered Species Act, the Occupational Safety and Health Act, and the Consumer Product Safety Act. The memo surely anticipated, and perhaps contributed to, today's toxic turn. At a time when Congress voted for the landmark Clean Air Act of 1970 with only a single dissenting vote cast across both houses, Powell's embrace of a friends-vs.-enemies, us-vs.-them vision of American politics was jolting to say the least.

Powell's proposal that members of the American Establishment sharpen their tone and rhetoric—he titled an entire section of the Memo "A More Aggressive Attitude"—likewise seems perfectly suited for the era of MAGA Republicanism. Today's right-wing politicians, pundits, and pastors employ overheated and often hateful, deceitful, or vulgar language to describe not just political opponents but also teachers, journalists, civil servants, lawyers, immigrants, minorities, women, and others.

Powell also identified the few pivotal institutions—notably, universities, public schools, and the media—that he deemed durable and credible threats to American business interests, and he prescribed an agenda for controlling, weakening, or transforming them. Powell realized that by the time Americans got around to debating specific regulations or court cases, the battle was already won or lost. To effect the societal transformations he aimed for, what was needed was to change how people saw the world. To do that, key institutions had to be wrested away from problematic leftists and bent to capitalism's will.

Intentionally or accidentally, the Powell Memo conflated the interests of corporate America with those of culturally conservative America.

The future justice renowned for his moderation did so by railing against threats to traditional values with the same breathlessness as threats to profits. That not otherwise obvious conflation of interests helped forge what we now understand as a powerful alliance between so-called social conservatives and big business. And it has been this Powell alliance that has buoyed the electoral prospects of generations of Republicans and also made it near impossible for corporate executives to oppose the excesses of today's culture warriors, no matter how distasteful they might find their Christian nationalist zealotry.

And behind it all would be the resources of big business. Powell identified corporate money as the key to funding pro-business and pro-traditional values advocacy in the courts, in the corridors of the Capitol, in the classrooms, in the media, and in family living rooms across the country. He thus called into service a class of elite lawyers and businessmen and encouraged them to mobilize and partner with the large and heretofore untapped cohort of white working-class and evangelical voters. The organizations that those partnerships spawned—among them the Heritage Foundation, the Manhattan Institute, the Alliance Defense Fund (now Alliance Defending Freedom), the Family Research Council, and the Claremont Institute—have become essential players, providing MAGA Republicans with the talking points, policy arguments, legal strategies, legislative templates, and foot soldiers to wipe out the era of democratic liberalism and replace it with a full-fledged Vigilante Democracy.

Viewing these developments in hindsight, it's clear that MAGA Republicanism owes quite a debt to Powell and his 1971 blueprint. Again, this isn't to say that Powell foresaw, let alone wanted, Vigilante Democracy. Far from it.

Perhaps the most unanticipated and consequential decision made by the second-generation inheritors of the Powell agenda was turning on their corporate benefactors. Most notably and impactfully, Heritage and Manhattan have drifted far from their focus on business deregulation and dismantling regulatory agencies and embraced aggressive state control over everything from social media companies to Wall Street to hospitals to middle school soccer teams.[9]

In preparation for a second Trump presidency in 2024, Heritage isn't looking to shrink government and deregulate the marketplace. Instead, the organization has published a nine-hundred-plus-page manifesto. Called *Project 2025*, the plan is to exert fuller—we'd say authoritarian—control. This includes tighter White House control over the federal government (including the vast regulatory bureaucracy and the defense and intelligence agencies), purging and possibly prosecuting individuals and groups who stand in the president's way, and replacing the United States' liberal policies with Christian nationalist ones. (Among them, Heritage advocates promoting "biblically based" policies as they relate to marriage and family.[10]) Referring to Heritage's own heritage, aligned as it used to be with Reagan Republicanism, journalist David Corn observes, "For a movement once defined by its cries against the evils of big government, this is quite the turnabout. It is a sign of how deeply Trump's authoritarian impulse has penetrated into the conservative cosmos."[11] The same holds for the Manhattan Institute, whose leadership in the 1970s and 1980s prioritized libertarian aims such as deregulation, privatization, and tort reform but now obsesses over transgender rights, elementary school curricula, and corporate DEI programs.

This generation of right-wing activists are demanding more, not less, state regulation to enforce reactionary family values and look askance at Fortune 500 companies and white-shoe corporate law firms, purportedly for going "woke." They're promoting conspiracy theories about bankers, industrialists, and scientists and wouldn't dare tolerate elected officials, government administrators, or jurists who seek compromise with those in the center, let alone on the left. And they're partnering not with corporate boards but rather mom-and-pop vigilantes.

FROM CORPORATE RAIDER TO CULTURE WARRIOR

Just as Wayne Gretzky famously skated to where the puck was going, Glenn Youngkin hustled to catch Heritage and Manhattan just as those think tanks were swinging hard to the American Far Right. The soon-to-be governor did so by promising to address a traditional Republican concern using novel MAGA tactics.

Youngkin zeroed in on public education, insisting, as Lewis Powell did a half century earlier, that our schools had been "captured." Youngkin vowed to wrest control of the public schools from woke bureaucrats and teachers who he said were indoctrinating (white) children in critical race theory (CRT) and making kids feel shame and guilt over America's racial sins. Youngkin also took exception to county and school districts' public health mandates, specifically those concerning Covid vaccines and masks. He assured voters that, if elected, he would ban CRT from Virginia schools.[12] (Youngkin offered no evidence that CRT had ever been taught in any of the commonwealth's public schools.) Youngkin also announced that he would establish a hotline for parents to report educators who schooled students on "inherently divisive" matters. And, last, he advised parents that he'd give them the authority to defy local school districts' public health directives.[13]

This "Parents Matter" approach worked. What Fox News called Virginia's "anti-woke rebellion" led Youngkin straight to the governor's mansion.[14]

REGULATORY SWORDS IN THE HANDS OF VIGILANTES

Once in office, it was time to deliver. This would be no easy feat. Many of the policies that Youngkin railed against had been put in place by democratically elected county or school boards, or by public agencies exercising authority granted to them by the Virginia General Assembly. A governor, no matter how popular, had only so much power to unilaterally override duly enacted programs and policies. But Youngkin was working with MAGA's vigilante playbook—and thus could rely on deputized private parties to achieve outcomes that couldn't be realized using the regular levers of government power.

The most radically and creatively antidemocratic of Youngkin's MAGA policies was his day-one executive order permitting parents to bypass local directives requiring masking.[15] At first blush, the Youngkin order may have seemed mere bluster—fiery rhetoric without substantive import. After all, Virginia already had a parental opt-out: Families objecting to their district's masking requirements could request home-school accommodations.[16] That traditional opt-out and others like it functioned as shields, insulating families against what they saw as intrusive government regulation. *So long as those families withdrew from public spaces, the government wasn't going to chase them down.*

Youngkin's stunning innovation was to invert the relationship between dissenting families and the larger community. The dissenters would no longer have to withdraw. They could remain in public spaces notwithstanding their refusal to comply with health directives. As a result, the dissenters' kids would be admitted to school mask-less. They thus would be setting policy for everyone else, no matter how numerous the "everyone else" cohort was, and no matter how strenuously that cohort's elected representatives embraced the health directive.

By refashioning parental shields into swords, Youngkin empowered small groups of parents to go on the offensive, imposing their views—and inflicting their germs—on democratic majorities. We term this transformation from the old right to opt out (and withdraw from public spaces) to the new right to opt in (and dominate those public spaces) "dissenter vigilantism."

Like the other forms of legalized vigilantism we describe, dissenter vigilantism entails the state relying on private parties to stymie democratic engagement, negate democratic policies, and further subordinate already vulnerable and marginalized individuals and communities. In this specific instance, all sorts of jurisdictions—municipalities, counties, and school districts—had carefully fashioned public health rules requiring masking during a designated public health emergency. Those rules most directly benefited those who were chronically ill, disabled, or otherwise had compromised health—or who lived with family members who fit into those categories. Not surprisingly, the demographic groups disproportionally aided by masking rules were Black, brown, and/or poor students. Those students and their parents and relatives had higher than average incidences of Covid comorbidities; further, they were more likely to live in multigenerational homes and thus endanger, say, elderly relatives.[17] Nonetheless, dissenters were given their way, forcing the most vulnerable children to take extraordinary precautions of the very sort that elected officials said they wanted to avoid.

We recognize that masking may seem like old news. Few among us are eager to start wearing an N-95 again, and communities across the United States have rescinded their mask mandates. But the Youngkin innovation—turning shields into swords—surely helped accelerate the abandonment of masking rules, especially in progressive cities and counties within red states. After all, what value is there in maintaining community mandates if a governor like Youngkin can deputize a single dissenter to flout the democratically promulgated mandate and endanger those whom the rules were designed to protect?

More to the point, the weaponization of parental opt-outs has now been employed in other contexts, too, ones even more important to the MAGA movement's broader antidemocratic agenda: school curricula and library books.

LESSONS AND LIBRARIES

Back in the day—literally, just a couple of years ago—parental rights laws generally meant some form of excused absence from a particular lesson or reading. As with public health mandates, parents could opt *out*. Say you found the sixth-grade Sex Ed talk a little too racy? Fine, your child could go to study hall for the hour. Or say you found some books on the shelves of the school or town library objectionable? Fine, no one was going to force you or your children to read them. But now, as with masking policies, simply having an opt-out regarding course instruction or library materials isn't good enough. Opting out is seen as far too accommodating, even conciliatory—and, often, too respectful of majoritarian preferences. There's humility associated with opting out, an acknowledgment that majorities prevail and dissenters must defer to the majority or retreat from public spaces.

Humility. Deference. Retreat. Those words are verboten in MAGA-land.

Here, some history may be useful. Up until a hundred years ago, it wasn't at all apparent that there were any constitutionally guaranteed parental rights. In 1923, *Meyer v. Nebraska* recognized a limited form of them. In that case, Nebraska had criminalized teaching foreign languages to schoolchildren, meaning that families couldn't enroll their kids in, among other things, German-language schools.[18] The Court struck down the nativist law, reasoning that Nebraska lacked a rational reason for prohibiting instruction in German. Two years later the justices invalidated an Oregon law obligating all children to attend public schools. Writing for a unanimous bench, Justice James McReynolds rejected the assertion that children are "mere creature[s] of the state," and with it, that states have the power to force children "to accept instruction from public teachers only." Parents, the justices added, have rights, too.[19]

These two cases are canonical, occupying storied positions in American constitutional jurisprudence. But their combined reach is far from sweeping. As subsequent cases made clear, parents do not have a constitutional right to control the content of public education. Nor do those enrolling their children in public schools have a constitutional right to opt out of certain lessons. A 1987 case from the U.S. Court of Appeals for the Sixth Circuit, which encompasses Michigan, Ohio, Kentucky, and Tennessee, insisted that families of public school children respect an attitude of "civil tolerance." In our pluralistic society, we must "live and let live," and that includes sitting through lessons some might find objectionable.[20] A 1995 case from the First Circuit, the federal appellate court for much of New England, expressed alarm over the chaos that would ensue if parents' rights were construed broadly to permit, among other things, specific families "dictat[ing] the curriculum at the public school to which they have chosen to send their children."[21]

To be sure, many—but hardly all—states have authorized statutory opt-outs, mainly for Sex Ed (and some for animal dissection units).[22] With statutory opt-outs, the burden has generally been on those families not only to justify the reason for requiring an opt-out but also to privately supplement their children's education so that the students don't fall behind as a result of their missing lessons or assignments.

Now, as with Youngkin's masking directive, states are turning defensive shields into offensive swords. Writing in the *New York Times*, Jamelle Bouie explained how the MAGA-fied parents' rights movement

> is meant to empower a conservative and reactionary minority
> of parents to dictate education and curriculums to the rest of
> the community. It is, in essence, an institutionalization of the
> heckler's veto, in which a single parent—or any individual,
> really—can remove hundreds of books or shut down lessons
> on the basis of the political discomfort they feel. "Parents'
> rights," in other words, is when some parents have the right
> to dominate all the others.[23]

Bouie certainly captures what's happening in red states today—and the illiberal, antidemocratic politics that motivate these new parents' rights laws.

Let's start with Indiana. Right-wing legislators there have been trying for some time to pass a law that empowers parents to remove books containing "harmful" material. After several failed attempts in prior legislative sessions, they finally succeeded in 2023. The new law requires every public school in Indiana to post on its website the full inventory of library books available to students and specifies a process by which parents may request that material be removed if deemed obscene or harmful to minors.[24] Educators and librarians describe the parental removal process as a bullying tactic.[25] In a moment of candor bordering on gloating, Indiana state senator James Tomes, who sponsored the bill, agreed with the critics' characterization: "I hope it does have a chilling effect."[26] And at the risk of burying the lede, we hasten to add that teachers and librarians may well be criminally prosecuted—and convicted of a Class 6 felony—for knowingly demonstrating, disseminating, or displaying objectionable content.[27]

Then there's Florida. In 2022, the Sunshine State's legislature enacted what is now commonly known as the "Don't Say Gay" law, which prohibits teachers from discussing sexual orientation or gender identity in any manner that is deemed not to be "age-appropriate."[28] A 2023 expansion of the law authorized parents to initiate book bans for material deemed inappropriate.[29] Legislators could have drafted a more modest bill; seemingly, one that granted parents the right to restrict their own children's access and borrowing privileges should have sufficed. Instead, Tallahassee went maximalist, privileging any one aggrieved family's desire to, in Bouie's words, "dominate" the rest of the community.

There are two important components to the new, more powerful version of the Don't Say Gay law. First, any books that parents object to are removed immediately from circulation pending review. The practical effect is to ensure that the books are unavailable to all students, quite possibly during crucial stretches of the school year (such as when those books are most pertinent to specific classroom lessons or assignments). As inertia plays a large role in American law and politics, the immediate withdrawal of the books during the pendency of review (rather than keeping them on the shelves) may result in school administrators simply agreeing to remove the books permanently, rather than incur another fight with angry, activist parents.[30]

Second, even assuming the school district rejects the parents' petition, the petitioning parents may appeal any adverse ruling. The appeal goes directly to the state board of education, whose review is assisted by a handpicked "special magistrate." (It is the responsibility of the school district to compensate the magistrate for time and expenses.[31]) In Florida, as in many states, the governor appoints state board members. When assigning appellate review responsibilities, state lawmakers knew full well that the board was, and would remain for some time, stacked with Governor Ron DeSantis's allies—specifically, culture warriors keen on stoking outrage, coddling Christian nationalists, and seemingly indifferent to the ongoing marginalization of racial minorities and members of the LGBTQ+ community. (This is, after all, the same board that drew the nation's side-eye when, in January 2023, it unilaterally decided to decertify the Advanced Placement course on African-American History.)

Once the state gets involved, DeSantis's right-wing cronies can side with the dissenting parent in a ruling that doesn't just override the will of the particular community where the challenge originated; it can have statewide effect, thus restricting the library offerings of even the most liberal districts where absolutely no one raised the slightest objections.

The communities whose decisions are challenged first by lone, likely unpopular dissenters and then by state boards feel the punishing effects of dissenter vigilantism. They know, or will soon learn, how the state works in conjunction with private deputies to surveil, confront, and ultimately countermand democratically determined policies. And they know, or will soon learn, how the state works in conjunction with private deputies to stamp out little blue patches of liberalism in otherwise monochromatically red states.

The existence of these blue districts, cities, or counties—assuming they have all the authority usually accorded to local governments to make public health and education decisions—has been recognized as vitally important.[32] It's what keeps liberal, diverse families and businesses from being forced to either relocate out of state or accept marginalization and de facto disenfranchisement. But here's the thing: In today's political climate, the residents and business owners in those blue cities and counties pose serious governance challenges to the Christian nationalists trying to maintain, if not tighten, their grip on state-level political and cultural power. And it's precisely why vigilante laws like Florida's Don't Say Gay and Texas's S.B. 8 (permitting private parties to enforce abortion bans even in blue cities such as Houston, where locally elected prosecutors refuse to do so) are so punishingly effective.

Meanwhile, in Tennessee, legislators heralded the passage of what was termed a compromise book-banning bill. This law allows parents, school employees, or other community members not only to challenge school library books as inappropriate, but—as in Florida—to appeal any unfavorable challenge to a state board.[33] When asked what should happen with the books the state bans, one of the law's sponsors dead-panned: "I would burn them."[34]

How exactly is the Tennessee law a compromise? Here, too, framing is everything. The original bill included a provision like Indiana's imposing criminal liability on librarians for shelving and lending material deemed inappropriate.[35] So, once the right-wing legislators agreed not to imprison librarians, their less draconian bill was deemed far more palatable.

Note that even the possibility of legislation motivates and embold-ens parents to pressure school officials to start culling their shelves and scrubbing their curricula. In 2022, some Oklahoma legislators sought to give parents and guardians authority to demand the removal of any school library books that incorporate themes of sex, sexual ori-entation, or gender identity. This proposal went further than the laws described above. School officials were obligated to pull any and all books that the families "believed" to be inappropriate. Officials who refused could be summarily fired—and districts that held out could incur fines in excess of $10,000 a day. Even though this bill didn't pass, its impact was felt. One Oklahoma town removed over three thousand novels based on a single parent's threatened lawsuit. The parent crowed, "I actually feel great, it's almost verbatim what I told them that I wanted them to add into the [book screening] policy."[36]

Oklahoma legislators also sent up a companion bill that would have fined teachers a minimum of $10,000 if they taught something—truly anything—that went against a student's religious beliefs.[37] Given the range of beliefs in our pluralistic society, such a law would load practically every school lesson with legal land mines. It would certainly narrow or distort the teaching of biology, ecology, literature, health education, and even certain discussions of history, civics, and economics. Again, so long as such bills are ping-ponging around the statehouse, instructors are undoubtedly going to self-censor their teaching.

Returning to Florida, an earlier law requiring schoolbooks to be approved by qualified school media specialists[38] invited speculation that distributing harmful materials would expose educators to criminal liability. As in Oklahoma, the mere threat of imprisonment led plenty of teachers and librarians to scrub their lessons and mothball their collections. In Florida's Manatee (population 412,000) and Duval (close to 1 million) Counties, school officials instructed teachers to "remove or cover all materials that have not been vetted"; administrators also advised classroom instructors that any new books would not only need to be reviewed by the abovementioned "media specialist" but also approved at a school meeting and "signed off" on by the principal.[39]

Let's be clear about exactly whom these laws empower. The individuals and groups prosecuting the culture wars, enforcing schemes of social and political subordination, and seeking to thwart democratic equality in America are relatively small in number. It is sometimes difficult to quantify precisely how small various vigilante efforts are. But not in this particular context. According to an extensive report by the *Washington Post*'s Hannah Natanson, a mere eleven people, whom Natanson dubs "serial" objectors, were responsible for 60 percent of all books challenged in 2021–2022 across 153 school districts around the United States.[40]

Eleven people.

VIGILANTES AND APPARATCHIKS

Parents' rights laws hardly operate in isolation. They're key components in the larger curricular censorship and book-banning movements.

Legislative or school board—initiated bans have swept up Toni Morrison's *The Bluest Eye*, Art Spiegelman's *Maus*, picture books profiling baseball greats Jackie Robinson, Hank Aaron, and Roberto Clemente—and even one of the Berenstain Bears offerings.[41] Sure, many of the books were re-shelved, a fact some invoke to argue that we shouldn't be too alarmed. But there's a huge administrative (and, for the staff, physical and emotional) toll in reviewing and reinstating books. Committees are formed, stakeholders consulted, and air-tight defenses of the challenged books composed and shared with families that lodged the complaints. One Missouri librarian described working through book challenges "as a complete professional nightmare." Others explain that even the books that are not ultimately banned are nonetheless restricted, kept behind administrators' desks or accessible only with express parental permission.[42]

Recall, too, that the existence of parents' rights laws leads school districts to preemptively pull books (and decline to order new publications), cancel courses, and sanitize lessons. It's not worth the hassle, let alone the legal and financial liability, if and when parents do raise objections.

We appreciate why some might assume parents' rights laws feel redundant in deep-red states and communities. After all, we just noted how state and county legislators and local school boards are likely ready and willing to do this work.

Still vigilante enforcement matters. A lot. The parents' rights laws reach deeper, blanket more ground, and instill a greater sense of fear and angst in the minds of teachers and administrators—not to mention students and parents supportive of how their schools are being run. These laws serve as force multipliers, positioning parents who already are paying close attention to their children's education as sentries to make sure no "woke" lesson or "groomer" reading goes unchallenged. By allowing these sentries to formally challenge school decisions, the vigilante enforcement scheme has the added advantage of insulating the state government. It's not Ron DeSantis (or faceless and often reviled bureaucrats) skulking around your local library and dictating curriculum choices. It's your friends and neighbors, on their own initiative, maintaining community standards.

What's more, the state's deputization of ready-and-willing culture warriors signals to these partisans that they matter, that they are valued, and that they should remain tethered to the MAGA Republican Party (notwithstanding the movement's dismal track record when it comes to governing competently). Deputizing culture warriors for some missions may pave the way for these partisans to be more forceful participants in local governance—and even run for office.

As we mentioned above, the most oppressive and politically impactful effects of parents' rights laws are felt in Democratic-leaning cities and counties within red states. Principals and school superintendents there are far less inclined to prohibit teachers from speaking candidly about race, gender, and sexuality in the classroom. And, if left to their own devices, democratically elected local school boards would be unlikely to mandate the removal of books from libraries.

Right-wing families agitating for change in those communities are unlikely to find much success through local elections. Under an opt-out regime, they'd be forced to go along with the majority or withdraw from public spaces. But under new opt-in schemes, they can override that majority. The mere act of complaining will likely result in the scrubbing of lessons and the censorship of reading material—especially in states like Florida and Tennessee where appeals are brought directly to the state capital.

The effects aren't pretty. Some communities are already considering closing their public libraries—it's simply not worth the constant gotcha surveillance and ever-present threat of financial ruin, if not physical violence.[43] Families who want—or whose children truly need—more inclusive education may be forced to enroll in private schools or relocate to less suffocating communities. And that's why, once again, Florida's and Tennessee's parents-and-state-boards tag teams are so crushingly effective. One can no longer move a few

towns over and hunker down in Democratic strongholds like Orlando or Memphis; families unnerved or threatened by Christian
nationalist programming in public schools will have to relocate out
of state (and quite likely out of the region). Faced with those choices,
it's little surprise, then, that red state school privatization movements
are gaining so much momentum. As we'll discuss in Chapter 9, even
overwhelmingly liberal supporters of public education may now have
ample reason to rethink that support.

EDUCATING YOUNG CULTURE WARRIORS

We feel confident in saying that this is not the future Lewis Powell envisioned. Red states are not trying to mold staid conservatives
who will assume positions of leadership and responsibility in business,
law, and the arts. They are aiming to turn out MAGA-fied Christian
nationalists emotionally and intellectually unprepared for the wider
cosmopolitan world. But that's all according to the plan. It will be these
students' responsibility to join in the culture war that their parents
and grandparents are currently waging, fighting against indecent ideas
and justifying the ongoing marginalization, humiliation, or effective
expulsion of another generation of Black and LGBTQ+ kids.

We described how, in Florida, the governor's highly politicized
board members reinforce the work of vigilantes on the ground.
Now consider how similar boards are busy attempting to subject
the state's public colleges and universities to the same types of constraints that have been imposed on K–12 schools. One college in
particular, New College, the popular and well-respected state liberal
arts college in Sarasota, seems to be DeSantis's testing laboratory.
There, his hand-selected board has been working to engineer what
can only be described as authoritarian control over the college's
curriculum and pedagogy. To the extent there are any Lewis Powell
Republicans still alive (and still calling themselves Republicans),
they would surely say that DeSantis's transformed New College

looks foreign and grotesque—an institution better suited to Viktor Orbán's Hungary than their own United States.

And they'd be 100 percent right.

Orbán, Hungary's voraciously autocratic prime minister, is a favorite of Donald Trump, Tucker Carlson, and Steve Bannon. (Bannon refers to him as "Trump before Trump.") One of Orbán's first moves—and one that put the world on notice of his designs to consolidate power, weaken the civil and political rights of his fellow Hungarians, and "re-Christianize" the nation—was to push the dynamic, liberal, and cosmopolitan Central European University out of the country. To fill that void, Orbán and his supporters poured money into a right-wing and tightly controlled outfit, Mathias Corvinus Collegium.[44]

MCC, as it's known, and Budapest more generally, have become important destinations—pilgrimages of sorts—for right-wing Americans who see Orbán's Hungary as a model for the United States to follow. Orbán thunders against Europeans "becoming peoples of mixed race," peddles his own version of white replacement theory, cozies up to Vladimir Putin, and has been condemned by the EU Parliament for spearheading Hungary's decline from a democracy to what Strasbourg calls "a regime of electoral autocracy."[45] Before he was fired from Fox News in 2023, Carlson traveled to Budapest, where he spent a full week fawning over Orbán and touting Hungary's commitment to Christian nationalism. The following year, the influential American Conservative Political Action Conference (CPAC) chose Hungary as the site for its first European conference.

Like those on the far right, we, too, look to Hungary; for in it we likewise see the future of New College and, perhaps, other American universities. DeSantis's plan for New College—to purge professors, administrators, and entire academic departments deemed "woke"[46]— owes an obvious debt to Orbán, to the point that it might as well have been conceived in Budapest. It's being shepherded by Christopher Rufo, the self-appointed hall monitor of elite institutions whose plagiarism allegations against Harvard's president Claudine Gay led to her resignation; a professor from the stridently right-wing Hillsdale College; and a third trustee affiliated with the Claremont Institute.

As this book went to press, DeSantis was pushing to remake the internal governance of other state colleges and universities, and aiming to cut departments, curtail DEI programs, strip scholars of academic tenure, and push out leftist professors at even the flagship state universities.

DeSantis may have flopped as a presidential primary candidate in 2024, but he and his brain trust have a keen understanding of the mutually reinforcing relationship between state-powered authoritarianism and vigilantism. Top-down control by state officials needs to be paired with the energy, outrage, and oppressiveness of vigilante activism. It's one thing to mandate instruction that pushes a Christian nationalist agenda. It's something altogether different to empower and mobilize partisans to demand conformity with such teachings. So the tone is set at the top, but then parents, community activists, and—soon enough—"right-thinking" students themselves are expected to help surveil, investigate, and enforce compliance.

THE INDIVIDUALIZATION OF AMERICAN LAW

Back when Justice Powell was rallying corporate America to fight communists and New Leftists, he outlined a multipronged strategy to inculcate students in the values of capitalism. Powell's program relied heavily on careful, quiet outreach to powerful Establishment figures in business, law, and finance.

But, as we discussed, the American Right has completely turned on the Establishment, attacking not just liberal or partisan ideas and policies but also mainstream and heretofore uncontroversial ones pertaining to public health, basic science, and irrefutable facts about American history, politics, and law. Whereas Powell sought to rely on elites to mobilize the American majority, who would then close ranks against the far left, the new breed of MAGA Republicans is seeking to empower regular folks on the far right to close ranks against the American majority.

Powell's faith in the Establishment and fear of fringe, radical activism led the future justice to go so far as to deride Dr. Martin Luther King's "Letter from a Birmingham Jail"—and specifically, Dr. King's position on civil disobedience. In a lecture delivered at Washington and Lee's law school, Powell argued: "Whatever may be said for the idealism of a view that permits each man to apply his own predilection as to a higher natural or moral law, it affords no basis for a system of organized society." This individualization of American law was, to Powell, "simply a doctrine of anarchy."[47]

Contrast Powell's warning about radicalism with Youngkin and DeSantis's eagerness to encourage the "anarchy" that inevitably occurs when people decide for themselves whether and how the law must be respected. Youngkin, DeSantis, and their ilk want to empower individuals to reinforce social and political hierarchies (and be legally authorized to do so). Rather than protest serving as a tool primarily for those effectively disenfranchised to highlight injustice and press for legal change, it becomes an instrument for factions and groups fearful of losing their positions of privilege and power.

Like other species of vigilantism we explore in this book, dissenter vigilantism is explicitly antidemocratic. Grievance warriors get the legal authority, legal tools, and in some instances public plaudits and monetary incentives to wield coercive power over democratic communities and public institutions of trust and responsibility. Their impact is, as elsewhere, profound and suffocating. Even where there are constitutional limits on the state's power to censor (and contractual limits on the state's power to, say, rescind faculty tenure), the deputized vigilantes can push so hard and so aggressively as to make it effectively untenable for school districts to continue offering lessons or providing access to books on race, sex, or gender themes—and, increasingly, for teachers to remain in the districts.

FROM THE CLASSROOM TO THE COURTS

In the current right-wing ecosystem, it's not just elected officials leaning into dissenter vigilantism. Perhaps even more disheartening to someone like Lewis Powell, today's "doctrine of anarchy" is also endorsed by a new generation of judges largely unbeholden to legal precedents and seemingly unbothered by laws empowering private actors to enforce the MAGA agenda. In the past few years alone, courts have sided with litigants objecting to public health mandates, housing protections, climate change measures, student debt relief, and antidiscrimination laws. Such objections are hardly novel, but throughout the long decades that constituted the era of democratic liberalism, they were regularly turned aside by judges who accorded deference to democratic decision-makers and politically accountable (and expert) regulators.[48] It's particularly revealing to look at how a doctrine of anarchy is beginning to penetrate even the realm of national security.

Across all eras in American political and legal history, the courts have been especially solicitous of the government on matters pertaining to national security, often quite explicitly acknowledging that claims of individual rights and liberties must necessarily take a back seat to military needs. Within this already privileged domain of state power, regulations in furtherance of morale, cohesion, and readiness have been accorded the greatest judicial deference. Perhaps not at all surprising, none other than Justice Lewis Powell insisted in the 1976 *Greer* case before the Supreme Court that the military "stands apart from and outside of many of the rules that govern ordinary civilian life in our country." Quoting an academic authority on the subject, Powell added that a "military organization is not constructed along democratic lines and military activities cannot be governed by democratic procedures. Military institutions are necessarily far more authoritarian" than other institutions of our government.[49]

That the Court means what it says regarding challenges to military policy should be even more evident from the 1986 case *Goldman v.*

Weinberger.[50] The Goldman in the case caption was one Dr. Simcha Goldman, an Orthodox Jewish psychologist. Commissioned as a captain in the air force and stationed stateside in sunny California, the doctor challenged a military regulation requiring him to remove his yarmulke indoors, including while seeing his patients at the health clinic on the base.

Goldman, who was also an ordained rabbi, took his challenge all the way to the Supreme Court. There, he lost. Writing for a majority that included Justice Powell, William Rehnquist explained that the military's commitments to "unity" and to fostering an "esprit de corps" invariably take precedence over "the desires and interests of the individual."[51] General regulations must be followed even if particular applications may seem excessive or unjust.

Fast-forward to the present day, and to the courtroom of federal trial court judge Reed O'Connor. MAGA partisans often file their suits in Fort Worth, Texas. They do so because they know there's a 90 percent chance that their cases will be heard by Judge O'Connor or his colleague Mark Pittman, two of the most stridently MAGA jurists in the nation.[52] Over the past several years, O'Connor has sided with litigants challenging federal gun laws, same-sex marriage, antidiscrimination laws, and key provisions in the Affordable Care Act.[53] Pittman canceled a Biden administration student debt relief program, determined that a federal entity created under Richard Nixon to support Black and brown entrepreneurs must provide the same services to white clients, and struck down a Texas law prohibiting eighteen- to twenty-year-olds from carrying concealed handguns.[54]

The case that's most pertinent to our discussion is a 2021 suit brought by a handful of Navy SEALs who refused direct military orders to receive a Covid vaccine. Prior to the onset of the Covid pandemic, the Pentagon already had directives in place requiring all entering members of the armed services to receive seventeen other vaccines. But the SEALs were strategic in selecting their venue, and the odds favored them. They drew Judge O'Connor, who struck down the military order while avoiding any mention of the Supreme Court's *Goldman* or *Greer* decisions.[55]

So did the U.S. Court of Appeals for the Fifth Circuit, dubbed by legal commentator Ian Millhiser "The Trumpiest Court in America."[56] These judges, with appellate jurisdiction over cases brought in Texas, Louisiana, and Mississippi, sided with the anti-vax SEALs, notwithstanding the seemingly far greater imperative for Navy SEALs not only to stay healthy during (and in preparation for) sensitive missions but also to avoid infecting those on their teams.[57] Among the court's explanations for invalidating the military vaccination order was that the SEALs incur great dangers—armed conflict, parachute accidents, diving in polluted waters—as if that justified individual SEALs *deciding for themselves* whether to put their entire unit at risk with no corresponding strategic or tactical upside, and for reasons entirely unrelated to their operational missions.

Ultimately, the Supreme Court reversed the Fifth Circuit and sided with the navy. We nonetheless think the case is noteworthy because powerful federal judges on the district and appellate benches were willing to abandon precedent, buck common sense, and imperil national security—all in the service of permitting culture war partisans to impose their dissenting views on everyone else. We also emphasize this case because three Supreme Court justices were willing to back the SEALs and the Texas judges. For Justices Clarence Thomas, Samuel Alito, and Neil Gorsuch, their colleagues' decision to uphold the navy's health mandate and thereby deny a small number of SEALs the power to dictate health and safety conditions for everyone else in their squads, including their commanding officers, was a "great injustice."[58]

We don't want to give the Supreme Court majority too much credit. The plaintiffs were ill-informed, and the remedy they sought, unlike Captain Goldman's, would quite literally have endangered national security. And, as we'll see in Chapter 6, the Court is already endorsing what we call courthouse vigilantism. Extending that endorsement to the regulatory sphere will be leagues easier when the context is public schooling (and parents' rights) rather than the military.

Of course, just because the public-schooling issues that are the chief targets of dissenter vigilantism do not rise to the level of national security does not mean we shouldn't treat those instances of dissenter vigilantism as a full-blown threat to democratic equality in America. Simply put, encouraging numerically small clusters of radicals to impose their Christian nationalist beliefs on democratic majorities allows MAGA politicians to override progressive policies and programs, subordinate vulnerable individuals and communities, and retain plausible deniability if and when private culture warriors go overboard.

Dissenter vigilantism is expanding day by day. Indeed, by the time you read this chapter what we've described above may seem tame. And, as we'll continue to explore, dissenter vigilantes are hardly working alone. Their efforts are complemented and supplemented by vigilantes working in the courthouses, on the streets, and throughout our electoral system.

CHAPTER 6

"You're Just Gonna Have Your F-cking Life Destroyed"
Courthouse Vigilantism

Anna Zargarian didn't plan her pregnancy. But when she and her fiancé, Scott, "got a little surprise" in September 2021, the Austin, Texas, couple couldn't have been happier.[1] Anna had always wanted to be a mom, and the couple were at a point in their lives where they were ready. Some months later, Anna felt a gush of fluid between her legs. Knowing that her water had broken, she and Scott rushed to the emergency room, where tests confirmed a condition known as PPROM—preterm premature rupture of the membranes— that affects about one in two hundred pregnancies.[2]

Late in a pregnancy, PPROM can be managed. But Anna was only nineteen weeks along. Even with top-flight neonatal care, a fetus at that stage of development couldn't survive. "My heart broke into a million pieces," Anna recalled. "I didn't even know a pain like that could exist until that moment."[3]

And yet there was more bad news to come. Anna's condition put her at risk of developing a fatal blood infection. The doctors at the hospital recommended terminating the pregnancy. But because Texas had recently enacted S.B. 8, which authorized any person to sue medical providers performing abortions, the doctors refused to assist.[4] Their hands were tied.

One member of Anna's medical team stated what those who tried to defeat S.B. 8 in the state legislature already knew: "You're wasting your time trying to obtain help here"—meaning, in Texas.

Going elsewhere was easier said than done. Out-of-state clinics were flooded with Texans who had been denied medical care and were given the same advice Anna received. But, after some effort, she and Scott found one in Colorado that promised to treat her. After a nail-biter of a flight—had she gone into labor en route, Anna could easily have died from sepsis or loss of blood—doctors in Colorado terminated her pregnancy. The experience devastated her. Texas had robbed her and those like her of the "time to grieve, to breathe, to take in what had happened to us" at the lowest moment in the women's lives.[5]

We're all familiar with the criminal abortion bans that have taken effect since the Supreme Court in *Dobbs v. Jackson Women's Health Organization* erased the long-standing constitutional right to reproductive autonomy.[6] But it wasn't a *criminal* abortion ban that struck fear in the hearts of Anna's medical team. Nearly one year before the Court overturned *Roe v. Wade*, Texas enacted S.B. 8, authorizing what we call *courthouse vigilantism*. S.B. 8 deputizes private parties to bring punishing lawsuits against not only physicians who perform abortions but also the vast network of supporting actors and institutions modern healthcare depends on—hospitals, insurance companies, even friends or rideshare companies offering transportation to or from the clinic.[7]

Private parties bringing such suits are often called bounty hunters for a reason. Taking on the work of surveilling, harassing, threatening to sue, and actually suing any and all people involved in affirming a woman's reproductive rights can be quite profitable. But it's not always about money. For some, this work is a religious calling. For still others, it's about power, a welcome opportunity to put women exercising control over their bodies (and thus also their lives) in a position of subordination and despair.

State lawmakers throughout the South and in other solidly red jurisdictions are picking up on courthouse vigilantism, using similarly minded bounty hunters to police and punish LGBTQ+ participation in schools and in public life more broadly; to restrict teachers' lessons and reading assignments; to censor the books school librarians keep on display and available for lending; and to penalize people and institutions in other parts of the United States who may try to help women like Anna get the healthcare they need in blue states, where abortions remain legal.

These courthouse vigilante laws are different from anything we're familiar with in our lifetimes. During the era of democratic liberalism, regimes like the ones we're describing had all but died out. But they were a signature feature of the antebellum period. The comparison may be a discomforting one, but the Fugitive Slave Acts of 1793 and 1850 were not very different. As we described in Chapter 2, those laws empowered bounty hunters to track down and recapture Black people who had fled lives of bondage. Pursuant to federal law, northern courts were obligated to facilitate the slavers' work and issue arrest warrants, recognize ownership claims over Black people alleged to be fugitives, sign papers authorizing bounty hunters to ferry those fugitives back to southern plantations, and levy fines against white abolitionists who dared help fugitives.

Then, as now, architects of courthouse vigilantism leveraged the antidemocratic impulses of ordinary Americans. Legislators, governors, and judges empower those folks to act out their base impulses. No longer limited to just griping to the regulars at the barbershop or firing off missives into the social media vortex, legally empowered culture warriors can take it upon themselves to enforce traditional hierarchies. And, more to the point, it ought not be surprising that we're seeing the resurrection of courthouse vigilantism now. Now is the time when the forces of democratic equality are seriously threatening to topple the last of those hierarchies. By empowering courthouse vigilantes, those longing to preserve white Christian political, social, and economic power are establishing a beachhead from which they can fight the forces of change.

Again, we can't help but point out the parallels to the antebellum Fugitive Slave Acts. Congress enacted the original 1793 law at a moment when it wasn't clear that the southern slavocracy could or would endure in the new national republic. And it amended the law in 1850, right as the combination of westward expansion and a surging abolitionist movement threatened not only to make it easier for runaway slaves to find sanctuary but also to recalibrate north-south power in ways that disfavored southern interests.

THE TARGETS OF COURTHOUSE VIGILANTISM

In the antebellum and Jim Crow eras, courthouse vigilantism (like other forms of legal vigilantism) was used to maintain and reinforce white supremacy. Today the threats to the ancien régime are more varied. Race still matters, but so do women's rights, LGBTQ+ rights, and the rights of religious minorities.

Abortion

It's impossible to overstate how doggedly the Christian right has worked to ban abortions in America. We'd compare the decades-long campaign to something out of *Les Misérables*, but of course Inspector Javert never would have collaborated with vigilantes. Not so Texas Republicans, who turned to them just ten months before the Supreme Court overruled *Roe v. Wade*.

Had no one anticipated the Court's *Dobbs* decision, it would be fair to say the anti-choice activists deputized private actors as the only available means of targeting abortion rights. As we learned in Chapter 2, during Reconstruction the Supreme Court prohibited state and local officials—*and only state and local officials*—from infringing on the constitutional rights of Black Americans in the postbellum South. Those officials then turned around and colluded with private actors, who were deputized to do the work of constructing and enforcing Jim Crow. Even while *Roe* was still on the books, Texas would rely on the same formalist legal distinction. That is, the state could deputize private actors to infringe rights that the state itself was duty bound to honor.

```
                                                    S.B. No. 8


 1                      AN ACT
 2   relating to abortion, including abortions after detection of an
 3   unborn child's heartbeat; authorizing a private civil right of
 4   action.
 5        BE IT ENACTED BY THE LEGISLATURE OF THE STATE OF TEXAS:
 6        SECTION 1.  This Act shall be known as the Texas Heartbeat
 7   Act.
 8        SECTION 2.  The legislature finds that the State of Texas
 9   never repealed, either expressly or by implication, the state
10   statutes enacted before the ruling in Roe v. Wade, 410 U.S. 113
11   (1973), that prohibit and criminalize abortion unless the mother's
12   life is in danger.
13        SECTION 3.  Chapter 171, Health and Safety Code, is amended
14   by adding Subchapter H to read as follows:
15        SUBCHAPTER H.  DETECTION OF FETAL HEARTBEAT
16        Sec. 171.201.  DEFINITIONS.  In this subchapter:
17            (1)  "Fetal heartbeat" means cardiac activity or the
18   steady and repetitive rhythmic contraction of the fetal heart
19   within the gestational sac.
20            (2)  "Gestational age" means the amount of time that
21   has elapsed from the first day of a woman's last menstrual period.
22            (3)  "Gestational sac" means the structure comprising
23   the extraembryonic membranes that envelop the unborn child and that
24   is typically visible by ultrasound after the fourth week of


                                1
```

Texas Senate Bill 8 (2021).

But anyone paying the least bit of attention to the Court knew *Roe*'s days were numbered. So why go to the effort to create a vigilante regime? The simple answer is that reliance on vigilantes is about more than just circumventing judicial precedents. Vigilantes are needed in liberal-to-moderate cities and counties, whose locally elected officials have made clear they won't enforce anti-abortion laws.[8] They're also needed in far-right communities where government officials would be eager to prosecute but have limited staff resources to devote to surveillance and investigations. Vigilantes are motivated, numerous, and don't cost the government any money (bounties are paid by the offending parties). And it's precisely because they can be anywhere—perhaps, everywhere—and because they can take any form (a nosy neighbor, a disgruntled records clerk, a self-righteous taxi dispatcher) that they serve to instill far more fear, even dread, both in pregnant persons and anyone remotely considering supporting reproductive rights in those jurisdictions.

Worse still, because vigilantes are not government actors who are subject to discipline for violating professional codes of conduct, they can push beyond the limits of reasonable surveillance and civil litigation. And that means they may be so intrusive that they deter people from engaging in lawful activities. For instance, Texas pharmacists have been reporting that they're afraid to sell Plan B (which prevents rather than terminates pregnancies), and Lone Star doctors have indicated that they're even hesitant to prescribe methotrexate to their female rheumatology or oncology patients, as that staple drug may also be used to treat ectopic pregnancies. Someone, somewhere—a pharmacy clerk, an insurance agent, or a customer milling about the cash register—could always decide to tip off lawyers who would file suit.[9]

Courthouse vigilantism begets more aggressive civil litigation, too. The connection we're drawing is, we think, straightforward enough. Prior to passage of S.B. 8, random individuals had no business litigating someone else's healthcare decisions. But now that anti-abortion activists can sue their neighbors and coworkers, these emboldened morality cops might try to bring other causes of action, too. In one rather stunning instance, two of the architects of S.B. 8 helped gin up a multimillion-dollar wrongful death suit against the friends of a woman who chose to pursue a self-managed abortion (which S.B. 8 doesn't target).[10] In their eagerness to pursue the case, the attorneys overlooked that the plaintiff, Marcus Silva, promised to drop the suit if his ex had sex with him. Silva also threatened to send intimate videos of her to family members and coworkers. "You're just gonna have your f-cking life destroyed in every f-cking way that you can imagine to where you want to blow your f-cking brains out," said Silva in a recording that was submitted to court.[11]

The lawsuit, alleging that the friends helped Silva's ex termi-
nate her pregnancy, is not the slam dunk that S.B. 8 cases are. But,
again, defending even the most frivolous of suits is terribly costly
and stressful—and, in this case, the complaint implies that the de-
fendants are baby killers. The message is unmistakable: *Don't bother
looking for loopholes in S.B. 8. We'll still come after you.*[12]

It's hard to step back from the visceral terror of vigilante lawsuits.
But we need to do so, lest we risk downplaying the powerful political dimensions of courthouse vigilantism. Simply stated, S.B. 8 and
copycat laws being enacted in states like Idaho and Oklahoma are
affronts to democratic equality.

Abortion rights empower women. They empower women in the
workforce, in educational settings, and in domestic spaces, particularly
those where an unwanted pregnancy can shackle women to abusive
family members and partners. Women forced to yield autonomy over
their bodies to others are far less likely to be politically engaged,
politically empowered, and politically influential (which generally
requires money, time, good health, and education), especially in ways
that challenge the Christian nationalist worldview central to MAGA
Republicanism today. So, when we talk about abortion vigilantism
as antidemocratic, we mean it. Literally.[13]

LGBTQ+ Rights

Perhaps as threatening to right-wing identity, and power, is increased
public acceptance of LGBTQ+ people and their families. Whereas just
a decade or so ago, mainstream Democrats including President Barack
Obama were hesitant to endorse same-sex marriage, now more than
70 percent of Americans nationwide report that they're perfectly fine
with it.[14] And, when Clarence Thomas suggested in his concurring
(non-controlling) opinion in *Dobbs* that the Supreme Court could reverse its 2015 decision recognizing same-sex marriage as a constitutional

right, congressional Democrats and Republicans did what they almost never do these days: teamed up to pass the Respect for Marriage Act. The 2022 law provides federal statutory protection for same-sex marriages; it will remain in place even if the Court disclaims its earlier constitutional ruling.[15]

Perhaps because the public is so fully accepting of gay and lesbian individuals and couples, the religious Right has focused its legal attacks on transgender persons—kids, in particular—arguing (baselessly and irresponsibly) that according these children equal status in society endangers everyone else. Right-wing activists claim that transgender people shouldn't be allowed into bathrooms that match their gender identity. They further insist that transgender kids—principally, transgender girls—shouldn't be allowed to play on scholastic sports teams that match their gender identity, as that would give them an unfair advantage over cisgender girls.

MAGA states can and have passed laws in furtherance of the activists' goals. But here, too, state enforcement by government officials is incomplete, largely for the same reasons that state enforcement by government officials of abortion bans is incomplete. Vigilantes can be everywhere, at all times; they can operate even within school districts that take pains to be especially supportive and solicitous to transgender students; they can operate from the visitors' bleachers, as fans of the opposing team may be keen on disqualifying anyone who doesn't *look like a real girl*, as it were.

The net effect is substantially the same as with abortion vigilantism. These laws deputize morality police to, in effect if not also intent, humiliate, marginalize, and possibly banish transgender students. Transgender kids won't use the bathrooms that match their identity. They won't play sports. Already quite possibly struggling with peer bullying or other stressors, they may drop out of school altogether.

As evidence of the extent to which states prioritized vigilante enforcement, consider the following. In 2021 and 2022, elected officials across nearly two dozen states filed anti-transgender sports bills re-quiring scholastic teams to segregate squads according to sex as deter-mined at birth. Ninety-seven of the bills that were introduced—and nine of the ten bills that were eventually enacted into law—included vigilante enforcement provisions.[16] These provide monetary awards and attorney's fees to individuals who take it upon themselves to sue coaches and school districts that allow transgender girls to play alongside cisgender girls.

It's worth looking in depth at an Ohio bill. As originally crafted, H.B. 151 allowed anyone to dispute a student athlete's gender. (In the Buckeye state, an athlete must be slotted onto teams based on what gender they were assigned at birth.) Once someone—again, it could be *anyone*—registered a complaint, the "disputed" athlete would be forced to undergo a medical examination of their "internal and external reproductive anatomy," submit to testosterone testing, and partake in genetic screening before they'd be permitted to play again.

This ghastly bill aimed to transfer tremendous power to people with the worst possible motives in mind, including cutthroat coaches of rival schools, parents who will pull out all the stops to get their kid more playing time, school bullies, and awful interlopers who want to embarrass a girl for looking just a little too "mannish." The sponsors of the bill were (and still are) perfectly happy to use these private enforcers for their own ends—namely, to terrorize and traumatize transgender kids and their families, relegating them to the literal sidelines and metaphorical margins of their communities.

Eventually, the medical exam component of the bill was removed. But most of the other provisions, including those restricting gender-affirming care, stayed in. Although Republican governor Mike De-Wine (whom the *Atlantic* called the "Last Establishment Republican"[17]) vetoed the bill, the MAGA stalwarts in the statehouse overrode his veto.[18]

Then there are the vigilante-enforced bathroom laws, which

Tennessee, Oklahoma, and Alabama have instituted. In March 2021, Tennessee authorized students, teachers, school staff members, and district parents to bring a lawsuit if they (or their children) encountered a transgender person using a multi-occupancy restroom that matched their gender identity, not the sex they were assigned at birth. Plaintiffs may recover attorney's fees as well as "monetary damages for all psychological, emotional, and physical harm suffered."[19]

Outside of the school context, eight states so far have enacted S.B. 8–like laws authorizing private actors to sue medical providers who provide gender-affirming care to youths. (Given how difficult it is for random people to access medical records—and that's been by design, as the feds and states have generally endeavored to protect patient privacy—several of those states "allow lawsuits to be filed from 10–30 years after the patient reaches 18 years of age."[20]) And there are even vigilante laws, such as Tennessee's H.B. 1, authorizing suits against parents of transgender children who consent to their child receiving gender-affirming care.[21] So much for parents' rights.

Laws like these force queer students and their families to keep their heads down, know their place (of inferiority), or move far away. (They also put constraints on straight and cisgender kids—looking *a little too gay* or, particularly for female athletes, looking *a little too muscular* and thus inviting intrusive surveillance and even litigation.)

As with abortion restrictions, lawsuits targeting LGBTQ+ students are, of course, deeply and devastatingly personal. We know, for instance, that transgender children are already more likely to be bullied and harassed at school; they are also at high risk of committing suicide.[22] We also know that welcoming environments and participation in sports tend to improve all students' self-esteem considerably. As we stated from the outset, cruelty is not the point. It's a means to an end. And that end is political domination. Politically active LGBTQ+ persons and their allies pose not the fantastical, absurdist threats that the Christian Right claims—for instance, turning straight people gay or turning cisgender people trans. But they may well challenge

MAGA Republican political projects and the long-standing political dominance of Christian nationalists. And so we see these laws passed now, in this moment, precisely because the MAGA Republicans know that their hold on positions of power in government is precarious at best—and, of course, that LGBTQ+ voters and officeholders skew overwhelmingly Democratic.

Educational Gag Laws

The MAGA Right insists that the public education system, from kindergarten to the nation's most prestigious graduate programs, is at war with traditional American values.[23] Though debates and clashes over schools go back decades, we can trace the current panic, and corresponding turn to vigilantism, to the summer of 2020. With books like Ibram X. Kendi's *How to Be an Antiracist* topping the bestseller charts, Christopher Rufo, a then-obscure right-wing gadfly, hatched a plan to make every parent in America fear critical race theory (CRT). This was no easy feat given that CRT was, and remains, an esoteric academic project—and was not a part of K–12 scholastic curricula. (It's so niche that few college or graduate students study it in any depth.) But Rufo did what many presumed was unthinkable, making parents around the country more panicky about the scourge of CRT than the then-still-raging Covid pandemic when it came time to reopen schools.

His plan was to elevate CRT's importance, insist (backed by shaky evidence) that it was pervasively taught in American schools, and then conflate CRT with the BLM movement. Later, he'd draw a link to corporations' and schools' push for diversity, equity, and inclusion in order to discredit that project, too.

Rufo soon convinced others, including then-president Donald Trump, Tucker Carlson, and executives at powerful right-wing think tanks, that CRT was a significant threat. They were attracted to his central premise—namely, that CRT is wrong and dangerous because it emphasizes the central role race and systemic racism have long played, and continue to play, in American law.[24] And they were persuaded by, or at least willing to go along with, his unsupported claim that CRT "has pervaded every institution in the federal government."[25] In short order, Russell Vought, Trump's director of the powerful Office of Management and Budget, called for an audit of federal agencies' training programs, with a view to canceling those that instructed that the United States is an "inherently racist or evil country."[26] Meanwhile, the Manhattan Institute (where Rufo is a senior fellow), the Heritage Foundation, and Citizens for Renewing America got busy drafting model legislation to ban teachers, counselors, and other public employees from providing instruction related to so-called woke ideology of the sort they associated with Kendi's work, the *New York Times'* 1619 Project, and even literary classics or early reader books that dealt honestly with the brutality of race in the United States.[27]

Legislation along these lines has proven immensely popular across vast swaths of the red states. In 2021, lawmakers in 22 states introduced 54 educational gag laws. In 2022, 36 states considered 137 gag order bills.[28] And though these measures originally zeroed in on race— Florida's "Stop WOKE" Act[29] is a particularly salient example— legislators wasted no time adding gender and sexuality to the list of divisive subjects that were banned in libraries and classrooms.

Courthouse vigilantism figures prominently in these new legal regimes. Slightly more than one-third of all gag order bills authorize citizens to take the lead in policing what teachers say, what materials they assign, and what books school librarians shelve and display. Like anti-abortion and anti-LGBTQ+ private plaintiffs, they are expected to do the states' work—surveilling, investigating, and filing civil suits against teachers and school districts. Courts in turn are instructed to honor the grievances of these litigious vigilantes, punishing schools that run afoul of vague prohibitions on such things as teaching "divisive subjects."

Florida's "Don't Say Gay" law is a prominent example. Under the law, parents may sue and receive damages, attorney's fees, and an in-junction ordering the school to stop teaching the material in question. While the constitutionality of Don't Say Gay and other such laws is being challenged in federal courts, their impact is felt immediately by cash-strapped and conflict-averse teachers and districts that don't want to run the risk of being sued (and would rather not deal with intrusive members of the community crying foul every time a teacher cracks open a poetry or history book).

Again, we ask: What's the goal? Ostensibly and quite hurtfully it's about denying essential truths and, in doing so, erasing certain groups and their histories. Glossing over the horrors of slavery, the immorality of the Confederacy, and the lasting and progressively debilitating effects of postbellum white supremacy signals to all children that distinctively Black experiences don't matter—and that any present-day struggles ought not be attributed to past racial injustices. Likewise refusing to speak about LGBTQ+ persons, families, and experiences sends sig-nals to schoolchildren that there is something wrong, problematic, or inferior about those members of their community.

All of this is inescapably political. By shielding yet another generation from unvarnished lessons on American culture and history, architects of these laws are conditioning future voters to lack appreciation for past and ongoing injustices. Obviously Black and LGBTQ+ students feel the effects most acutely. Their families may remove them from the public schools or possibly relocate to more liberal states. But let's not lose sight of the effects these laws have on potential allies, too. Those deprived of the opportunity to wrestle with unsettling truths about the United States and the broader world may grow up insensitive to the harms visited upon their neighbors, classmates, and work colleagues. Last, there are the instructors themselves who, rather than teach in states where parents and colleagues are playing *gotcha vigilantism*, feel compelled to leave the profession and quite possibly relocate to blue states.

The impact is to dilute the voting power and weaken the political resolve of those most likely to challenge Christian nationalist orthodoxies—allowing MAGA stalwarts to maintain power and influence notwithstanding the increasing unpopularity of their positions.

GASLIGHTING GAMES
Where's the Avalanche of Suits?

We've spent this entire chapter describing the passage of a whole suite of new laws and lamenting the rise of a new class of vigilantes ready and willing to haul doctors, nurses, coaches, and librarians into court. The fact of the matter, though, is that there hasn't been a flurry of litigation. Far from it.

Maybe, some might surmise, there really isn't much thirst for courthouse vigilantism—and, if so, maybe we're making much ado about nothing. That's certainly the impression some state sponsors of vigilantism want you to have.[30]

But here's the thing: When surveillance is pervasive and punishments are crushingly punitive, laws are rarely broken. When S.B. 8 took effect in Texas, it was widely known that vigilantes could be lurking anywhere and everywhere—waiting to pounce. And it was just as widely known that, were the vigilantes to bring lawsuits, the fines levied on healthcare providers, insurers, and the like would be financially ruinous. So, in truth, it should not have been at all surprising when abortion clinics closed rather than fight off suits that could bankrupt them. Nor should it have been at all surprising that scholastic curricula were scrubbed, lessons censored, library holdings culled, and transgender-inclusive school polices reversed before any number of anti-LGBTQ+ and anti-CRT bills were signed into law.

In short, because risking prosecution is a losing proposition, everyone complies. Seemingly (but only seemingly) voluntarily.

Fake Precedents and False Equivalences

Courthouse vigilantism's apologists have a few more tricks up their sleeves. A popular one is to insist that what they're doing—that is, authorizing private citizens to sue medical clinics, teachers, coaches, and school districts—is no different from what civil rights, consumer rights, and environmental laws empowered private citizens to do some fifty years ago. As they see things, what was good enough for the liberal goose in the 1960s and 1970s ought to be good enough for the right-wing gander today.[31]

There is an element of truth in what they're saying, but let's not kid ourselves. Civil rights, consumer rights, and environmental laws do not encourage or empower employees, students, home renters, or homebuyers to surveil anyone and everyone in the community. Those who might bring suit using these laws aren't looking for trouble—trouble has already found them. They have been directly and specially affected by some instance, pattern, or practice of discrimination, exploitation, or pollution.

By contrast, laws like S.B. 8 put targets on the backs of a broad range of community members—medical professionals and other caregivers, as well as teachers, coaches, and students. To gain the information needed to enforce today's suite of courthouse vigilante laws, would-be plaintiffs need to intrude in the intimate affairs of pregnant persons, into safe spaces such as classrooms, locker rooms, and medical records. Laws that deputize anyone to pry will, for sure, attract those keen on prying and will, especially when there are monetary bounties up for grabs, ensure an overabundance of such prying.[32]

Of greater importance, when we consider the relative effects on democratic equality, the contrast between the laws of the 1960s and 1970s and the laws of today couldn't be any starker. The former laws all had pro-democratic effects. The Civil Rights Act of 1964, the Voting Rights Act of 1965, the Fair Housing Act, the Clean Air and Clean Water Acts, and the various consumer protection laws that Congress and state legislatures enacted around the same time deputized citizens to make the nation a more equal and inclusive democracy, in which an ever-increasing group of people could claim a robust set of political, civil, and economic rights.

Throughout American history, those victimized by employment, housing, and education discrimination have lacked power. So, too, have those who've quite literally been denied the franchise. Likewise, members of the public disproportionately affected by harmful environmental conditions and dangerous consumer products tend to be those with the fewest resources at their disposal to protect themselves against such harms. That's why we are characterizing the civil rights, environmental, and consumer protection laws differently. They all spoke to the state's recognition (in the heyday of democratic liberalism) that more had to be done to reduce societal inequality.

Laws like Texas's S.B. 8 and Florida's Don't Say Gay cut in the opposite direction. Far from *expanding* civil, economic, and political rights, and thus helping to level the political playing field, they authorize private citizens to *restrict* the rights of others—particularly those who are just beginning to exercise political power. And just as the civil rights and environmental laws reflected the political mood of the 1960s and 1970s—again, democratic liberalism—so, too, do today's anti-abortion, anti-LGBTQ+, and anti-CRT laws reflect the current political mood. And that mood is aggressively Christian nationalist.

The False Promise of "Voting with Your Feet"

Courthouse vigilantism's defenders claim to have one more ace up their sleeve. American federalism is designed to allow, even encourage, rather extensive experimentation at the state level. So, they say, we shouldn't fret too much if and when state policies are deemed by some to be odious, even intolerable. *Those sufficiently distressed can always simply relocate to a blue state.* This is what political scientists and economists term "voting with your feet."[33]

For sure, people move all the time and do so for any number of reasons. But moving isn't always feasible. Let's start with the easiest case, relocating just for a day or two, to secure an abortion. Piece of cake, right? The truth is that many lack the ready funds necessary to travel out of state for reproductive healthcare. They may not have an understanding boss and can't risk losing their job. They may have childcare or eldercare responsibilities—or they are minors and have school and unsupportive, possibly abusive parents or boyfriends—and thus can't simply pick up and leave.

We're not quite done. Consider, too, the fact that undocumented persons may need abortions. Especially if they're trying to travel from states like Texas, they're going to encounter checkpoints at mass transit depots and along the highways. And there are issues of timing and health. Again, we're reluctant to say Anna Zargarian got lucky. But, comparatively speaking, she did. She could have been too sick to travel, or she could have hemorrhaged or died from an infection en route to Colorado.

And abortions are the easy cases. What about the kids who can't use the bathrooms that match their gender identities or can't play sports? What about the children denied access to books and lessons that speak to their and their families' experiences as, say, Black Americans? They can't make quick trips from Tennessee to California each time they want to kick a soccer ball or learn about Sojourner Truth. No, that needs to be a permanent move, and of course that's significantly harder. It's expensive to move. It requires leaving family, friends, and work behind. And it requires a leap of faith that, on the whole, life will be better elsewhere.

We could rest our case here. The logistics are absurdly difficult, if not impossible—and travel to sanctuary jurisdictions places the greatest burdens on those who are the most vulnerable within already vulnerable classes of people. But we ought not to get sucked into debates on feasibility when there are overriding dignity and equality issues at stake.

One shouldn't have to *escape oppression or marginalization*, regardless of the expense. We're okay with people moving towns or even states because they prefer the weather, or like one jurisdiction's tax regime or school system over another. But they shouldn't have to move in order to be treated as full and equal citizens.

It's perhaps only fitting to bring Anna Zargarian back into the discussion—this time, to explain things from her perspective:

> As a human being and a patient, I felt like I had no choice during this nightmare. What I needed most in that moment was the choice Texas lawmakers robbed me of—the choice to lose my child with dignity and with respect for my body and well-being and future.[34]

Anna is of course correct in placing the lion's share of blame on Texas state officials. Recall, though, that state officials were not in Anna's hospital room when her doctors informed her that they wouldn't perform the procedure they agreed she needed. The doctors weren't afraid of the Texas Rangers busting into the ER. Perhaps if it had been the Rangers, or local police, the doctors could have pleaded with the officers, who might have been willing to compromise, show compassion, or look the other way (knowing that their politically elected boss would not be happy with this nightmarish standoff making it onto the nightly news).

But, no, the doctors must have been afraid of those in their immediate presence—namely, nurses, orderlies, other patients, and perhaps even one another. Every one of them was a potential vigilante, and any one of them, by their lonesome, could have brought a financially punishing lawsuit against the hospital—and its employees.[35] That's what makes these regimes so harrowing and so brutally, inexorably effective.

CHAPTER 7

"You Can Run Them Over. DeSantis Said So!"

Street Vigilantism

PHILADELPHIA, MISSISSIPPI

Ronald Reagan knew that to win the presidency in 1980, he'd have to break President Jimmy Carter's hold over what Carter and others proudly proclaimed the "New South"—a geographic and civic community eager to distance itself from its insurrectionist and segregationist past. Four years earlier, drawing support from Black and white voters alike, the peanut farmer from Plains, Georgia, had won all but one of the states of the old Confederacy and captured all of the Civil War's so-called border states.[1] Indeed, given Carter's strong showing during the nation's Bicentennial, perhaps Richard Nixon's successful 1972 "southern strategy"—steeped in racial resentment and segregationist nostalgia—had been just a fluke.[2]

Reagan was determined to prove otherwise. Having secured the Republican nomination, he journeyed to the Neshoba County fairgrounds in Philadelphia, Mississippi, of all places, to kick off his general election campaign. Transitions from primaries to general elections usually involve candidates moderating their views as they seek to bring swing voters into the fold. Not so in Reagan's case.[3]

The fairgrounds were hardly an obvious choice for a major political event. The population of the entire county numbered around twenty-three thousand, and Neshoba County was hundreds of miles from even modest-sized cities such as Birmingham and Memphis. What *was* close by was the specter of white supremacy. In June 1964, three Freedom Riders had been arrested in Philadelphia (Neshoba's county seat), "released," and then trailed, abducted, and viciously murdered by a gang made up of townies, sheriff's deputies, Klansmen, and even a Baptist preacher.[4]

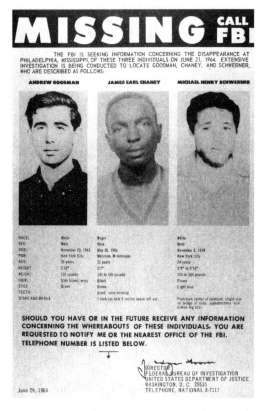

FBI *missing persons poster for Andrew Goodman, James Earl Chaney, and Michael Schwerner.*

The vigilante slayings of James Chaney, Andrew Goodman, and Michael Schwerner—a Black Mississippian and two Jews from New York—were among the last punches that Jim Crow landed. In short order, President Lyndon Johnson and Attorney General Robert Kennedy dispatched the FBI to blanket Neshoba.[5] The swift arrival of federal agents frustrated local law enforcement's efforts to cover up the brutal crimes, not to mention any of their officers' complicity. Just days after the killings, Congress passed the Civil Rights Act.[6] A year later, it followed up with the Voting Rights Act.[7]

Against that historical backdrop, Reagan's visit posed a challenge to the post-1965 political consensus that relegated unreconstructed southerners to the margins of American civic life. He associated himself not with the Freedom Riders, or the storied leaders of the civil rights movement, but rather with the state and local institutions that, for generations, had coddled racist vigilantes.

Reagan campaigned on the promise that America would once again be a "shining city on a hill." Yet, to kick off his campaign, he took us back to a place of darkness and terror. It was a move born of desperation. Carter and a new generation of southern Democrats aimed to permanently bridge long-standing racial and regional divides. If they succeeded, they'd dominate national elections for the foreseeable future. Reagan arrived in Philadelphia to blow up that bridge. As longtime *New York Times* columnist Bob Herbert later wrote: "Reagan was the first presidential candidate ever to appear at the fair, and he knew exactly what he was doing when he told that crowd, 'I believe in states' rights.'"[8]

The gambit worked. His speech drew raucous cheers. And being, as Herbert put it, "elbow deep [in] race-baiting" helped Reagan's party claw back almost the entirety of the old Confederacy.[9] Only Carter's home state of Georgia cast its Electoral College votes for the incumbent.

Reagan's speech marked a turning point in the Republican Party's (and post-1965 America's) approach to the legacy of Jim Crow. Still, for all his dog-whistling and race-baiting, Reagan respected respectability. He may have played footsie with white supremacists, but he certainly wasn't bringing them home to meet the parents—or, in his case, the cabinet. Reagan was an honest-to-goodness politician of the twentieth-century Right, which meant being tethered to the very same Establishment extolled by the likes of Lewis Powell in his 1971 memo. His cabinet, filled with mainstream fixtures from business, law, public administration, and the military, reflected as much. Little surprise, then, that the B-movie actor turned corporate pitchman turned transformative politician rejected a KKK endorsement in 1980 and did the same again in 1984.[10] Nor was it a surprise when he denounced Bernhard Goetz, even though Goetz's defenders championed a racialized account of law-and-order politics that Reagan and his surrogates had helped resurrect.

The old Republican elite held the line for years. George H. W. Bush, Reagan's vice president, whose family pedigree, education, and public service marked him as the very embodiment of the American Establishment, sought to make the United States a "kinder, gentler, nation." As president, Bush took a strong stand against Louisiana's David Duke, the telegenic onetime grand wizard who abandoned the Klan's costumery but clung to its views. Even Bush's son, George W., who very much defined himself in opposition to country club Republicanism, denounced private border Minutemen as meddlesome and dangerous vigilantes.

Later, when George Zimmerman shot unarmed Black teenager Trayvon Martin in Sanford, Florida, the leading Republican officials of the time condemned the 2012 shooting. That year's Republican presidential nominee, Mitt Romney, called it a tragedy. Jeb Bush, the Florida governor who had signed the "Stand Your Ground" law that was in effect when Zimmerman shot Martin, scoffed at the claim that Zimmerman was acting in self-defense. Self-defense, Bush argued, "doesn't mean [you] chase after somebody who's turned their back."[11]

Yet, unlike Goetz, Zimmerman became a minor celebrity, championed by those likewise eager to "fight back." He sued Trayvon Martin's family for $100 million; the converse happened in Goetz's case, where the *victims'* families sued the subway vigilante.[12] Zimmerman even auctioned off the gun he used to kill the child—a sick stunt that ultimately netted him $250,000.[13] (Sheriffs in the Jim Crow South used to auction trinkets incident to lynchings—and townspeople used to gobble up these testaments to white supremacy.)

Zimmerman's brashness coincided with the profound changing of the guard in Republican circles. Within just a few years of George Zimmerman's acquittal, old-school Establishment Republicans were too busy being chewed up and spit out to have the wherewithal, let alone political clout, to condemn Zimmerman's antics. Donald Trump walloped Jeb Bush in the 2016 Republican primary, and right-wing fury at Romney runs so high that the longtime GOP statesman reportedly spends $5,000 a day in private security to protect his family.[14]

CENTRAL PARK

Of course, even back in the 1980s and 1990s, not everyone was abiding by Establishment norms of decency and justice. Among those seemingly never at peace with the post–Jim Crow political consensus was a certain New York real estate developer. In 1989, Donald Trump placed a full-page ad in four New York papers, including the *Times*, calling for the execution of the five Black teenagers accused of, and later wrongfully convicted of, raping a white twenty-eight-year-old banker who had been jogging in Central Park.[15] Trump claimed that New York is "a world ruled by the law of the streets, as roving bands of wild criminals roam our neighborhoods." His solution was more violence: "I want to hate these muggers and murderers. They should be forced to suffer. . . . I want them to understand our anger. I want them to be afraid."[16]

While New York's crime rate has been on a steady and near-continuous decline since the prosecution of the so-called Central Park Five, Donald Trump has become more belligerent, vindictive, and lawless, setting the tone and quickening the tempo for the vigilantism to come. Throughout the 2016 campaign, Trump promised legal support if his loyalists got arrested or sued for assaulting hecklers.[17] (In time, he'd start offering a more tangible assurance for would-be vigilantes: pardons, including for, among others, insurrectionists.)

CHARLOTTE, NORTH CAROLINA

In September 2016, Glenn Reynolds was monitoring the highly charged presidential election. But he also had an eye on what was happening one evening in Charlotte, North Carolina. Protesters there had taken to the streets after local police shot and killed a forty-three-year-old unarmed Black man. Reacting to the protesters blocking the I-277 highway, Reynolds, a tenured law professor, then-columnist for *USA Today*, and proprietor of an extremely popular right-wing blog, took to Twitter. His advice: "Run them down."

Jeered by many, and temporarily suspended from *USA Today*, Reynolds apologized for his statement, explaining his words were poorly chosen and that, of course, he didn't mean them literally.[18] Still, his succinct, declarative tweet seemingly prescribing vehicular violence was a harbinger of what lay ahead.

CHARLOTTESVILLE, VIRGINIA

On August 12, 2017, James Alex Fields, Jr., lost patience with racial justice counterprotesters.[19] The site was Charlottesville, Virginia, home to Thomas Jefferson and the world-class university he founded. This postcard-perfect college town drew the nation's attention that summer when white supremacists, neo-Nazis, preppy antisemites, fascists, paramilitary types, and Christian nationalists convened to show their strength, resolve, and solidarity—but mostly their outrage—over the city's decision to remove a statue of Robert E. Lee.

Fields was among those who wanted the Confederate monument to remain in place, so much so that the then-twenty-year-old traveled from Ohio to make his opposition known. At one point during the day, Fields was photographed carrying a shield bearing the symbol of the self-described fascist group Vanguard America.[20] (A high school teacher of his later described Fields as having "white supremacist views."[21]) Others who assembled bore Nazi and Confederate flags, carried tiki torches, and shouted such slogans as "white lives matter," "blood and soil," and "the Jews will not replace us!" Aware of what was brewing in town, members of civil rights organizations; religious congregations; university faculty, staff, and students; and plenty of locals confronted the hatemongers.

As the day progressed and the counterprotesters continued to express their disgust—and snarl traffic—Fields returned to his car. Counterprotesters penned him and countless other motorists in, preventing anyone from driving away. This didn't sit well with Fields, who barreled his Dodge Challenger into a group of pedestrians. The collision sent several people "through the air."[22] Fields hit other cars, too—and those cars smashed into yet more counterprotesters. Fields then threw the Challenger into reverse and floored the gas, hitting even more people. After this final collision, Fields drove away, only to be stopped and arrested several blocks from the scene.

In due time, the nation learned the true extent of his rampage. Blood and flesh had been splattered all over Fields's car. Thirty-five people were injured in the attack. One of them, a young woman named Heather Heyer, did not survive.

Naturally, the national media sought Donald Trump's reactions. Trump first emphasized that the violence in Charlottesville had emanated from "many sides."[23] His second time commenting was, perhaps, worse: "We condemn in the strongest possible terms this egregious display of hatred, bigotry and violence on many sides."[24] His third attempt surely wasn't a charm. But it was better. "Racism is evil. And those who cause violence in its name are criminals and thugs, including the KKK, neo-Nazis, white supremacists, and other hate groups that are repugnant to everything we hold dear as Americans."[25] While some took heart in Trump's naming specific right-wing groups, others worried that Trump's mention of "other hate groups" was yet another gesture in the direction of bothsidesing the show of right-wing force. On a fourth occasion, Trump reverted to casting aspersions on "both sides," while also recognizing that there were "very fine people" among the white supremacists.

But even as Trump blustered and prevaricated, he never got

anywhere near defending Fields. To the contrary, Trump acknowledged the possibility that Fields's actions could be construed as "terrorism"; the president also volunteered that Fields "is a murderer and what he did was a horrible, horrible, inexcusable thing."[26]

Attorney General Jeff Sessions concurred. He, too, indicated that Fields's attack met the definition of domestic terrorism. Referring to ramming protesters as "unacceptable" and "evil," Sessions promised to pursue "the most serious charges that can be brought."[27] With Sessions professing that the "indictment should send a clear message . . . that we aggressively prosecute violent crimes of hate that threaten the core principles of our nation," and with FBI leadership underscoring that "peaceful protest without intimidation, without the threat of violence, is every American's birthright," federal prosecutors charged Fields with thirty counts of violating two hate crime statutes.[28]

Lacking both public sympathy and political backing, Fields pleaded guilty, sought mercy on the grounds of his difficult childhood and history of mental illness, and received a life sentence. The federal prosecutors hailed the sentence, announcing that "calculated" and "coldblooded" attacks motivated by "deep-seated racial animus" have no place in American society—and that the results of this case made clear how the nation would respond when confronting violent white supremacy and domestic terrorism.[29]

OWNING THE STREETS

If only that were true. Fields had gone too far—or, rather, he'd gone too far *too soon* (or *too fast*). Going forward, our response would be very different. We'd not only respond to right-wing political violence with greater leniency. We'd also devise any number of legal strategies to legitimate, validate, and even reward it.

These strategies shape what we're calling *street vigilantism*—what's surely the most intuitive form of legal vigilantism in the American

Right's playbook. It's also the most sweeping, thanks to its architects and practitioners' ability to draw upon a range of existing assets (including guns and vehicles), popular cultural and political tropes about freedom and self-defense, and supportive state actors.

Stand Back and Stand By

In late September 2020, at the first Trump-Biden presidential debate, moderator Chris Wallace asked Donald Trump whether he was "willing, tonight, to condemn white supremacists and militia groups and to say that they need to stand down and not add to the violence."[30] Wallace was referring to the right-wing outfits that had been brandishing firearms and at times violently confronting Black Lives Matter marchers. Trump, in his inimical way, hemmed, hawed, and sputtered. Wallace kept the pressure on—as did Biden, who interrupted to likewise demand that Trump condemn white supremacist violence. With Wallace and Biden sounding like Nike pitchmen urging Trump to *just do it*, Trump finally responded.

"Proud Boys," he began, "stand back and stand by."

In the four years since that September 2020 debate, Trump has dropped all pretense of tact and decency. But, in 2020, his response to Wallace and Biden might have satisfied some Americans. The Proud Boys, however, understood exactly what the president was saying. Far from disavowing them, he was explaining how they could be most useful. As if the direction to "stand by" wasn't enough of a wink-wink to the extremists who'd become increasingly influential within the MAGA movement, the president added: "Somebody's got to do something about Antifa and the left because this is not a right-wing problem, this is a left-wing problem."

On social media, the Proud Boys crowed "Standing down and standing by sir."[31] Megan Squire, a computer scientist who studies online political extremism, reported that the social media posting captured the general mood on the far right. "To say Proud Boys are energized by this," Squire remarked, "is an understatement. . . . They are absolutely over the moon. Their fantasy is to fight Antifa in [Trump's] defense, and he apparently just asked them to do just that."[32]

Trump's mafioso-like intimations that *someone ought to do something about so-and-so* were amplified by right-wing surrogates. His then attorney general, William Barr, called BLM protesters "outside radicals and agitators [who] pursue their own separate, violent, and extremist agenda." (One need not think too hard about why Barr viewed Black Americans and their allies as "outside[rs].")[33] Furious that BLM protests had not been put down, Rush Limbaugh bemoaned, "If there's no pushback, then—and if the pushback isn't seen, then people are going to get dispirited and think that nobody cares about this assault on the country."[34] Just like in the movies, pointed musings by the godfather and his capos preceded actions carried out by the soldiers on the streets. This seems to match the understanding of Joe Biggs, a senior member of the Proud Boys and convicted January 6 rioter. Biggs interpreted the "stand by" message as the president directing militias "to go f-ck them up."[35]

Armed and Confrontational

You saw the militia walking down the street, you would have thought they were an army. . . . [They] had better equipment than our State Police had.

Virginia governor Terry McAuliffe, August 13, 2017[36]

Terry McAuliffe was the furthest thing from a political naïf. A longtime, battle-tested confidant to both Bill and Hillary Clinton and a former chair of the Democratic National Committee, the governor had a preternatural understanding of American political culture.

In August 2017, as the Unite the Right Rally heated up in Charlottesville, McAuliffe knew the nation was awash in guns. He knew gun ownership had taken on near-religious status for a substantial number of Americans. And he knew right-wing extremists were increasingly bold, increasingly well organized, and armed to the teeth. Yet, still, seeing them strolling around what was ordinarily considered one of the friendliest and most welcoming of college towns threw him. More importantly, it threw the Virginia State Police, whom McAuliffe noted were outgunned.

Today's gun culture and militia activities are tied up with a particularly strident and not necessarily obvious, let alone careful, reading of the Constitution's Second Amendment. They're also deeply connected to this nation's founding mythology, which continues to influence how many Americans view government (that is, warily). But these readings and understandings haven't always been codified by legislatures, recognized by courts, or endorsed by sheriffs, mayors, governors, or presidents. Reasonable restrictions on firearms have been a near constant in American history.[37]

Particularly given the absence of expressly enumerated Second Amendment rights to wield guns outside of a "well regulated Militia" (by which James Madison certainly did not mean to include gangs like the Oath Keepers or Proud Boys), the Supreme Court could have stood on the sidelines while some states expanded gun rights and other states (and the federal government) maintained their traditional gun control laws. The Court instead has jumped into the fray. The justices in the solid right-wing majority have adopted a position, purportedly grounded in "history and tradition,"[38] that threatens to gut even the most modest of gun restrictions.[39]

The result is not just the presence of guns everywhere. More than that, the Court's reckless and ahistorical mythologizing links American gun culture with a distinctively American distrust of the government (and, quite possibly, a corresponding duty to take up arms against the government if and when the state wrongs its citizens). As if this already toxic mix of readily available guns and revolutionary mythology weren't dangerous enough, we have to further reckon with the fact that so many Americans (including Americans in positions of trust and authority) are quick to label even the most sensible and necessary of government regulations as tyrannical. The end result? It's no longer just a cool flex to hit up the neighborhood Dairy Queen with an AR-15 slung across your back. For some, it's now a constitutional imperative to bring your guns to school board meetings, political rallies, legislative assemblies, and the polls.[40]

Working in tandem with expansive gun rights, conspiracy theories about government tyranny, and, of course, fears that white Christian culture is threatened by Black Americans, immigrants, Jews, and LGBTQ+ persons are "Stand Your Ground" laws. Though their champions might insist otherwise, these, too, are largely creatures of the twenty-first century.

Under age-old English law, which the United States adopted at the time of its founding, the "Castle" doctrine governed the use of violence in self-defense. This legal rule requires an individual to retreat from an armed confrontation, if at all possible. The sole exception: if you're on your own property. Unlike Castle states, Stand Your Ground states (only one of which had codified the doctrine prior to 2005) allow people to use lethal force whenever and wherever confronted. As the anti–gun violence Brady Center reports, Stand Your Ground is premised on a "shoot first, ask questions later" model that "serves to embolden vigilantes . . . while threatening all Americans' public safety."[41] Notwithstanding evidence indicating that the shift from Castle to Stand Your Ground increases the rate of firearm homicides and does nothing to deter or prevent crime, at least twenty-seven states have switched to Stand Your Ground.[42]

As the old infomercials used to boast, *but wait, there's more.* We're at a moment when Americans are expressing less and less faith in democracy. Even apart from government tyranny, there is just less of a commitment to democratic outcomes. Study after study suggests as much, but the enduring popularity of Donald Trump and his complete and overt disdain for the democratic process should tell us all we need to know.[43] We mention this here, though, for a specific reason. For those not beholden to democracy, there's no inherent reason why majority voting rules, rather than demonstrations of force, should guide how we resolve disputes and render collective judgments.

That claim may sound overheated, but consider how quick some of our fellow citizens are to resort to violence in situations that need not escalate in that fashion. Consider, too, how openly contemptuous some of those folks, including individuals in positions of trust and power, are when a legislature or judge tells them no. We've all seen the ads and threatening tweets authored by right-wing politicians posing with their guns and daring Democratic politicians to *come and take 'em*. That understanding—*GUNS > VOTES*—has made today's turn to street vigilantism so much more probable, more expansive, and more lethal. Every regulation they find burdensome, every book they find offensive, every protest they find objectionable, every public hearing or legislative session that they believe has been captured by those who don't have real Americans' interests at heart, provides a predicate for angry activists to carry and, if need be, discharge their weapons with confidence that they will not be punished.

Back(ed by) the Blue

Though, as we've just shown, the laws are increasingly favorable to those who own, carry, and yes, brandish weapons, the confidence we just mentioned runs even deeper. And for good reason. Scholars, journalists, and some government officials have been sounding the alarm over what they characterize as a too-cozy relationship between those carrying weapons in public spaces for political purposes and members of many police departments around the nation. (Importantly, if ironically, the very purpose of modern police forces is to maintain law and order precisely so ordinary citizens need not bear such awesome responsibilities.)

In his reflections in the immediate aftermath of Charlottesville, McAuliffe posited an "us vs. them" story—namely, the police were matched up against violent armed protesters threatening public order. McAuliffe's account is, however, a little too clean. Mounting evidence points to the conclusion that police and vigilantes regularly share the same political and cultural values and inhabit overlapping social spaces (real and virtual). There's a 2006 FBI report that raised all the red flags;[44] there's a 2015 FBI counterterrorism policy guide that draws links between law enforcement officers and "militia extremists, white supremacist extremists, and sovereign citizen extremists"[45]; a 2020 Reuters investigation tying such groups to police instructors, who play an especially crucial role in socializing and acculturating new classes of police recruits;[46] an account of organizations working to "connect citizens to sheriffs" in service of disrupting the orderly workings of the 2022 elections;[47] and a 2023 scholarly report on successful efforts to recruit sheriffs into right-wing extremist movements.[48] By these reckonings, it's at the very least not always clear where police stand—a source of confusion and frustration for everyone, including some of the January 6 insurrectionists who expressed shock and dismay when it became clear that the Capitol Police were not going to give them a free pass.

We'd like to think that there was absolutely no reason to doubt the integrity and professionalism of the Capitol Police, and that the insurrectionists—so wrong about so many things—were entirely delusional when they thought the force would be on their side. But the insurrectionists witnessed what so many others witnessed in summer and fall 2020: law enforcement officers across the nation employing especially harsh tactics when confronting BLM protesters, while treating right-wing vigilantes with kid gloves.

Throughout 2020, Albuquerque—like many other American cities— experienced waves of protests. Folks there, as elsewhere, were fed up with racism, police brutality, and lingering vestiges of white supremacy. On June 15, 2020, protesters rallied in the Old Town neighborhood in opposition to a public statue valorizing a Spanish conquistador. There the protesters encountered stiff opposition, including armed members of the right-wing paramilitary group that called themselves the New Mexico Civil Guard.

One of the counterprotesters was Steven Ray Baca. Video recordings show him shoving a woman from behind; she fell to the ground, injuring her legs. The videos also capture Baca barreling into another female protester (again from behind). He "grabbed her shoulder and slammed her into a concrete sidewalk where she hit her head."[49]

Some protesters then confronted Baca, who sprayed them with Mace and drew his .40-caliber handgun. Among those challenging Baca was Scott Williams, who attempted to use a skateboard to disarm Baca. Baca fired at Williams, shooting him four times in the torso. It was then that Baca's allies in the New Mexico Civil Guard leaped into action. They quickly surrounded and shielded him from the irate protesters. Then, when the police intervened, Baca directed them to call his family—Baca's uncle was with the Bernalillo Sheriff's Office. (Albuquerque is Bernalillo County's largest city.) Baca's dad, too, had been a Bernalillo County sheriff's deputy.

Contemporaneous reports noted that "the police handled the New Mexico Civil Guard and [Baca] very gingerly, with care to make sure they didn't get injured."[50] This especially considerate treatment made all the more sense once it came to light that just two weeks prior to the shooting, an Albuquerque city cop was filmed "encouraging men in tactical gear [who were] preparing to guard property against police brutality protesters." Members of the Civil Guard were among those who conferred with the police and who were told to "take care of each other and take care of the people of Albuquerque." (And lest one think that exchange with the police was an isolated event, during the incident when Baca shot Williams, Albuquerque police were overheard on a police scanner "describing 'armed friendlies' posted on rooftops near the protest."[51])

This explicit characterization of militiamen as "armed friendlies" is jarring; it also offers some insight into what else was going on and carries forward to this day. A few weeks before the Baca shooting in New Mexico, Constable John Shirley of Hood County, Texas, posted a "Call to Action" on an Oath Keepers Facebook page. Shirley, elected to oversee county law enforcement matters, was summoning members of the Oath Keepers to provide protection to businesses that were defying pandemic shutdown orders promulgated by Governor Greg Abbott. Shirley's specific plea was for active and former law enforcement officers to mobilize, armed of course, and ready themselves. Lest there be any doubt who or what Shirley was fighting against, the constable explained that "We are now in a Global War on Antifa."[52]

The sheriff of Canadian County, Oklahoma, similarly called for volunteers to join his "posse" to help him protect "lives and property" and to support "the Constitutional rights of innocent, law abiding citizens of Canadian County."[53] Reviving the chilling Jim Crow–era practice of using mass-media outlets to amplify calls to bully civil rights agitators, local ABC affiliate KOCO 5 News hyped the sheriff's call as "breaking news" and posted information on how viewers, too, could join the posse.

One might hope and expect things would be different in New Mexico—at least in heavily Democratic Bernalillo County. But even there, officials struggled for years to bring charges against Baca. Three years passed before the county appointed a special prosecutor. Only in the summer of 2023 was there any progress. In June 2023, Baca pleaded no contest to aggravated battery and guilty to battery and unlawful carrying of a deadly weapon.[54] As part of his plea deal, prosecutors agreed to drop the charges relating to the shooting. Perhaps influenced by the fact that the women he attacked asked that he not be given jail time, the presiding judge gave Baca a suspended sentence—meaning Baca won't serve any time so long as he doesn't further run afoul of the law.[55]

Friends in High Places

Steven Ray Baca's calling in a favor because he had some relatives on the force looks downright amateurish compared to the connections the McCloskeys summoned to get out of their own jam. Mark and Patricia are a well-known St. Louis power couple. They became infamous the world over when they rushed outside their sprawling manse to confront BLM protesters marching peacefully through their gated neighborhood. Far from militiamen decked out in tactical gear, Mark appeared barefoot and sporting a pink polo and rumpled khakis. Far more significantly, he brandished an AR-15 while shouting, pointing, and gesturing menacingly at those in the procession. Patricia, likewise barefoot, was decked out in a pair of black capris and a striped top. She ventured farther from her porch, where she screamed at the marchers while pointing a silver .380 pistol straight at the passersby.

At first, it seemed as if the McCloskeys would face justice for threatening BLM marchers, and charges were promptly filed against the couple.[56] But then MAGA bigwigs got involved. Donald Trump announced he was taking a keen interest in the case, and Missouri governor Mike Parson vowed to "do everything he could within his powers to help" the McCloskeys.[57] The McCloskeys pleaded guilty, and Parson—true to his word—promptly pardoned them. Far from chastened from the experience, the McCloskeys announced that they'd do it again if "faced with a similar or same situation."[58] Said Mark: "That's the whole point of the Second Amendment. We stood out there with guns, and that placed them in imminent fear of physical injury, and they back[ed] off."[59]

Republican leaders were so taken by the McCloskeys that they made them featured speakers at the 2020 Republican National Convention. Though the couple used the opportunity to rant about Democrats "abolish[ing] the suburbs,"[60] their words didn't matter much at all. Their very presence was message enough: *Right-thinking*

Americans across the nation, the Republican Party has your backs. Just as importantly, the message for those who dare clamor for racial justice was equally clear: *Get used to powerful guns being pointed in your faces—and impunity for those doing the pointing.*

Connecting those two messages and paying heed to the racial dynamics of the standoff in St. Louis bring us to a deeper, even more dispiriting maxim: (Black) protesters exercising their First Amendment rights may be curtailed by (white) gun owners menacingly exercising Second Amendment rights.

We're told that everything is bigger in Texas, and that seems to include pardons. And Greg Abbott's pardon of army sergeant Daniel Perry is a whopper. Incensed by a gathering of those protesting racism and police brutality, Perry rammed his car into a crowd of protesters. Then he repeatedly shot Garrett Foster, a Black air force veteran who cared for his wife, a quadruple amputee. An Austin jury found Perry guilty of murder,[61] and the presiding judge sentenced him to twenty-five years in prison.[62]

The day the verdict came down, Tucker Carlson tore into the prosecution, insisting that Perry acted in self-defense against a "mob of rioters."[63] Invoking a depressingly common antisemitic trope, Carlson blamed Austin's "Soros-funded" district attorney for bringing a politically motivated case.[64] The chair of the state GOP and the state's attorney general both bashed the verdict, too. The next day, the governor tweeted, "I am working as swiftly as Texas law allows regarding the pardon of Sgt. Perry."[65]

In May 2024, the state pardon board, which is stacked with Abbott appointees, recommended a full pardon for Perry.[66] Abbott quickly agreed, and the convicted murderer walked free.[67]

DRIVER'S LICENSE TO KILL

We've seen in several instances that the vigilante weapon of choice is measured in horsepower as well as caliber. And now, running down protesters is a statutory right in several states. The legalization of vehicular attacks on protesters goes to show how quickly things have changed over the past eight years, especially in red America. Spurred by what they see as righteous acts of self-defense, right-wing legislators have rushed to immunize drivers who ram into protesters.

Take Oklahoma. When Ryan Knight and fellow citizens ventured onto I-244 to protest police brutality, the state had yet to codify a "right to ram" in its statute books. Perhaps Knight thought the law would protect *him*. Or perhaps the notion that anyone, under any circumstance, would drive their car into a crowd of peaceful protesters never even crossed his mind. Whatever Knight was thinking, he and other protesters did indeed stop traffic on an elevated portion of the highway that runs through Tulsa's Greenwood District, the city's largest Black neighborhood.

Just as we don't know what legal calculations, if any, Knight was making on May 31, 2020, we also don't know anything about the state of mind of the driver of a red Dodge pickup pulling a horse trailer. Nor do we know if the driver was aware of the vicious race massacre that had occurred in Greenwood some ninety-nine years prior.

What we do know is this: This particular driver pulled out a gun and threw it onto the dashboard for the nearby protesters to see.[68] Seeing that the truck was going to barrel into them, the protesters attacked it. Inching forward at first and then gaining speed, the driver drove straight into the crowd.[69] We also know that, because of that red truck and its driver, Ryan Knight never made it across the bridge. The truck crushed a throng of people, hurling Knight off the elevated stretch and onto the ground below. When he awoke in the hospital, Knight initially couldn't swallow or breathe on his own or move his fingers. Due to his spinal cord injuries, he lost his job and was confined to a wheelchair.[70]

According to an in-depth report by the *Boston Globe*, in the sixteen months immediately following George Floyd's murder, motorists rammed their vehicles into protesters at least 139 times, killing three and injuring at least one hundred. (There were only three documented rammings between August 2017, when James Fields killed Heather Heyer in Charlottesville, and December 2019.[71]) As of late 2021, when the *Globe* published its series, felony charges had been brought against the drivers in fewer than one-quarter of the cases; and in only four instances did prosecutors secure felony convictions. To make matters worse, in some cases, district attorneys brought charges against the injured pedestrian-protesters, on such risible grounds as jaywalking or disorderly conduct.

Based on this record, it's a fairly safe bet that protesters could be rammed with near impunity. That bet certainly paid out in the Tulsa case. Still, state lawmakers weren't content to rely on the good judgment of elected district attorneys, especially in cities where Democrats tended to prevail in local elections. Refusing to leave anything to chance, the Oklahoma state legislature quickly enacted a law immunizing drivers from criminal prosecution and civil damages for hitting and even killing protesters, so long as the drivers were fleeing a riot and reasonably believed fleeing was necessary to protect themselves.[72] Following Oklahoma's lead, at least thirteen other states have considered or are considering similar *run them down* bills authorizing vehicular rammings.[73] Experts interviewed by the *Globe* observe that these laws "may be the permission some angry [constituencies] are seeking to transform their hostility to BLM and other liberal protesters into violence."[74]

So far, Iowa and Florida have joined Oklahoma. But regardless of what legislatures do, motorists are feeling emboldened. Back in the summer of 2020, months before Florida passed its law, St. Petersburg motorists were held up by BLM marchers blocking a roadway. One passerby shouted to the drivers, urging those caught up in the melee to ram the protesters. Her words reflected the astonishing extent to which vehicular homicide seems like a sensible and justifiable tool against those nonviolently clamoring for racial justice. Raising her voice for all to hear, she announced: "You can run them over. DeSantis said so!"[75]

KEEPING UP WITH KYLE

One cannot talk about legalized street violence without considering a figure we've already mentioned: "American Vigilante" Kyle Rittenhouse.[76] On August 24, 2020, the then-seventeen-year-old left his home in Antioch, Illinois, and drove north, crossing the state line into Wisconsin.[77] Rittenhouse was headed to Kenosha, where a white police officer had just shot Jacob Blake, a Black resident, seven times in the back and side as he attempted to get into his car. The shooting, captured on video, prompted outrage and drew protests. Right-wing social media took note as well. Triggered by the fires and other forms of property damage incident to the protests, posters urged citizens to "take up arms to defend [Kenosha] tonight from the evil thugs."[78]

Rittenhouse heeded the call. During the day of August 25, he helped remove graffiti. That night, carrying both a med kit and an AR-15, Rittenhouse stood guard with other armed men protecting a used-car dealership; he conversed with Kenosha police, one of whom told the boy that "We appreciate you guys. We really do."[79] And then, about an hour after that exchange with a cop, Rittenhouse mixed it up with some of the racial justice protesters.

One of these individuals baited Rittenhouse and his armed comrades, screaming at them. This man then chased Rittenhouse and threw a plastic bag containing toiletries at him, then lunged for Rittenhouse's gun. Rittenhouse fired four times, killing the protester.

When he discharged his weapon, Rittenhouse didn't reach for the med kit he was carrying. He didn't dial 911. Instead, he stood over the man, called a friend, and exclaimed, "I just shot somebody!" Then he ran down the street, where protesters who'd witnessed the shooting tried to disarm him. Rittenhouse tripped and fell, then fired at one protester who had hit him with a skateboard. This shooting was fatal, too. Then a third protester, this one armed with a handgun, continued the pursuit. Rittenhouse shot him as well, severing the victim's biceps.

As police arrived at the scene, Rittenhouse approached a police cruiser. One officer reportedly told him, "No—*go.*" Rittenhouse then made his way back to Illinois and had to be extradited to face prosecution in Wisconsin.

At trial, the prosecution emphasized that Rittenhouse, whom they labeled a "chaos tourist,"[80] had crossed state lines to confront protesters. Buoyed by a friendly Wisconsin jury and a seemingly brazenly sympathetic judge who insisted prosecutors could not refer to Rittenhouse's victims *as victims*, Rittenhouse was acquitted on all charges.[81]

Moments after the verdict was announced, Rittenhouse pivoted into celebrity vigilante mode. He made a beeline to the Fox News camera crew waiting outside the courthouse. We'd later learn that the gunman had already entered into a deal with Fox to produce a documentary hosted by Tucker Carlson.[82] In the months that followed, Fox News continued to provide a steady stream of pro-Rittenhouse content.

Trump also took a shine to him, speaking favorably about him on Sean Hannity's show and welcoming Rittenhouse and his mother to Mar-a-Lago. Rittenhouse was "adopted as an informal mascot" by the Proud Boys, who "serenaded" him at a bar.[83] The group's leader, Enrique Tarrio, was photographed wearing a T-shirt that read, "Kyle Rittenhouse Did Nothing Wrong!"[84] (Since then, Tarrio has been found guilty of seditious conspiracy for his role in the January 6 insurrection and is serving a twenty-two-year prison term.) Far-right members of Congress proposed to arm wrestle over who would get the privilege of recruiting the high school dropout to join their staff[85]—and Marjorie Taylor Greene introduced a bill to award him the Congressional Gold Medal.[86]

To this day, Rittenhouse continues to milk his fame. He has an online store selling merchandise, does public events (where a $275 VIP pass gets you some face-to-face time and a selfie), has a video game called *Kyle Rittenhouse's Turkey Shoot*, and has his own YouTube channel.[87] His book, titled *Acquitted*, is dedicated to his therapy dog.[88] Rittenhouse, who according to his attorney is broke,[89] remains a regular on the fringier right-wing media platforms and has appeared on Donald Trump, Jr.'s show, where he offered up wild antisemitic conspiracy theories.[90]

BACK TO TULSA AND ON TO WACO

Forty years after Reagan's dog-whistling speech in Philadelphia, Mississippi, another Republican presidential candidate, this one an incumbent, journeyed to Tulsa, Oklahoma, to jump-start his campaign.

The Tulsa Race Riot, June 1, 1921. (Library of Congress)

The year 2020 was a tough one for Trump. After months of hunkering down amid the worsening Covid pandemic, the GOP base was restive. They were incensed over government officials' decisions to prioritize community health over individual liberty; they were agitated by (false) reports that the coming election would be "stolen"; and they were furious over the burgeoning BLM movement.

Like Philadelphia, Tulsa drips with symbolism. As we mentioned above, Tulsa is the site of one of the most devastating race massacres in American history. In 1921, rabid white residents—some operating with tacit, others with explicit, state support—burned the homes and businesses of Black families in the city's Greenwood District. They rounded up thousands of Black residents, beat hundreds, and killed perhaps hundreds more.

Trump initially scheduled his rally for June 19—*Juneteenth!*—the holiday commemorating the end of slavery. Tremendous local opposition to the timing—even Tulsa's Republican mayor announced he'd skip the event—prompted the campaign to push the event back a day.[91] In hindsight, it's clear why the stubborn and usually shameless Trump agreed to reschedule. He knew the content of the speech would be sufficiently incendiary.

Whereas Reagan dog-whistled through Dixie, Trump hollered through what Republicans insist is America's Heartland. Trump insisted Black BLM protesters were a threat to honest, law-abiding (white) citizens—the "forgotten men and women" for whom he campaigned. Hardly "conservative" in the way Reagan was, and unmistakably resentful of the Establishment that had dominated the postwar Republican Party, Trump had long been palling around with the kind of white supremacists who would make David Duke blush.

That day in Tulsa, Trump laid it on thick. He championed symbols of the Confederacy (accusing Democrats of working to "vandalize *our* history" and "desecrate *our* monuments"). He warned his base that a "President" Biden would seize Republicans' guns and "prosecute [them] for going to church." In "Joe Biden's America," Trump added, "rioters, looters, and criminal aliens have more rights than law-abiding citizens." And in Joe Biden's America, "we'll lose everything."[92]

Trump continued to gripe about Black protesters, equating them with violent criminals and accusing them of ravaging cities and perpetrating mayhem. He congratulated his base—"our people"—for not being "nearly as violent." Turning on a dime, he added, "but if [his MAGA loyalists] ever were [to respond with violence], it would be a terrible, terrible day for the other side. Because I know our people. I know our people. . . . We will never submit to their threats, and we will never let them destroy our nation." Indeed, he said, "when you see those lunatics all over the streets, it's damn nice to have arms. Damn nice."[93]

Of course, Trump did not prevail in November 2020. Nor in December 2020 or January 2021, despite all sorts of desperate and violent gambits to cling to power. But neither his resounding defeats at the polls, in the courts, and on January 6, nor his second impeachment has stopped him from celebrating vigilantism and seemingly embracing it to further both his political campaign and his criminal defense.

Already a noxious mix of party boss and cult leader, the volatile MAGA leader had to go to even greater extremes to kick off his bid for the 2024 presidency. His choice of venue was Waco, Texas, and the date would be March 2023, precisely thirty years after the gruesome, seven-week-long standoff that occurred there between the heavily armed, apocalyptic Branch Davidians and federal law enforcement—a standoff that, for many who run in far-right militia circles, marked a turning point in American history.

Trump's rally in Waco began with the playing of a song recorded by, get this, the *January 6 Prison Choir*. Trump then proceeded to rant about transgender activists, Ron DeSantis, the prosecutors leading the varied investigations against him, elected Democrats, and the Deep State.[94]

Even to those long accustomed to his coarse, vulgar, and menacing tirades, Trump's language was jarring. He called the upcoming presidential race "the final battle," insisting either "the Deep State destroys America or we destroy the Deep State." And he professed: "I am your warrior, I am your justice." Tapping into the fury that he himself has been manufacturing and stoking for the better part of a decade, he announced: "For those who have been wronged and betrayed . . . I am your retribution."[95]

As much as Trump's political surrogates urge mainstream audiences not to read deeper, let alone sinister, meaning into campaign slogans and the candidate's turns of phrase (including the vile claim that immigrants are "poisoning the blood of our country"), we all know exactly what the man intends to convey to his MAGA base. There's every reason to believe that's just as true when it comes to venue selection. And it's worth contrasting the Waco event not only with most ordinary campaign events but also with the 2020 Tulsa kickoff. The Tulsa race riots exemplified the fusion of right-wing, racist private and public power. Waco, where heavily armed antigovernment cultists made their bloody, fiery stand, represents an inflection point where members of the radical Right turned against the FBI and any other form of federal law enforcement.

In between Tulsa and Waco was, of course, January 6 at the U.S. Capitol. On that day, when the Capitol Police made clear they weren't backing the insurrectionists' play, approximately 140 officers were physically assaulted, one of whom was fatally wounded, and countless more were physically menaced and verbally abused. Four officers have since taken their own lives, a good number still suffer from physical and psychological trauma, and no shortage of the corps continue to endure threats and other forms of harassment.

After the FBI raided Mar-a-Lago in August 2022 (in conjunction with the investigation of Trump's alleged mishandling of classified information), Congressman Ronny Jackson tweeted, "Tonight the FBI officially became the enemy of the people!!!"[96] And as that tweet was making the rounds, a gun-wielding man wearing body armor—and who had ties to January 6—sought to penetrate the FBI building in Cincinnati. The man, whom law enforcement officers killed after a series of standoffs, had taken to social media to call for violence against the feds. More recently, MAGA faithful have been engaging in sustained and increasingly violent campaigns harassing and threatening prosecutors, sheriffs, judges, and court staff across the various jurisdictions where criminal and civil proceedings against Trump are underway.[97]

We've said before that the Republican Party keeps marching further and harder to the right with every single election cycle. With indictments, civil judgments, and at least one guilty verdict hanging over the former president's head, Trump may well frame his war against the government as a religious, messianic, perhaps even eschatological imperative.

Appreciating that, with or without Trump, MAGA Republicanism isn't going anywhere anytime soon—and that everything about the political movement is getting more violent, more erratic, and more antagonistic to the state—we must ready ourselves for the possible arrival of a newer, truer, even more chaotic phase of Vigilante Democracy. This new phase would be one in which private violence may be legitimated by the Republican Party as well as the state. And if that's the phase we're entering, then our relevant points of comparison are no longer to Jim Crow America but rather to National Socialist Germany.

CHAPTER **8**

"We're Going to Be Watching"
Electoral Vigilantism

I t was December 2020, and Kacey Rae Bowers's days were numbered. The punishing impact of liver cancer had brought the forty-two-year-old Arizonan back to her parents' modest home in the suburbs of Phoenix. It was a home that had long welcomed children and grand-children, fellow members of the Mormon church, and everybody and anybody in Arizona Republican politics. Rusty, the family patriarch and Speaker of the state's House of Representatives, was a tireless campaigner for Republican candidates, Donald Trump included.[1]

Yet neither Rusty's Republican bona fides nor compassion for his dying daughter protected the family from the hordes of vigilantes who descended on—and, as the *Washington Post* described it, "practically occupied"—the Speaker's neighborhood.[2] The reason? Rusty wouldn't help Trump invalidate the 2020 election.

Raucous and monstrous protests featured "Trump trains." For days on end, drivers formed caravans, blaring their horns and waving MAGA flags. Trucks carrying video billboards baselessly, and scurrilously, labeled Rusty a pedophile. Inside, Rusty's wife tended as best she could to Kacey Rae.

Thanks to permissive firearms laws that Rusty himself had helped pass, just about anyone in Arizona can openly carry weapons, no permit needed.[3] In one episode during the protests, Bowers confronted an armed man associated with the Three Percenters. Fearing the man, who was screaming obscenities, would go for his gun, Rusty stayed close so he could wrestle it out of his hands if necessary.[4]

It wasn't just street thugs applying pressure. Donald Trump, Rudy Giuliani, and John Eastman all pushed Rusty to back their scheme. One of Rusty's colleagues in the state legislature doxed him, posting the Speaker's home address and cell phone number on Twitter.[5]

Rusty stood firm, and Arizona awarded its eleven electoral votes to Joe Biden, as the voters had directed. But, of course, the MAGA world was far from willing to move on.

After the failed insurrection on January 6, Republicans knew they needed to clean house. Rusty was quickly disposed of: The Arizona Republican Party censured him, and in 2022 the party threw its support behind a far-right primary opponent, who routed the veteran legislator.[6] In that election cycle and the ones that followed, the MAGA machine would back extremists with little regard for democracy or the rule of law. The machine would do so not only for candidates seeking statewide office but also for those vying for seats on local boards or municipal councils.

The marshaling of private power to control who votes, determine how elections are conducted, and manipulate the counting of the votes falls under the umbrella category we call *electoral vigilantism*. It's perhaps fitting that this last type of legalized vigilantism derives its tremendous potency from pulling together elements of our first three—namely, dissenter, street, and courthouse vigilantism. After all, political power is ultimately what it's all about: the forceful assurance that a privileged, minority faction can implement its cultural and moral agenda without building or sustaining a popular mandate.

"ELECTIONS ARE NOT WON BY A MAJORITY OF PEOPLE, THEY NEVER HAVE BEEN"

Remember Ronald Reagan's incendiary 1980 "states' rights" speech? Just weeks after Reagan whistled Dixie in Neshoba County, Mississippi,

Paul Weyrich, cofounder of the Heritage Foundation, the Moral Majority, and the American Legislative Exchange Council (that's right, all three) was eager to share his thoughts on how to turn back the clock to before the era of democratic liberalism. Speaking to the "Religious Roundtable,"[7] whose members included powerhouse evangelicals like Tim LaHaye and Pat Robertson, activists such as Phyllis Schlafly, and the Gipper himself, Weyrich rebuked faith leaders who championed civil rights and democratic equality. "Many of our Christians have what I call the goo-goo syndrome—good government," he sneered. "They want everybody to vote." This, Weyrich insisted, was a mistake. "Elections are not won by a majority of people, they never have been from the beginning of our country and they are not now. As a matter of fact, *our* leverage in the elections quite candidly goes up as the voting populace goes down."[8] In other words, in order to win elections, the Christian Right needed to make sure those other Americans didn't vote.

It took decades for Weyrich's message to go mainstream, no doubt because any threat to white Christian political power back then seemed (and was) remote. Now, of course, things are very different, and we're seeing a marked uptick in efforts to keep people—mainly people of color—from registering to vote, deter those registered from voting, and manipulate election results. After Trump's loss in 2020, red state legislatures went into overdrive, enacting a wave of voting restrictions.[9] The stated rationale was to prevent another election from being "stolen"—or as Weyrich might put it, from being won by a majority of the electorate.

These so-called election integrity measures are largely enforced by government bodies, like election boards, secretary of state offices, and state governors' offices. The more draconian measures are even enforced by police and prosecutors, who are charged with rooting out illegal voting. But state enforcement is not necessarily ideal. Government efforts to block people from voting or discard their votes are deeply unpopular; actions undertaken by state officials are, as we've explained in earlier chapters, subject to far more searching constitutional scrutiny; and indications that the state is interfering with voting rights are likely to galvanize targeted communities, increasing voter turnout and raising awareness among those voters to make sure they're fastidious when casting their ballots (to guard against challenges). So, as they've done in other contexts, here, too, right-wing leaders have turned to vigilantes for critical support.

THE PLAYBOOK
Go Local

America's election system is jaw-droppingly decentralized. There is no federal election authority that delineates district lines for federal office, administers nationwide elections, and ensures votes in those elections are counted fully and fairly. Subject to limited federal protections against, for example, racial discrimination and poll taxes, the states are otherwise free to run elections as they see fit. And because the states typically delegate to counties and other localities much of the work of administering elections—and because many localities rely heavily on part-time employees and heaps of volunteers (who are generally not well trained and are unlikely to be held legally accountable for abusive or careless work)—opportunities for voting irregularities are rife. But, curiously enough, there is very little election fraud, certainly not of the sort Donald Trump convinced a huge number of Republicans happened in November 2020.[10] What we have in spades is a long history of voter intimidation, voter suppression, and voter disenfranchisement campaigns, which of course were devastatingly successful during Jim Crow and which are making something of a comeback today.

The stakes, of course, couldn't be higher. Presidential races now turn on a handful of districts in a handful of swing states. If vigilantes can interfere with even a small subset of the ballots cast in those districts, they can radically change the course of not only this nation but the entire world.

DIY Voter Disqualification

In the resulting state-level battles, Georgia has been host to some of the most hard-fought and consequential contests in recent years. Democratic victories by Joe Biden and Senators Jon Ossoff and Raphael Warnock signaled that the Peach State, long considered solidly red, was increasingly competitive.[11] Recognizing that demographic changes continue to favor the Democratic Party—and that their days in office may be numbered—the state's MAGA leaders have been working on strategies to hold on to power. They're not doing so by, say, abandoning far-right policies and rhetoric in an attempt to woo centrists and even moderate Democrats and bring them into the Republican camp. Rather, they're prioritizing voter disqualification and suppression. Over the past few years, they've even criminalized get-out-the-vote efforts and banned folks from handing out water or food to voters queued up and waiting their turn in Georgia's scandalously lengthy poll lines.[12] And, as we've seen time and again, they're doing plenty to leverage the power (and implied terror) of citizen enforcement.

A case in point is Georgia's voter challenge law. This law invites "any elector [that is, voter] of the county or municipality" to "challenge the right of any other elector of the county or municipality, whose name appears on the list of electors, to vote in an election."[13] Though some version of the law had been on the books since 1994, Georgia supercharged the power of challengers in 2022, eliminating restrictions on the number of objections any one challenger may lodge.[14] Given the difficulties with voting and the already sky-high tensions around politics these days, the threat posed by a few people bringing wholesale objections as a form of electoral sabotage is real. Even if these objections just gum up the works, making already slow lines that much slower, they may deter some percentage of voters from staying in line. The hassles, conflicts, and risk that a confrontation turns violent may also keep those likely to be targeted for suppression far away from the polls.

Jennifer Jones felt the pressure.[15] A med student at Morehouse, one of Atlanta's storied historically Black schools, Jones arrived at her precinct in Fulton County, Georgia, to vote in the 2022 midterm elections. "When I handed in my ID, the poll worker said I was being challenged," she told the *Guardian*. "The poll worker didn't tell me why I was being challenged, even after calling someone else for assistance. . . . They just kept telling me I would have to vote with a provisional ballot." Jones "wasn't really comfortable doing that." As she reports: "I didn't get to cast my ballot that day."[16]

Like Georgia, Virginia has become something of a swing state. So there, too, every vote is of utmost importance. Virginia also deputizes citizen-enforcers, who by law can hang around any polling place and challenge people as they walk in to vote.[17] Though the laws of Georgia and Virginia are written in terms that suggest Black city dwellers are just as capable of journeying out to the exurbs and challenging white voters as the other way around, we know legal vigilantism won't play out that way. And let's face it: In practice, white voters are generally going to be able to get far more traction as citizen-enforcers than Black ones will. Just as importantly, we suspect Black voters—all too familiar with the dangers of standoffs with both white civilians and police officers—are going to be more readily and easily deterred from voting even when challenges to their voting status are beyond frivolous. Jennifer Jones may be an ace student well on her way to becoming a top surgeon. But a dumb dispute over her voter registration runs the risk of derailing those life plans. And that's precisely why these vigilante statutes are so devastatingly effective, not to mention one-sided.

And where are these challenges going to come from? MAGA world is not leaving things to chance. National leaders are providing considerable encouragement and institutional support. Not long after assisting Donald Trump in his various attempts to overturn the 2020 election, Trump lawyer Cleta Mitchell published a handbook encouraging right-wing activists to "purchase or acquire a current copy of the voter registration database" in their home counties, and "learn the process used by your local election office for removing invalid registrations."[18] The objective, Mitchell said, was to create "a volunteer army of citizens" to police elections.[19]

In 2021, True the Vote, the Houston-based group behind Dinesh D'Souza's misinformation-riddled propaganda flick *2000 Mules*, filed pre–Election Day challenges to some 360,000 voters in Georgia's crucial Senate runoff elections—the races that would determine which party controlled the Senate.[20] The following year, right-wing groups challenged 65,000 voter registrations across eight counties in Georgia. A Michigan activist group challenged 22,000 primary ballots from voters who had requested absentee ballots.[21] By 2024, right-wing citizen-activists in practically every presidential swing state were employing a variety of measures—everything from comparing voter registration and lease agreement addresses to using a mobile app to detect any discrepancies between voter-disclosed addresses and postal service change-of-address listings—to challenge the eligibility of sizeable numbers of disproportionately young, immigrant, urban-dwelling, and/or lower-income (likely Democratic) voters.[22]

It's true that these challenges for the most part haven't succeeded in removing large numbers of voters from the rolls. But, again, the hassles and headaches are real, and they have a secondary effect of perpetuating the lie that voter fraud is rampant in America. Said one former elections director in Michigan: "They are just going to beat the system into the ground."[23]

DIY Poll Watching

Voters who manage to stay on the registration rolls must still manage to actually cast their ballots and then hope their votes are properly counted. Tragically, vigilantes have targeted these steps, too.

Some of their attacks are little more than updated versions of Jim Crow–style terrorism. In 2022, an Arizona-based "patriot group" with links to the Oath Keepers organized armed, round-the-clock surveillance of ballot drop boxes during the midterm elections.[24]

Other campaigns are far more organized and appear more respectable. That same year, the Republican National Committee made a multimillion-dollar investment, hiring eighteen state "election integrity" directors and nineteen state "election integrity" lawyers across the nation. They recruited more than five thousand poll watchers and nearly twelve thousand poll workers. Along with Cleta Mitchell's "army of citizens" and Steve Bannon's *War Room* listeners, whom Bannon urged to fill any and all local precinct offices,[25] the GOP committed itself to keeping fraudulent (read: Democratic) votes from being cast and counted.[26]

Vigilante Ballot Subversion

The U.S. election administration regime is not only decentralized; it's also rather amateurish. That's not to impugn the integrity or competency of this crucial workforce. To the contrary, these capable and diligent workers are all the more admirable given that many are part-time or seasonal employees, while still others are volunteers and partisan observers.

And, until recently, they have had some help. Throughout the era of democratic liberalism, widespread buy-in to free, fair, and secure elections helped ensure that we didn't experience anything approximating rampant fraud, sabotage, or acts of intimidation. Because everyone for the most part played by the rules, our amateurish system didn't seem especially vulnerable, let alone cry out for a massive upgrade.

Unfortunately, not everyone still wants to play by the rules. And a regime that relied on good-faith participation presented a soft, easy target for politicos and their deputized vigilantes intent on sabotage.

One of the most notorious incidents took place during the 2020 election in Fulton County, Georgia. Initial reports based on partial vote counts had the incumbent Trump leading Joe Biden by a small margin. But most understood that mail-in ballots, predicted to skew heavily Democratic, were yet to be tabulated. The Trump team decided its best, win-at-all-costs move was to insist that Georgia stop counting ballots and declare its candidate the winner. For that ploy to work, the campaign had to make the public believe that the not-yet-counted ballots were surely fraudulent.

All eyes turned to State Farm Arena. Known to many as the home court for the Atlanta Hawks, the mega sports and entertainment facility had been repurposed by Fulton County to process the flood of mail-in ballots cast during the Covid pandemic.[27] The morning of the election, a clogged urinal caused a small flood that necessitated a temporary pause in the counting of the votes. Plumbers quickly fixed the issue, but the disruption gave Republican campaign operatives an excuse to peddle conspiracy theories about election fraud in the largest Democratic county in the state. Notwithstanding the chatting and griping, the officials at State Farm Arena continued processing ballots until approximately 10:30 p.m., when the county elections director told the workers to go home for the night; they could pick up where they left off in their tallies the following morning.

Shaye Moss and Ruby Freeman had worked for the Fulton County Department of Voter Registration and Elections for years. Moss is Freeman's daughter and had gotten the idea of working for the elections office from her mom, who had long picked up temp work helping to tabulate ballots.

When their boss advised them to stop counting and go home, Moss and Freeman sealed the yet-to-be-processed ballots in a plastic container and placed the container underneath a table in their workspace. But before Moss, Freeman, or any of their colleagues had a chance to leave, word came down that the Georgia secretary of state had countermanded the county director's order. The state wanted them to keep working.

Heeding the new instructions, Moss and Freeman retrieved the box, unsealed it, and went back to work. No big deal, right? Moss and Freeman knew that their every move was being recorded by closed-circuit TV cameras but thought nothing of it. That was just how elections worked.

Fast-forward to early December.[28] By then, all the votes had been counted, and Biden had been declared the winner in Georgia and was entitled to the Peach State's sixteen electoral votes. Team Trump, however, wasn't about to concede. On December 4, 2020, Rudy Giuliani appeared before a committee of Georgia state senators to argue that they should disregard the popular vote in the state and certify a slate of Trump electors to the Electoral College. The justification for this shocking proposal? A supposed plot by Shaye Moss and Ruby Freeman to rig the election for Biden.

As video of the State Farm Arena played, one of Giuliani's lieutenants explained how Moss (the "lady with the blonde braids") and Freeman (an "older" woman with the "name of Ruby" on her shirt) ferreted "suitcases" of fake Biden ballots into the ballot counting room. The mother-daughter duo then processed the fake ballots during the time when election observers, misled into believing that ballot counting for the night had concluded, were not present. Video of the hearing went viral. On the night of December 4, Sean Hannity devoted time during his Fox News broadcast to portray the Giuliani presentation as a "bombshell"— one that showed "what appears to be extensive law violations."[29] Other outlets had already identified Ruby Freeman by name.[30]

That's all Trump-loving vigilantes needed to initiate a campaign of violent, racist terror against Freeman, Moss, and their family. Soon Freeman's Facebook Messenger inbox was flooded with death threats and messages calling her the N-word. Trump enthusiasts combed the Internet for more personal information and found the cell phone number of Moss's fourteen-year-old son, whom they relentlessly harassed, preventing him from using the phone for online classes.

Trump and either his White House or campaign staff could have called off the mob, but instead, they joined in. Trump appeared at a Georgia rally in support of Senator David Perdue, who was in the midst of a tight runoff election against Jon Ossoff. In a rambling December 5 speech in Valdosta, Georgia, Trump played right-wing "news" clips featuring Moss and Freeman that repeated the entirely fabricated allegation that the pair had perpetrated massive ballot fraud.[31] A few days later, in a Zoom call with Georgia lawmakers, Giuliani served up a heavy dish of outlandish conspiracy theories, which he seasoned with a dash of old-school racism.[32] Giuliani claimed that some breath mints passed between Freeman and Moss were "USB [data] ports" that the pair treated "as if they [we]re vials of heroin or cocaine." He alleged that Moss and Freeman were the masterminds of the early-morning plumbing problems in the men's room. They created a distraction, he baselessly claimed, in order to sneak in the suitcases of fake ballots.

With Trump and his surrogates whipping the MAGA base into a frenzy, it didn't take long for the verbal harassment of Moss and Freeman to turn physical. A crowd of election deniers spouting QAnon nonsense showed up at Moss's grandmother's house (where Moss and her teenage son lived), attempted to break in, pushed the grandmother, and sought to effect a "citizen's arrest." Freeman, too, was directly targeted. By the time Congress was set to convene on January 6, both Moss and Freeman had gone underground. "We know where you live, n-----, we coming to get you," Freeman recalled messages saying.[33]

The attacks on Moss and Freeman made national news, led to a $148 million defamation judgment against Giuliani, and are described as elements of the alleged criminal enterprise that has led Georgia to indict Trump and more than a dozen of his confederates. But what Moss and Freeman experienced wasn't unique. Ballot counters were menaced in key counties in several swing states. On November 4, 2020, one day after the election, Trump diehards descended on Detroit's downtown convention center. Knowing Wayne County voters, particularly those in Detroit proper, were casting their ballots for Joe Biden (and presuming some sort of voter fraud), these partisans sought to keep election workers from tallying the votes.[34]

A group called Michigan Trump Republicans took to Facebook to summon a posse: "Who is available to go to [the Detroit convention center] right now to help monitor the vote? 35K ballots showed up out of nowhere at 3 am. Need help."[35] By 1 p.m., 227 Republican "observers" had made their way onto the counting floor, succeeding at least temporarily in thwarting the workers' efforts to count the votes. Democratic election observer Khaliluh Gaston recalled hearing one of her Republican counterparts instruct other Republicans to "challenge every single ballot."[36] "Even before a ballot hit the table, they were saying, 'We're going to challenge every ballot at this table.'"[37]

As word got out that Biden's lead in Michigan was widening, the Republicans in downtown Detroit pressed harder. They formed a circle around tables where election workers were tabulating votes and began chanting, "Stop the count! Stop the count!"[38] As if those already on the floor weren't doing enough to harass and intimidate the election workers, more MAGA observers were clamoring to get into the counting room. Finally, county officials had to lock the doors, denying admission to newcomers.

Chaos ensued. Trump boosters denied admission screamed at police and banged on the windows overlooking the counting room. Under Wayne County rules, only members of the media were authorized to photograph the counting process. With a menacing mob glaring in, county officials decided to cover the windows. This further enraged the crowd. The journalists in attendance turned their cameras on the mob, showing the entire nation the terrifying scene of ordinary suburbanites wildly, furiously pounding their fists on the windows while howling at the ballot counters and the police alike.

Against all odds, the election workers in Detroit and Atlanta completed accurate counts of their respective counties' ballots. (Multiple recounts and independent audits corroborated the original tallies.) But it doesn't take much imagination to realize how much worse things could have been had the vigilantes had the law on their side—that is, if they had more capacious rights to challenge, interfere with, or menace vote counters; if the police didn't back the election officials pleading for order to be restored; or if, as he has since done, Donald

Trump promised to grant federal pardons to any and all who advanced his election interests.

Purging and Capturing Precincts

Similar but slightly different versions of these 2020 sagas played out in Maricopa County, Arizona,[39] and Clark County, Nevada—both key urban (and heavily Democratic) counties located in swing states.[40] The medium- and long-term damage to our electoral system from these chaotic spurts of mayhem is still being tallied. "Can you imagine what it's like to feel responsible for your grandmother, your mother, your teenage son being threatened and lied about over and over again, to be singled out as a criminal, to be accused of treason in the only country you've ever called home?" asked Georgia's Shaye Moss, explaining why she had no plans to resume her work as an election official.[41] "Because of the lies," she told investigators, "I've lost who I was, and I'll never be again able to do the work that I felt called to do."[42]

Unsurprisingly, others have arrived at the same conclusion. According to surveys compiled in spring 2023, about 23 percent of all election workers on the job in November 2020 have already resigned or will resign before November 2024.[43] By fall 2023, CNN had reported that fifty-three of North Carolina's one hundred chief county election officials had left their posts[44]—no small loss especially as strategists suggest North Carolina may be competitive in 2024.[45]

The battleground state of Arizona has lost several key election officials. In her resignation letter, Pinal County's election director expressed frustration that the county leadership was capitulating to extremists in the Republican Party and did nothing to protect her from "intimidation."[46] Similar resignations occurred in Yavapai County, where both the county recorder and elections director quit.[47] Yet a third county in Arizona, Cochise County, saw a committed public servant forced out of her job. Lisa Marra, the county elections director, had endured unceasing pressure by local Republican officials to release ballots for a full hand count (something that's prohibited by state law) and, barring that, simply to invalidate the fall 2022 election results. Though she stayed in place long enough to preserve the integrity of that election cycle, she left soon after, citing an "outrageous and physically and emotionally threatening" workplace.[48]

Even solidly red states like Texas are a breeding ground for election tumult. In 2022, the entire senior election administration staff in Gillespie County, Texas, resigned. The chief of the office's resignation letter cited "the threats against election officials and my election staff, dangerous misinformation . . . and absurd [voter suppression] legislation."[49] And in Tarrant County, home to the city of Fort Worth, the now-former head of elections had been targeted by doxing campaigns, death threats, and racial attacks. Despite these attacks beginning in the November 2020 election—and despite her seemingly unanswered pleas to Congress to provide greater protection for election workers nationwide—Heider Garcia remained at her post until 2023. What pushed her to finally retire was the creation of a new election integrity task force (of the sort we described earlier in the chapter) to even more aggressively police supposed voter fraud.[50]

Similar stories can be told in Buckingham County, Virginia, where the entire election staff quit in response to relentless attacks and (entirely unsubstantiated) allegations of voter fraud by county officials. One such official, calling for audits and accusing the staff of not knowing the law, advised the elections director: "I am putting you on notice—for treason!"[51] Much the same thing happened in Lincoln County, Montana, where the entire election staff resigned due to wild allegations of fraud and abuse raised by the local elected officials. One of the resigning officials indicated that "election staff are fearful of attending [county] commissioner meetings, and rightfully so. There is zero support from the commissioners. [My colleagues] are leaving their positions under severe distress and anxiety."[52]

Most of these departures occurred either just as or soon after Donald

Trump started to ramp up the violent rhetoric that has become a staple of his campaign speeches. In 2023, Trump was vowing "retribution" for the supposed travesties perpetrated by his enemies in the federal government.[53] And he was securing his status as GOP front-runner by insisting: "Either the Deep State destroys America or we destroy the Deep State."[54] In that environment, even metaphorical allusions to violence—like Ron DeSantis's promise to "start slitting [the] throats" of federal civil servants on his first day in the White House—can't be written off as mere rhetoric.[55] Certainly not once we turned the calendar to 2024 and the claims intensified and became more explicit. In March, Trump assured his rallygoers that he will pardon the January 6 Capitol rioters (whom he calls "hostages")[56] and bring charges against members of the January 6 Committee and their witnesses.[57] He also warned his base—and, even more so, anyone thinking of voting against him—that there will be "a bloodbath" if Joe Biden prevails in November.[58]

Certainly, Rusty Bowers's state is taking these threats seriously. Charles Pierce of *Esquire* calls the Maricopa County vote-counting center "ground zero for potential election-related violence."[59] In many respects, Arizona is in better shape than other must-win jurisdictions. The governor, secretary of state, and attorney general are all Democrats committed to safeguarding American democracy. And Maricopa has a host of county officials who've proven to be serious and responsible (so much so that they incurred barrages of threats in both 2020 and 2022). Steeling themselves for November 2024, they're turning the county tabulation center into a fortress.

As reported in *Talking Points Memo*, the center "now has permanent fencing, a badge requirement to even enter the parking lot as well as additional badges to enter the building, metal detectors upon entering the building, and netting on the temporary fencing in the parking lot so that voters cannot take pictures of election workers or their license plates."[60] One county supervisor expressed some regret that they can't secure polling places to the same degree, underscoring that they don't want to "unintentionally creat[e] an environment where voters feel intimidated."[61] Undercover law enforcement officers will, however, be strategically situated throughout the county.[62]

While the greater Phoenix metro area readies itself for intense political violence of the sort normally associated only with failing, if not failed, nation-states, we are reminded of Harry Dunn, the Capitol Police officer. The question he asked his colleague on the afternoon of January 6, 2021, is the same one that haunts us to this day: *Is this America?* Given how far the January 7 Project and Vigilante Democracy have advanced in the intervening three-plus years, we're forced to answer in the affirmative.

VIGILANTE CAPTURE

With each passing campaign of harassment, despoilment, and chaos, the chances increase that vigilantes and their allies will be on the *inside*. They will have pressured current, conscientious government officials to resign; deterred potential competitors from applying or running for office; and, having cleared the field, seized positions as election administrators, city council members, and even county supervisors. Once in place, these officials will essentially function as Jim Crow politicos for the twenty-first century, commingling state power and vigilante violence to ensure that groups who challenge the white Christian nationalist agenda are systematically denied political power and civil rights.

Perhaps sooner than anyone expected, this is already happening.[63] Drive north a few hours from Sacramento, and you'll find yourself in the rolling foothills of Shasta County, California. Living amid a trio of national forests, the people of Shasta are just as striking as the landscapes. Shasta is much whiter and considerably further to the political right than the rest of California. In 2016, Shasta County's voters broke two-for-one for Donald Trump.[64] Four years later, Trump's share of the vote was essentially unchanged.[65]

Enthusiasm for Trump in Shasta has had a lot more to do with his do-it-yourself approach to justice, which we described in Chapter 4, than with, say, his policies on taxes or trade. Shasta is awash in guns, and far-right militia groups are prevalent. Commitments to private law enforcement run deep there, too. Robert Ellickson's seminal study *Order Without Law* explored how Shasta residents relied principally on self-policing methods (rather than on the police or courts of law) to resolve property disputes.[66]

One could read Ellickson's account as one of virtue, or at least a particular kind of virtue. The people of Shasta had tight, cohesive bonds to one another, so much so that they took it upon themselves to handle any problems that arose. They didn't need to lawyer up or run to the police for help. But, it's hard to overlook the potential for serious, even lethal, bullying—for ganging up on those who couldn't or wouldn't conform to the dominant ethos of a community unreceptive to new ideas and perspectives.

We certainly can't draw a direct connection between the crews of Shasta cattlemen Ellickson studied in the 1980s and those that came together to form the Cottonwood Militia shortly after the 2008 presidential election. But, in the Cottonwood Militia, we see a similar distrust in (or disregard for) democratic processes and institutions, and a corresponding faith in the leading residents of Shasta to develop and enforce their own moral code.

Right around the time America elected its first Black president, a Shasta County barber named Paul "Woody" Clendenen helped launch the Cottonwood Militia.[67] Clendenen likes to emphasize the militia's political activities.[68] But what passes for political activism in Shasta might just as easily be mistaken for campaigns of intimidation, coercion, and violence. When Black Lives Matter supporters marched through Shasta's county seat of Redding in 2020, for instance, armed militia members mobilized, ostensibly to protect local businesses from the peaceful protesters.

But even before the modest BLM rally, the militia members were restive. Clendenen and his crew were furious at the Shasta County

Board of Supervisors. The Cottonwood Militia insisted that the supervisors—Republicans all—weren't doing enough to defy the state's aggressive public health measures instituted to protect Californians from the then-raging pandemic.

They also were angry at townspeople who complied with those measures. That same summer, militiamen threatened residents with retribution if any of them complained about businesses that did not enforce the then-extant masking or social distancing regulations: "Don't think," Woody Clendenen said in one video posted to social media, that "we are going to forget who you are because we are not going to. We know who you are."[69] Clendenen had a sidekick in this video, a man named Carlos Zapata. Zapata chimed in to warn that the Cottonwood Militia was keeping tabs on residents. "We also have people on the streets. We know where you live. We know who your family is. We know your dog's name."[70]

At an August 2020 board of supervisors meeting, the Cottonwood Militia's presence was unmistakable. They loomed particularly large in part because many residents were still wary of crowded, public gatherings, and thus they stayed home. But residents had an additional reason to steer clear. They knew that the Cottonwood Militia resented the board members for capitulating to the liberals running things in Sacramento; they recalled, too, the militia's anger at the townspeople who complied with state or county rules.

When it came time for public comments, Zapata spoke up. Last seen on video seemingly threatening to whack his neighbors' dogs, Zapata was an ex-Marine, local restaurateur, and rowdy presence around town. After a violent bar fight in May that led to the issuance of an order requiring Zapata to turn over his guns, Zapata bragged, "There is not a person in this county who is going to serve that f-cking thing." At the meeting, Zapata demanded countywide defiance of state orders and regulations. "I've been in combat," he announced, "and I never wanted to go back again, but I'm telling you what, I will to save this country. If it has to be against our own citizens, it will happen, and there's a million people like me, and you won't stop us."[71] If that weren't explicit enough, he added, "It's not going to be peaceful much longer."[72]

The militiamen have kept the pressure on fellow residents. They've targeted the very few local journalists in the county, threatening them with violence. They've also attacked business owners (often on the mere suspicion of being anti-militia), using vandalism and violence to secure their fidelity to the militia. As one outward display of cooperation, businesses posted statements in their storefront windows. These statements noted that attempts by government regulators to impose or enforce regulations would "be met with resistance."[73]

The Cottonwood crew and others also continued to threaten the county board. At a January 2021 meeting—which was opened to the public in response to angry, menacing opposition to a virtual convening[74]—one woman told the supervisors that a "civil war is brewing." Another woman likened pandemic masking rules to the Nuremberg Laws and told her elected representatives that she, too, was ready and willing to fight in a civil war. A middle-aged man then announced to the board that the "days of your tyranny are drawing to a close, and the legitimacy of this government is waning. . . . When the ballot box is gone, there is only the cartridge box."[75]

By September 2021, the far-right elements in Shasta had gathered enough signatures to trigger a recall election for Leonard Moty, the chair of the board. Online trolls smeared Moty as a pedophile.[76] Townspeople who supported the lifelong Republican and former Redding police chief were themselves subjected to vicious, violent threats. With an infusion of almost one million dollars from a former resident who harbored a grudge against the board of supervisors over a land-use dispute, Zapata, Clendenen, and their pals launched a slickly produced propaganda series called *Red White and Blueprint* to document their efforts to take over county government.[77]

There's little question that their campaign of intimidation worked, inhibiting those otherwise inclined to back Moty from doing so.[78] In

February 2022, with just 42 percent of registered voters voting,[79] Moty was recalled. Tim Garman, an antivax MAGA loyalist, took his place. Observers emphasized how exceedingly low the turnout was. Shasta turnout for the 2020 presidential race was 85 percent; even the similarly off-cycle September 2021 recall of Governor Gavin Newsom brought 65.7 percent of the electorate to the polls. In one account of the Moty recall race, the *Washington Post* interviewed local officials who surmised that many voters "probably stayed away out of fear."[80]

Moty's recall was just the beginning. The arrival of Garman meant that the board was pivoting closer to the militiamen's positions. Personnel moves reflected as much. In May 2022, the board fired the long-standing county health officer who had supported the state's Covid measures.[81] The same month, county chief executive Matt Pontes resigned, citing threats by one of the far-right supervisors who had been clamoring for his ouster.[82]

That fall, two board members who weren't aligned with the militiamen announced they'd be running for reelection. But they didn't stay in the race very long. Those believed to be affiliated with the militiamen started knocking on doors—they claimed to be part of a "voter task force"—and harassing residents.[83] The county clerk told the *New York Times* that she and her colleagues had been stalked, yelled at, and accused of "treason," as well as experienced "bullying and aggressive behavior."[84] Still, it wasn't as bad as the "direct threats that election officials in some states have gotten."[85]

Soon afterward, the two incumbents bowed out, and their replacements solidified the extremists' hold over the levers of democratic governance. Having already replaced key personnel, the board's next major move was to scrap the county's (perfectly reliable) Dominion voting machines and mandate hand counts, a move that smacked of QAnon conspiracy nonsense and would create scores of new opportunities to manipulate the vote.[86] They also voted to permit concealed weapons inside local government buildings, a measure that violates state law but nonetheless sends a strong signal to the community and law enforcement alike.[87]

Shasta is hardly a model for the nation. In fact, the extremists are running the county so poorly and stridently that they're falling out of favor almost as quickly as they forced their way onto the board. In March 2024, voters ousted Patrick Jones, one of the militia-friendly supervisors installed on the board during the hard-right takeover, in favor of a more moderate candidate. Still, what's been going on there, and what's likely to persist for some time, is troubling and instructive.[88]

Years of escalating threats visited on residents, business owners, and government officials were not met with denunciations, arrests, or even mild rebukes. They were, instead, rewarded with a mandate to govern. Obviously, at least some were deterred from speaking out, voting, and even standing for reelection. Others have been worn out. Some two years after the Shasta county clerk told the *New York Times* that things were rough but not terrible, she has been forced to retire. She's experienced "heart failure," a condition exacerbated by stress.[89]

Shasta may not be a model. But intimidating would-be rivals and critics surely is. Intimidation, silencing, harassment, and bullying are all staple features of Vigilante Democracy. They're what MAGA strategists are hoping will ensure that white Christian political power perdures notwithstanding the demographic and cultural changes pushing America down a more liberal and inclusive political pathway.

And as we see the MAGA strategists' plans to prop up a Vigilante Democracy come to fruition, the question we must ask is this:

What can we do to stop it?

PART III

The Stakes

CHAPTER 9

"The Very Definition of Lawlessness"
How Legal Vigilantism Suffocates Democracy

I n the preceding chapters, we've shown how legal vigilantism has led to individuals being injured, if not killed. We've also shown how targets have been forced to conceal who they are, change what they do, and alter whether and how they inhabit public spaces. But focusing on specific harms and discrete attacks runs the risk of failing to capture legal vigilantism's larger effects on democratic society. To fully appreciate those effects, we need to consider the ways these ecosystems of violence, intimidation, subordination, and disenfranchisement extend into every corner of civic, political, economic, and family life.

Our starting point is that true democracy requires assurances not just of a formal right to vote, but of *equal and inclusive citizenship 365 days a year*—in accessing schools, in civic spaces, and, yes, in doctors' offices.[1] That's why the resurgence of legalized vigilantism is so suffocating. The January 7 Project never takes a day off, and it never looks the other way. The surveillance, the harassment and threats, the confrontations, and the litigation wear down and scare off those otherwise inclined not just to peaceably protest, but to protest without fear of being shot or run over; not just to vote, but to vote without concern of being disqualified on partisan grounds; and not just to submit comments at hearings, but to submit comments without being harangued, stalked, or doxed. Today's new vigilantes go so far as to rattle those merely seeking free, public education not circumscribed by partisans fighting a one-sided culture war. And they intimidate those seeking personal autonomy over gender and reproduction.

And yet legal vigilantes aren't necessarily depriving their targets of their constitutional rights, especially as those rights are understood by the right-wing majority that controls the Supreme Court. The architects of Vigilante Democracy are sabotaging the conditions that make it possible to participate as equals in a democracy. And they're doing so in a manner that is both devastatingly effective and constitutionally permissible. Like a crime syndicate that employs safecrackers, assassins, numbers runners, crooked cops, drug dealers, and corrupt union officials to control communities, Vigilante Democracy deploys lawyers, gunslingers, thugs, parent associations, snitches, podcasters, influencers, keyboard warriors, and QAnon trolls to bend every pillar of American democracy to its will.

Three conclusions follow. First, there is an organizational sophistication and strategic coherence to what today's MAGA bullies are doing. Legal vigilantism might come off as chaotic, messy, ill-conceived, and ill-executed. But appearances can be deceiving and, perhaps, intentionally so. The energy and efficacy of legal vigilantism comes from elevating often long-standing cultural, racial, and religious grievances into de facto state policy of privately enforced, Christian nationalism. If anything, amateurish, shrill private enforcement gives the January 7 Project any number of benefits. The movement seems less threatening and less formidable than it actually is; it gives state actors political and legal cover if and when particular manifestations of vigilantism backfire; and it ensures organic experimentation, innovation, and further recruitment, as new MAGA warriors are encouraged and emboldened by those they see in action.

Second, legal vigilantism land-mines democratic spaces. Forcing racial and religious minorities, LGBTQ+ people, women, and their allies to the margins compromises those groups' ability to participate fully in our constitutional democracy. The result: MAGA Republicans wield outsize, perhaps controlling, influence over American law and politics. They can use that control not only to entrench a substantive anti–civil rights and anti-liberal agenda, but also to further expand and normalize vigilante initiatives, making it that much harder for the targets of vigilantism to resist.

This leads to our third and perhaps most maddening conclusion. With Christian nationalists firmly ensconced in positions of power—courts, legislatures, town councils, administrative boards, and more—they can do long-term and possibly permanent damage to the infrastructure of government. Knowing that antidemocratic, vigilante tactics are unlikely, by themselves, to work forever (especially given the shrinking percentage of Americans who count themselves members of the political Right), the architects of Vigilante Democracy are intent on gutting and delegitimating public institutions. The play here is as simple as it is diabolical. They want to starve, weaken, and privatize government programs and services. This way, once liberal and progressive candidates start winning major elections in red states, those victors will find themselves without the resources needed to govern effectively.[2]

ELEVATING CULTURAL GRIEVANCES INTO STATE-SUPPORTED CHRISTIAN NATIONALISM

Vigilante Democracy makes a mockery of everyday equality by perpetually, relentlessly, and when necessary violently subordinating the dignity and worth of some in order to more fully validate the privileges and preferences of others. You may be irritated by your neighbor's reproductive decisions; you may be offended that trans kids are allowed to use bathrooms and play on sports teams that match their gender identities; you may be annoyed, even angry, that teachers and administrators weigh in on what you deem to be sensitive, divisive subjects regarding race and gender and sexuality; and you may even be furious that protesters take to the streets advancing causes you find anathema.[3]

Without Vigilante Democracy, these feelings of frustration, even fury, would remain just that. You'd take a walk around the block, vent on Facebook, or at most donate to the campaign of your favorite politician. Without Vigilante Democracy, you'd never dream that your feelings of frustration, even fury, would rise to the level of legally protected rights (let alone give you a hall pass to engage in state-supported private violence and intimidation). For rising to that level—in court, before a regulatory body, or in any other civic space—would suggest that *your* feelings of irritation or annoyance or even fury ought to be given priority—*legal* priority—over others' identities, their most fundamental choices, and the heretofore protected speech and assembly rights of folks you find annoying. And yet, as we covered in Part II, quite a few states now allow you to sue, intimidate, and even inflict physical harm regardless of whether the "irritants" or "annoyances" have caused (or threatened to cause) you any physical or economic injury.

We shouldn't shut our eyes to what this means. When states assign to furious MAGA citizens the right to thwart women, LGBTQ+ persons, racial and religious minorities, and allies such as teachers and doctors, they're imposing duties—that is, affirmative obligations—on those groups to censor themselves. And this imposition of affirmative duties on folks doing little more than acting on their own deeply held beliefs and aspirations (or just being who they are) undercuts democratic equality.

This is why we reject any such characterization of today's right-wing power grab as *just* a culture war. We've used the term in this book because it's a convenient label for a certain kind of state policy that's a little too interested in people's private lives and convictions. But suggesting that this is just, or merely, *cultural* ignores how hateful and intolerant rhetoric is tethered to a powerful legal strategy of subordination and civic and political disenfranchisement.

Today's culture wars are worlds removed from isolated episodes like Vice President Dan Quayle's attacks on the fictional TV character Murphy Brown (who—gasp—decided to have a kid as a single mom); Bill Clinton's scapegoating of Sister Souljah (for her anti-white rhetoric); or Tipper Gore's demand that Prince's recordings have a parental advisory label. Today, people are acting on, and officials are codifying, wildly anti-Black, xenophobic, and anti-LGBTQ+ rhetoric. Exclusionary school policies—everything from transphobic bathroom and sports facilities to whitewashed curricula—result in actual, meaningful, and caste-reinforcing injuries. Family planning decisions aren't just commented on, as Quayle once did. They're being outlawed. (In his brief challenging abortion rights, S.B. 8 architect Jonathan Mitchell called the *Roe* decision protecting them "the very definition of lawlessness."[4])

And books containing frank discussions of history, gender, and sexuality aren't (just) slapped with warning labels, the way Tipper Gore wanted. They're being banned from classrooms and pulled from library shelves. In short, characterizing today's right-wing assaults as (just) cultural slights downplays the immense and undeniable impact of legalized vigilantism.

Under Vigilante Democracy, the hurt feelings of individuals discomforted by a diverse America are forged into legal and physical weapons. As a consequence, the roles of victims and assailants get reversed. Legal vigilantism forces people out of specific jobs and professions, compromises the physical and emotional health of patients and students, limits educational lessons and opportunities, and drives families to relocate out of vigilante jurisdictions.[5]

Victim inversion is so central to the vigilante project, it has even raised the eyebrows of the most MAGA of Supreme Court justices. During oral arguments on whether the federal courts should stop S.B. 8 from taking effect, Clarence Thomas asked Texas's lawyer how plaintiffs with no connection to either the patients or the medical facilities have grounds for suing physicians performing abortions. Judd Stone, Texas's solicitor general, replied that individuals bringing such suits have suffered "the tort of outrage": someone who "becomes aware of a non-compliant abortion" may experience "extreme emotional harm."[6] This threw Thomas for a loop. He stammered: "I—I—forgive me, but I don't recall an outrage injury. What would that be? You said extreme outrage, that would be the injury?"[7]

Whatever else one may say about Thomas, his memory was not failing him. Stone, too, should have known better. As a young lawyer, Stone clerked for another right-wing jurist, Antonin Scalia, whose hostility to inventive theories of injury was legendary.[8] Scalia's scorn was directed at environmentalists and animal-rights activists, who at the time were seeking relief for injuries far more concrete than Stone's tort of outrage.

Though Scalia's position regularly carried the majority of the Court, he never had occasion to entertain a speculative, even fantastical claim that, if recognized, could subordinate women's bodily, civic, and political rights with the precision and potency of S.B. 8. But it's quite possible that he (and others) would take pains to distinguish tree-hugging plaintiffs from anti-abortion plaintiffs. Disdain for the former and regard for the latter may have helped Thomas push his doubts to the side. When the Court's decision came down, Thomas said nary a word about the novelty of the "outrage injury" that S.B. 8 vindicates.[9]

Still, Thomas's initial skepticism reminds us of how radical this reassignment of rights and duties truly is—and of the political agenda it serves. Justice Stephen Breyer recognized this agenda when he mused that S.B. 8 plaintiffs aren't altogether different from the angry white parents who opposed desegregation in Arkansas in the 1950s.[10] Under Stone's reasoning in defense of S.B. 8, Arkansas could have passed a law validating the white parents' hurt feelings, legitimating their racism, and prioritizing their frustrations over the interests (and rights) of Black schoolchildren and their allies. Such a law would have empowered the white parents—and, really, anyone else distraught over Black and white kids learning in the same classrooms—to sue the Black children who had risked life and limb to integrate Little Rock's Central High.[11] But even the avowedly segregationist Arkansas governor Orval Faubus, who ordered state guardsmen to prevent Black students' access,[12] didn't have the audacity to deputize white supremacist mobs and give them the legal imprimatur of courthouse vigilantes. Had Breyer pushed further, he might have reminded Stone of something we've been saying all along: S.B. 8's best analogy is to antebellum times and the Fugitive Slave laws.

Vigilante Democracy's inversion of rights is hardly limited today to courts of law. Beyond the dramatic shift in rights and duties surrounding political protests, the rights-inversion seems closely tethered to a broader upheaval in how Americans think and talk about rights, as evidenced by the conflicts we're witnessing in neighborhoods, in retail stores, on commercial flights,[13] and between civilian and religious authorities.[14] These, too, are more than just symbolic. The assumption that society should cater to the angry and aggrieved has emboldened customers to assert (with some success) their inalienable "right" to shop while not only defying public health mandates but also disregarding private businesses' long-standing right to require shoppers to comply with store policies.[15] That assumption has led religious groups to assert with renewed energy (and some success) the "right" to special exemptions from generally applicable health and safety regulations.[16] And that assumption has led concerned citizens to claim (likewise with some success) the "right" to surveil fellow citizens as they cast ballots and to stand within spitting distance of election administrators as they count votes.[17]

ASSAULTING DEMOCRATIC SPACES

With rights and duties reassigned, the elite architects and lay practitioners of Vigilante Democracy have the tools, authority, and political cover to marginalize and intimidate those who threaten white

Christian supremacy in and across spaces recognized as meaningful and important. Chapters 5 through 8 took us to sites of considerable, sometimes unimaginable trauma, violence, and despair. Let's revisit some of those sites to appreciate the systemic, overarching effects of legal vigilantism—namely, its capacity to destabilize and commandeer *democratic* spaces.

The Schools. Public schools are the training grounds of democracy. It's here where we learn to be citizens, to find our voices, to respect one another, to understand the histories we share—as well as those that have divided us. And it's here where some of the most important battles for equality have been fought. *Brown v. Board of Education* wasn't the first time the Supreme Court declared segregation unconstitutional. In the years leading up to *Brown*, the Court had chipped away at Jim Crow in housing and higher education.[18] But *Brown*—and the Court's unanimous insistence on racial equality in primary schooling (and resounding outrage over the demoralizing social and psychological effects segregation had on Black children)—remains the Court's crowning achievement.

Brown also gave birth to a new era of racial integration and, yes, equal citizenship, giving hope to those listening to Martin Luther King, Jr.'s famous 1963 speech at the Lincoln Memorial that his dream was within reach. Likewise, the fervid opposition to *Brown*—cities, counties, and states continued fighting K–12 desegregation for years after the Court handed down its first ruling[19]—confirmed that integrated schools harbingered the demise of white supremacy.

So now here we are, seventy years after *Brown*, and state and local leaders are trying to reverse the effects of integration and reinstate the American caste system. And this time, unlike during the so-called white *flight* era of the 1960s and 1970s, when the integration of neighborhoods and schools prompted white city-dwellers to decamp to the suburbs,[20] we're witnessing white *fight*. Using overlapping and reinforcing vigilante regimes, states and communities are deputizing right-wing partisans to menace teachers, sanitize lesson plans, ban books, and stigmatize and endanger LGBTQ+ kids as well as any number of medically vulnerable students made even more so by parental opt-in laws. So, sure, the schools are nominally open to all—provided all are willing to accept an education system that increasingly reflects a right-wing ethos.

The Public Sphere. Democracy spills out of the schools and into town squares, public parks, and city streets. This was recognized by the founding generation, whose very first amendment to the Constitution guaranteed the freedom of assembly; by Tocqueville, who understood the freedom of association as absolutely necessary to support and enrich a democratic community;[21] and by Dr. King, whose "Letter from a Birmingham Jail" reminded a troubled nation that "freedom is never voluntarily given by the oppressor; it must be demanded by the oppressed."[22] Rallies, marches, and sit-ins have helped secure political equality for women, LGBTQ+ people, Black Americans, and more. Social movements in the interests of peace, economic security, and environmental protection have pushed those great causes forward. And, most recently, Americans have used street protests to demand racial and criminal justice, insist on reproductive rights, and decry subversions of democracy.

To be sure, the foot soldiers of the Christian nationalist Right are no strangers to marches and rallies. They tiki-torched their way through Charlottesville, bull-rushed municipal and county public hearings to voice outrage over Covid precautions, swarmed election boards demanding recounts, endeavored to "stop the steal" on January 6, and have protested LGBTQ+-friendly events everywhere from Texas to California.

In the romanticized characterization of the public square, everyone's free to show up, protest, and try to persuade their fellow citizens to support a cause. The American public square has long been compromised by, among other things, the distorting role money plays in our civic and political cultures. Vigilante Democracy provides yet another shattering jolt, making the public square physically dangerous.[23] Don't like abortion activists protesting Texas's draconian restrictions on reproductive choice? Don't like the way the county commissioners are discussing public health rules and regulations? Vigilante Democracy allows you to show up at the park or in the county boardroom, armed with military-grade weapons and decked out in tactical gear. (While some on the left have followed suit, they're so far the exception.)

Just who is allowed to exercise power, and who is not, is captured in the Right's response to Kyle Rittenhouse. Take then-candidate, now senator, J. D. Vance. A Yale Law grad who went on to work at a hedge fund owned by right-wing billionaire Peter Thiel, Vance first captured the nation's attention with the publication of his best-selling memoir, *Hillbilly Elegy*, a manifesto for rural white America's frustrations that anticipated the rise of MAGA politics.[24]

Commenting on the teen gunman's criminal trial, Vance claimed that "what's happening to Kyle Rittenhouse is one of the ugliest things I've seen in this country."[25] Rittenhouse stood for "basic, manly virtue"—the "virtues that we want our leaders to promote."[26] To Vance, the protesters Rittenhouse maimed and killed were, at best, an afterthought.

The end result? Though our public spaces are nominally open to all, the political and legal terrain has shifted to such an extent that those spaces heavily favor a particular set of activists and a particular set of views—ones that, it just so happens, track the MAGA agenda.

The Government. Vigilante Democracy is equally dangerous to the institutions and people charged with carrying out safety and health regulations, financial and consumer protections, transportation and energy policy, and law enforcement and national defense. The attacks here are informed by claims—repeated from the heights of the federal judiciary to the cesspools of the Dark Web—that government bureaucracies are undemocratic and that our civil servants are out of touch and untrustworthy. Some push even further, baselessly insisting that government civil servants are members of a Deep State cabal hostile to the people and to the Constitution.[27]

Like so much else that the MAGA universe treats as dogma, these claims are bizarre and reckless. The notion of rank-and-file bureaucrats as elite, aloof Beltway insiders is empirically untrue at the federal level and downright batty when we're talking about county health and election officials and school district personnel. These bureaucrats are not only very much a part of the communities they serve (with kids enrolled in the neighborhood schools and spouses who double as Little League coaches),[28] they're also highly accountable agents of the people and the people's democratic representatives.[29] Elections determine which officials will be given a mandate. Those elected officials can't do everything, or even most things, by themselves. So they use their democratic mandates to enact legislation and then direct bureaucrats to carry out programs and initiatives.[30] Those directions to bureaucrats continue to be reinforced or revised based on what the representatives hear at town hall meetings, in casual conversations between officials and constituents, and, if serious enough, during formal investigations or at street rallies or protests. For all these reasons, the idea that threatening or attacking bureaucracy *promotes* democracy is perverse. Because bureaucracy is an essential *part* of our democracy—a practical necessity to carry out the people's preferences for, among other things, law and order, safe drinking water, and banking regulations—undermining our system of public administration thwarts democracy.

There's no shortage of bureaucracy critics, and only some of them are MAGA loyalists.[31] So let's be clear what particular role Vigilante Democracy plays and how attacks on public administration advance the vigilantes' aims of reinforcing race, gender, and sex hierarchies and debasing government (in order to entrench right-wing political power). Consider all the ways in which individuals or small groups of aggrieved and incensed townspeople may thwart school administrators on matters ranging from sports eligibility to bathroom assignments to curricular design to library collections to masking or vaccine mandates. The same happens at election, public health, zoning, planning, and other county business meetings. This, too, is, at best, demoralizing for officials in charge and, at worst, opens officials to litigation, community ire (or violence), and express repudiation (when states authorize opt-ins to negate board decisions). When people show up to meetings dressed as if they're headed to the Battle of Fallujah, officials quite rationally shut those meetings down or simply refuse to participate. The presence of vigilantes constrains public comment, especially by citizens whose views are at odds with those of the menacing attendees. Democratic policymaking, let alone *reasoned* democratic policymaking, cannot be formulated under these circumstances.

The Family. Vigilante Democracy is similarly threatening to the family. Now, it's certainly true that for most of human history and in most societies and civilizations, family dynamics have done more to impede rather than promote true democratic equality. The over-whelming majority of family structures have been, and many re-main, patriarchal. In such contexts, women are regularly charged with (devalued) domestic responsibilities while men partake in civic, political, and economic life, and have freer license to pursue edu-cation and recreational diversions. Certain traditionalist strains of Christianity continue to demand that women be submissive to their husbands. Though this religious commandment—which one can find in Ephesians 5:22–24—isn't mentioned in campaign ads, legislative assemblies, or judicial opinions, the notion that we've lost our way and need to make America great again is undeniably part and parcel of the political theology coursing through the veins of Republican stalwarts today.[32] So, increasingly, is the commandment to bear chil-dren, with Christian nationalists invoking that imperative to ward off what they characterize as white replacement, to further demonize same-sex couples, and as a rebuke to what MAGA loyalists like J. D. Vance disparage as "the childless left."[33]

The sexual rights revolution of the 1960s and 1970s, protecting in-timate relations, guaranteeing abortion rights, and elevating women's rights, was momentous. Much of the discourse around the revolution centers on personal autonomy, privacy, and bodily integrity. But there is an important political dynamic, too, one well understood by the justices who recognized and sought to protect these rights. Justice Harry Blackmun, author of the *Roe* opinion, wrote some years later that the constitutional right to an abortion "has become vital to the full participation of women in the economic and political walks of American life."[34] Justice Ruth Bader Ginsburg, the leading women's rights lawyer in the 1970s, likewise saw the unmistakable link between reproductive rights and political equality. Dissenting in a 2007 case called *Carhart v. Gonzales* that upheld a federal ban on so-called partial-birth, or late-term, abortions, Ginsburg made clear that efforts to protect the constitutional right to abortion "do not seek to vindicate some generalized notion of privacy; rather they center on a woman's autonomy to determine her life's course, and thus to enjoy equal citizenship stature."[35] Blackmun's and Ginsburg's understandings of the relationship between bodily autonomy and equal citizenship are consistent with the controlling opinion in the 1992 *Planned Parenthood v. Casey* case, where a trio of Republican-appointed justices remarked that "the ability of women to participate equally in the economic and social life of the Nation has been facilitated by their ability to control their reproductive lives."[36]

During the nearly fifty-year run between *Roe* and S.B. 8 (and ultimately *Dobbs*, which overruled *Roe* and *Casey*), women made great strides in educational spheres, in the workforce, and in political life. They had greater license to chart their own life trajectories, exercise control over family dynamics, and escape poverty, violence, and other unhealthy domestic situations. And men have had to adjust their expectations (and demands) accordingly.[37]

In rolling back the world to a pre-*Roe* landscape—maybe one that (thanks to technological surveillance and the added boost from citizen enforcement) is in some respects now more oppressive than it was then—we can expect women to be forced into any number of more precarious circumstances such as dropping out of school or the workforce, marrying a less stable or desirable partner, or living at home with unsupportive or abusive parents. That's a huge blow to the liberty, health, and life choices of all pregnant persons. (It is also a brutal imposition on girls and women who are not pregnant but denied essential medicines such as methotrexate because of the possibility that those drugs might be used as abortifacients.[38]) The retrenchment of reproductive rights is a particularly brutal blow to women's political participation—and especially to the participation of women of color and poorer and medically vulnerable women. So the supposed boost to democracy that Justice Alito insists the *Dobbs* ruling provides[39] (ostensibly, by allowing voters in each state to decide whether to permit or prohibit abortions) and the populist, vigilante enforcement of laws like S.B. 8[40] need to be seen for what they are. These measures are inescapably (and we'd say intentionally) damaging to the long-term project of a truly inclusive majoritarian democracy. Disempowered, vulnerable women will be less able to mobilize to challenge Christian nationalist political candidates. And, presuming those candidates prevail, we can expect the continuation, if not intensification, of legislation that disproportionately harms women.

A similar story can be told about family, democracy, and LGBTQ+ rights. The right to form loving relationships, marry, have children, and participate fully in the educational, civic, and economic life of communities has been transformative. Here, too, rights that seem deeply personal and intimate have had dramatic spillover effects on political engagement and governance. The extent of these shifts is evidenced in the record number of openly queer and trans officials in all three branches of local, state, and federal government, as well as in the military.[41] The rollback of this progress is not just personally cruel and painful; it also subverts the entire project of building a majoritarian democracy open to all.

LAYING WASTE TO WHAT'S LEFT

Right-wing vigilantism will do, and already is doing, significant damage in the short term. Families are fleeing vigilante jurisdictions, at great cost and risk, physically and financially. For the vast numbers who remain, there is still a steep price to pay. In public spaces, they're self-censoring, assuming they dare to show up at all. Their LGBTQ+ kids may be pretending to be straight and/or cisgender or at the very least covering at school. And all children may well be learning a sanitized version of history.

This multipronged campaign of silencing and subordination is, without a doubt, the strategy of a coalition that's losing power and knows it. Vigilante Democracy's architects understand that they can't easily reverse the inevitable march toward equality and inclusivity. Demography is already pushing us closer and closer to being a majority-minority nation. And (white) Christian nationalism is losing younger adherents who reject the toxic politics that their elders preach and practice. Technology pierces community veils, exposing those raised in traditionalist congregations and communities to a broader world.

Legal vigilantism is far from a recipe for health and prosperity. Even non-targets (and ostensible beneficiaries) will have to deal with the long-term effects of losing talented, productive members of their civic and commercial communities. Teachers are already leaving. Those who stay may well be less qualified—and compelled to offer compromised and constrained instruction that leaves *all* children ill-prepared for a cosmopolitan and culturally and historically literate global workforce.[42]

We're also seeing signs that corporations struggle to recruit or retain employees to live and work in vigilante jurisdictions.[43] Doctors won't (or can't) practice in vigilante-friendly states; those who do practice there may disproportionately opt into "safe" specialties, leaving victims and champions of Vigilante Democracy equally bereft of, say, routine gynecological services and possibly even pediatric care.[44] And the laws of probability assure us that, in time, enough people loved by hardcore Christian nationalists will need abortions, come out as queer, or marry a racial or religious minority. Ongoing relationships with those people will, again, likely moderate the views of at least some of the bitterest adherents of white Christian nationalism. For these reasons, we might harbor hope that it's just a matter of time before the political tides change—and change drastically.

But here's the thing: Progressives, liberals, centrists, and even old-school Republicans can't just ride this out like a bad storm.[45] The Christian nationalists pushing vigilantism right now aren't just biding their time, clinging to power and prestige a little longer before handing over the reins of government to a more diverse, progressive contingent. They're using this time to sabotage democratic institutions. The aim seems to be to leave government barren and broken, tanking the very possibility of an effective, pluralistic democracy. This sabotage will also have a global impact in a world that depends on the United States being a steadying presence with respect to financial markets, climate and epidemiological risks, and global security.

Consider this scorched earth policy as some sort of reversal of General William Tecumseh Sherman's march across Georgia to destroy the South's capacity to keep fighting. The politics that motivates and sustains legal vigilantism is already prompting major cutbacks in funding to various government departments, agencies, school districts, and even libraries.[46] Legal vigilantism is pushing conscientious public school teachers, librarians, election workers, public health officials, and even prosecutors (among other government officials) to quit or retire prematurely. And legal vigilantism is shrinking or eroding public spaces by making them inherently unreliable, ungovernable, or dangerous.

This slash-and-burn campaign is an especially cunning one because it forecloses the use of public spaces that liberals have long deemed integral to American democracy. Now those same liberals may feel obligated to seek private educational, artistic, recreational, and residential (e.g., gated community) alternatives for themselves and their children. And once ensconced in private spaces, and forced to pay for privately provided services, they, too, will be less passionate advocates for public institutions.

This is all happening now. Already. And when the keys to government are eventually turned over to new, more progressive majorities, these new majorities will not be receiving a well-cared-for, regularly serviced, and durable vehicle. They'll be getting a neglected (if not intentionally degraded) jalopy—with little pep, limited range, and a decent chance of breaking down or catching fire. And once that happens, once this jalopy proves itself to be unreliable, there will be less enthusiasm across the political spectrum for upgrading it. Not only will the Right continue to oppose government spending, but as we just stated, it may now be joined by those in the center and on the left who've necessarily relied on and invested in private institutions while weathering the vigilante excesses of the interregnum—and may not have the resources or inclination to support an expensive overhaul of the debased public institutions.[47]

To be clear, this reversal of Sherman's March to the Sea isn't just a cartoonish revenge fantasy. It isn't just a matter of spite, "owning the libs," or anything so petty. It is about carving out more and more room for private governance *beyond the reach* of democratic elections and subsequent democratic control.[48] With public institutions stripped bare, the MAGA Republicans will have succeeded in weakening the regulatory power of progressive labor and environmental agencies, educators, and public health officials. Less money, fewer officials, and a more cowed group of holdover employees is going to hamstring the new generation of elected progressives who won't be able to get much done. The vicious circle of threats to officials, diminished funding, low morale, and subpar performance will spin so fast that, as we suggested, even dutiful Democrats will refuse to continue financing what amounts to a zoo full of paper tigers. Plus, the money "saved" by lowering tax expenditures will be funneled into private institutions—parochial schools, home ownership associations, as well as church-adjacent athletic, educational, and social enterprises—institutions that, although increasingly state-subsidized, will remain at least somewhat beyond the regulatory reach of the few state authorities that haven't yet been sabotaged. In short, if democracy can no longer be made to bend to the will of Christian nationalism, then Christian nationalism is going to first impede and then blow up democracy. It'll do so by shifting the locus of civic and social power out of the public domain and into private enclaves.

And, yes, we've seen responses of this sort before. Where white flight wasn't possible in the 1960s and 1970s, white majorities responded by closing public pools, libraries, in some instances even entire school systems. They did so rather than open their doors to Black children.[49] The white fighters of today know that history better than the rest of us—and they've already begun to repeat it.

PART IV

First Responders

CHAPTER 10

"Not Without Electoral or Political Power"
The Empty Promise of Voting Our Way Out of This Mess

On June 24, 2022, the Supreme Court decided *Dobbs v. Jackson Women's Health Organization*, erasing long-standing federal constitutional protections for reproductive autonomy. In his majority opinion, Samuel Alito couched the decision as one that returns power to the people: "Women on both sides of the issue [can] seek to affect the legislative process by influencing public opinion, lobbying legislators, voting, and running for office." Women, Alito explains, "are not without electoral or political power," adding that he and his colleagues in the majority find it "noteworthy that the percentage of women who register to vote and cast ballots is consistently higher than the percentage of men who do so."[1]

Just two weeks later, Joe Biden added his own gloss to Alito's passages: "That's another way of saying that you, the women of America, can determine the outcome of this issue. . . . It's my hope and strong belief that women will, in fact, turn out in record numbers to reclaim the rights that have [been] taken from them by the Court."[2] In the months that followed, Biden would return to this theme. In one June 2023 speech to a gathering of reproductive rights advocates, Biden said that *Dobbs* "practically dared the women of America to be heard."[3] And in his 2024 State of the Union Address, the president warned that "those bragging about overturning *Roe v. Wade* have no clue about the power of women in America."[4]

This of course is consistent with other calls to vote. Everyone from Frederick Douglass to Susan B. Anthony to Cesar Chavez fought for and celebrated voting as the most basic expression of political power. Just as important, they doubtless shared John Lewis's sentiment that voting is an "almost sacred" duty.

We don't quibble with the imperative to vote. And we embrace Lewis's characterization wholeheartedly. But we're realistic about why plain old voting, or even voting "like you never voted before"—another of Lewis's exhortations—may not be the answer on abortion. And if voting may not be the answer on abortion, an issue for which Alito concedes there's a strong political constituency, it's hard to fathom it protecting the numerically smaller populations of Black and LGBTQ+ Americans, educators, and their allies who are targeted by other aspects of the January 7 Project's campaign of oppression and subordination. This means that, while long-term solutions to the resurgence of state-sponsored vigilantism are undoubtedly going to require the exercise of power at the ballot box, a plan to "vote harder" alone isn't going to cut it. Voting is only one piece of what necessarily is a multipronged, and multifront, strategy of resisting legal vigilantism and building a strengthened democracy.

We're hardly alone in sounding a note of skepticism. Those focused on what's been going on across red America suspect that Alito is being daft or disingenuous—and that repressive anti-abortion laws weaken American women's economic autonomy and political power. As Wendy Brown has written, "While the Court is supposedly turning democracy back to the people in *Dobbs*, most of the states exalting over this decision are busily de-democratizing themselves by gerrymandering and restricting voting rights."[5] To Brown's list of status quo–reinforcing mechanisms, we'd add the various complementary regimes of state-sponsored vigilantism. And to those thinking the feds may, per Biden's suggestion, bail everyone out, we are afraid that the antidemocratic instruments and institutions operating at the national level present major, perhaps insurmountable, obstacles to democracy-reinforcing reforms.

RECLAIMING LOCAL POWER IN RED STATES

We might begin by considering the prospects for fighting Vigilante Democracy through local elections. Happily, not every locality is as extreme as Shasta County, California. But the Right would like to change that.

MAGA donors are pouring money into local races, spoon-feeding candidates talking points and policy positions, and working behind the scenes to control who votes—and who gets to count the ballots. As we've seen, the swell of political violence—enabled and emboldened by the passage of vigilante laws, law enforcement personnel who countenance if not endorse right-wing agitation, and the Supreme Court's opposition to most restrictions on gun ownership and open carry policies—chills progressive politics in innumerable ways. The bullying of election officials, too, is creating vacancies that are part of a right-wing strategy to promote partisan vote counting or, where that fails, encourage allegations that Democrats are perpetrating election fraud.

None of this is going to help swing communities back to the political center, let alone somewhere left of center.

But let's say we're overly pessimistic. Let's say progressives overcome Vigilante Democracy's obstacles to elect school board members, local judges, and city or county supervisors. Well, that's great, right? We'd see tolerant, inclusive sanctuaries that insulate individuals and families from the harsh, subordinating policies emanating from the statehouse.

Not so fast. Red state governments want to invade, subjugate, or bust up those sanctuaries. And they're doing precisely that.

Recall Chapter 5's discussion of educational gag laws, notably in Florida and Tennessee, that encourage parents whose local school districts refuse to ban books to appeal those decisions directly to a state board. If the state board sides with the parents clamoring for book bans, its ruling will preempt local districts' decisions on what materials districts assign or make available to their students. We see efforts of this sort, including ones not involving forms of vigilantism, throughout red America. They're a warning of the obstacles to enacting change through democratic victories at the local level.

Take Arkansas. Running a state that has long struggled with poverty, with meeting educational and public heath benchmarks, and with structural racism, Sarah Huckabee Sanders devoted the first few months of her governorship in 2023 to causes such as banning the term "Latinx" from state documents and establishing a "monument to the unborn" on the state's capitol grounds. Sanders's monument will stand not far from a sculpture commemorating the Little Rock Nine, the brave children who integrated Little Rock High.

Sanders's next big move was to warn schools against offering Advanced Placement courses on African-American history. Students enrolling in that course, her administration advised, wouldn't receive credit toward graduation, and districts that offer the class might run afoul of an executive order prohibiting "teaching that would indoctrinate students with ideologies."[6] Little Rock has come a long way since President Eisenhower had to deploy the 101st Army Airborne Division to secure the safe enrollment of nine Black children. In 2018, the city elected its first Black mayor, and soon after Sanders's broadside, the Little Rock School Board voted 9–0 to keep the college preparatory course in the district's curriculum. Still, the risk of penalties for teaching African-American History is a preemptive broadside against local progressive governance.

Arkansas may be overriding local control in a targeted fashion and on a piecemeal basis, but neighboring Texas is doing so in an indiscriminate and comprehensive fashion. Well aware of the large and powerful blue municipalities—Austin, Houston, San Antonio—and surrounding counties whose politics don't align with those of the governor or majority caucuses in the Texas House and Senate, the state legislature passed a blanket preemption law restricting localities from regulating above and beyond what's been authorized at the state level. This law, referred to as the "Death Star" bill, purports to block Houston from enacting labor laws that are more protective of workers than state regulations. By the same token, San Antonio may not be able to institute expansive environmental and sustainability measures. And Austin may be limited in efforts to deal with housing affordability issues. The Death Star bill prescribes private enforcement, and the individuals who sue to enforce it need not be residents of the communities whose laws or regulations they're challenging.

As Ana Gonzalez, a Texas labor activist, noted, "this is a direct attack on local democracy. . . . The state is coming in and completely eliminating" the power of towns, cities, and counties to shape community rules and regulations.[7] Yes, blue states have preempted local regulations in an effort to protect local communities from discriminating against marginalized groups. But whatever stance one takes on the optimal distribution of authority between state and local government as a philosophical matter, Texas's timing and tactics leave no question about the state's objective. The measures aim to disable local democracy (particularly in diverse communities) in the service of an illiberal, reactionary agenda.

Unsurprisingly, Florida has shown a similar hostility to local democracy. For better or worse, a bedrock feature of criminal justice in America has long been local, elected prosecutors who enjoy near-complete discretion when it comes to charging specific (alleged) criminals, as well as prioritizing or declining to enforce certain types of crimes. Yet in this current political moment—with the rise of a new generation of progressively minded district attorneys, and with the hardening of political divisions between Democratic cities and MAGA Republican state governments—locally elected DAs are under threat of removal by governors.

In August 2022, Florida's Ron DeSantis suspended popular, two-term progressive prosecutor Andrew Warren, who represented the large and diverse Hillsborough County. Warren had announced he wouldn't enforce the state's abortion ban and refused to commit to prosecuting individuals and families for defying anti-LGBTQ+ state laws.[8] DeSantis then appointed an interim replacement. Almost precisely a year later, DeSantis removed Monique Worrell, the only Black female elected prosecutor in the state, and hand-picked a successor to replace her.

Worrell, who represented the Orlando area, responded: "The country should be afraid of an individual who removes duly elected officials because they are not politically aligned with him. The country should be afraid of a man who dares to teach our children that slavery was somehow a benefit to the African Americans in this country."[9]

Meanwhile, Mississippi governor Tate Reeves must have been taking notes. The state's capital is the city of Jackson, with a population that is slightly more than 80 percent Black. Among the city's prodigious problems are widespread poverty and a devastating water crisis, largely attributed to state underinvestment and neglect. State officials, however, are zeroing in on something else.

In 2023, the state decided to enlarge what had been an autonomous district within Jackson. The new district would operate outside the authority of the duly elected city government. Oh, and this district would be drawn to sweep in Jackson's white population. To administer the district, the state created a new judiciary, vesting the appointment of judges not in the people of Jackson but rather in the state supreme court's chief justice, a white conservative.[10] The new district needed prosecutors and public defenders; those officials, too, were to be chosen not by the predominantly Black residents of Jackson but instead by the state attorney general (likewise a white conservative). And that district needed policing. Rather than rely on Jackson police, headed by a Black man who has lived in Jackson and served its people for decades, the state opted to broaden the policing role for the capitol police. The capitol police are led by a white man who was appointed by the Mississippi commissioner of public safety (yet another white conservative).[11]

To say this is a thinly disguised plan to free white Jacksonians from the clutches of Black elected officials is an insult to actual thinly disguised plans. As Cliff Johnson, a civil rights lawyer and University of Mississippi law professor, said: "No serious person can look at this map and this data and claim the proposed [special district] boundaries weren't drawn to make sure as many white Jacksonians as possible get the 'benefit' of a special police force and court filled with hand-picked judges and prosecutors."[12] Jackson's mayor, Chokwe Lumumba, called the state's move "an attack on Black leadership." This is, he explains, "a racist act. . . . It is apartheid in Jackson, Mississippi."[13]

Less brazen but similarly antidemocratic efforts to strip progressive communities of their ability to govern are happening in Tennessee. In 2018, residents of Davidson County, frustrated with ongoing police brutality directed at Black residents around the county seat of Nashville, endorsed a ballot initiative to create an independent body to monitor police interactions with the community. Called the Metro Nashville Community Oversight Board, this committee included Black and Latino members as well as women. Its director, Jill Fitcheard, herself a Black woman, said the board was "exactly what community oversight should look like."[14]

In 2023, the Nashville board issued its first report. The findings were staggering. Police and school security officers used force against Black kids ten times more frequently than against white youth. Police were three times more likely to unholster a firearm against a Black person than a white one. One might think that these injustices would have led the board to propose sweeping reforms, but the board announced only modest and technocratic recommendations. The board suggested changes to reporting requirements, de-escalation training, and greater efforts to recruit diverse officers. But even these baby steps were too much for the Republican-dominated state legislature. The lawmakers voted to dissolve the Nashville oversight board as well as a similar body established by Memphis residents. Noting that both cities are Democratic strongholds, Fitcheard remarked that the legislation disbanding the boards "feels very targeted."[15]

It's far from clear that progressive communities in deep-red states can stand as a bulwark against Vigilante Democracy. The message, rather, is that if they push back too hard, their power to engage in self-government will be cut out from beneath them.

TURNING RED STATES PURPLE . . . OR EVEN BLUE

With local governments disempowered, voters eager to follow Justice Alito's advice to exercise power at the ballot box might try to target Vigilante Democracy at its source—in red state legislatures. But they're unlikely to find much success there, either. Remember, vigilante laws are tactics. The strategy is to lock in right-wing control notwithstanding the demographic changes inescapably favoring more moderate and even liberal candidates. Vigilante laws not only make it more difficult for the groups they target to exercise political power; they're enacted by state legislatures that are structured to resist rather than facilitate efforts to hold lawmakers accountable.

Partisan Gerrymandering

We've discussed voter suppression and ballot subversion at length. Just as important is widespread gerrymandering that crams diverse and progressive constituencies into narrow legislative districts in order to dilute their power statewide.

Partisan gerrymandering gives rise to striking disparities between how people identify politically and who represents them. As law professors, we've long been familiar with the Supreme Court's 2019 decision in *Rucho v. Common Cause*, holding that the federal courts may not hear claims that partisan gerrymandering violates the federal constitution.[16] When we pulled the numbers, however, even we were shocked at what we found.[17]

In the reliably Republican state of Arkansas, careful survey data from 2022 suggest that the state's adult population is almost evenly split between Republicans and Democrats.[18] When we look at the partisan composition of both houses of the state legislature, however, we see that more than 80 percent of state senators and representatives are Republican. In Mississippi, Democratic residents actually outpace Republicans 44 to 43 percent.[19] Nonetheless, Republicans outnumber Democrats in the state senate by a 7-3 margin, and by a 2-1 margin in the house. Florida has more adults who are or lean

Democratic. Yet Republicans have a 70 percent majority in the state senate and a 69 percent majority in the house.[20] Small wonder that DeSantis's Christian nationalist agenda moves so quickly through the legislature. Texas, too, has a fairly surprising Democratic advantage among adults—46 percent to the 40 percent who identify as or lean Republican.[21] But its senate and house are, like the others, safely controlled by Republicans. Ohio is similar. There, 49 percent of all adults identify or lean Democratic.[22] Yet only 21 percent of all state senators and 32 percent of house members are Democrats.

Thanks to partisan gerrymandering, a groundswell of new Democratic voters would be needed for Democrats to win power—and that's before factoring in voter suppression, ballot interference, and the fact that reliably Democratic voters are being forced to flee to other jurisdictions by state-sponsored vigilantism.[23]

Expulsions

We'd be remiss if we didn't note that even these tremendous and disproportionate Republican advantages aren't enough for the architects and practitioners of Vigilante Democracy. Despite the fact that Tennessee has Republican supermajorities in both chambers of its legislature, Republican lawmakers felt compelled in 2023 to expel Justin Jones and Justin Pearson, two young, Black legislators who respectively represented parts of Nashville and Memphis. Both men are professed Christians—Jones is a Vanderbilt divinity student, and Pearson regularly preaches at Black churches. Their offense was to lead a gun control protest on the floor of the chamber. For taking exception to the legislature's failure to protect citizens from guns, they were accused and convicted by the necessary two-thirds majority of house members of bringing "disorder and dishonor" to the chamber. (A third legislator-protester, Gloria Johnson, who is white, survived the expulsion vote.)[24]

To regain admission to the house, Jones and Pearson each had to run for reelection. And though their home districts promptly and enthusiastically reaffirmed their support, the expulsions were costly and disruptive. And they're far from over. Having passed new rules of "propriety" during Jones and Pearson's absence, the legislature—called back into session by Republican governor Bill Lee to (belatedly) consider reforms in the wake of the 2023 Nashville school shooting—quickly prohibited Jones from speaking. Jones was gaveled out of order for allegedly straying from the topic of a proposed bill. Not long after silencing Jones, the house adjourned. Video footage appears to show a flustered and frustrated house Speaker, Republican Cameron Sexton, shoving Pearson on his way out of the chamber.[25]

Something similar happened in Montana, where the 2022 survey data showed adults favoring the Democratic Party over the Republican Party by a whopping twelve points.[26] Yet as we've seen in other red states, both legislative houses in Helena boast Republican supermajorities. Between Republican control of the legislature and a very Trumpy governor, MAGA-friendly politicians should feel quite confident of their hold on power.

But, as in Tennessee, Montana's GOP leadership is brittle and imperious. Zooey Zephyr, a progressive representative from Missoula, knows this all too well. In April 2023, just a few short months after becoming the state's first openly transgender state legislator, Zephyr was booted off the house floor—and banned for the remainder of the legislative session—for her vigorous opposition to the then-proposed ban on gender-affirming care for transgender youth. While Zephyr protested that she was asked to "be silent when my community is facing bills that get us killed," members of the Republican leadership accused her of fomenting an "insurrection." In the end, every Republican in the house voted to deny her the right to participate in the remainder of the session's proceedings, but they permitted her to vote remotely.[27]

MAKING A FEDERAL CASE OUT OF IT

So, how do we get out of this mess?

The easiest and best solutions would of course come from the federal government. As the feds stepped up during Reconstruction and again during the civil rights movement, the national government could, today, codify protections for abortion rights, interstate travel, and LGBTQ+ students and families. They could disrupt repressive school policies by conditioning federal funding on states and districts maintaining inclusive curricula, athletics, and library holdings. They could pass legislation to further protect voting rights and the safety and security of local and state government officials entrusted with election administration.

Thanks to the Supreme Court, which we'll get to below, the feds can't do much about rampant gun ownership or harrowing campaigns of intimidation by heavily armed militiamen. But the Justice Department could be more aggressive in prosecuting individuals or groups who violate the nation's civil rights laws. The DOJ could also do more to investigate and seek to enjoin local and state police forces that condone or themselves perpetrate civil rights violations. And, surely, it's easier to win at the federal level than in deep-red states.

Maybe, maybe not.

The Constitution Tends to Boost White, Rural Interests

Historically, the branch of government that's done the most to provide real protections for democratic equality is Congress. But while Congress has the constitutional authority to counteract the spread of state-sponsored vigilantism, its structure and procedures make securing new civil rights legislation a maddeningly difficult undertaking.

The challenges stem from the basic design of the institution. Even assuming the House of Representatives is either unproblematically majoritarian, or that gerrymandering by red and blue states cancels each other out, the big problem is (as it's always been) the U.S. Senate. Giving equal representation to states, not people, the Senate is intentionally and inescapably undemocratic. As political scientist Robert Dahl has noted, "the degree of unequal representation in the U.S. Senate is by far the most extreme" of all federal systems.[28] At the founding, this arrangement was explicitly understood as protecting the prerogatives of the slaveholding South.[29] That arrangement continued to benefit the South. The old Confederate states wielded disproportionate Senate power not only throughout the antebellum period but also the Jim Crow era and, seemingly, today as well.

An extensively researched report in the *Guardian* described today's Senate as "a firewall for a shrinking minority of mostly white, conservative voters across the country to block policies they don't agree with and safeguard the voter suppression tactics that shore up Republican power."[30] In 2021, the Senate was split 50-50 *even though* "Democratic senators represent[ed] nearly 40 million more voters than Republican senators." In 2023, states represented by Democratic senators had 99 million more residents than those represented by Republicans; the chamber was divided 51-49 Democrat to Republican.[31]

Things promise to get even worse with each passing decade. "By 2040, 70% of Americans are expected to live in the 15 largest states, and to be represented by only 30 senators, while 30% of Americans will have 70 senators voting on their behalf."[32]

The Senators Double Down

Given how embarrassing and destructive the representational inequities are—per capita, Wyoming residents have fifty-nine times more influence in the Senate than Californians do—you might think senators would do what they could on the margins to make the body more majoritarian.[33] And, once again, you'd be wrong.

Arguably the most distinctive feature of the Senate is its filibuster rule. The rule allows for forty-one senators—far from a majority of the chamber—to hold up most pieces of legislation indefinitely. In the olden days, a senator could stop the work of the Senate only by actually holding the chamber floor. And to hold the floor, that senator had to continue speaking—and standing.[34] Movie buffs surely associate such marathon speeches with Jimmy Stewart's triumphant one-man battle against political graft in *Mr. Smith Goes to Washington*; political junkies might gravitate instead to Strom Thurmond's twenty-four-hour filibuster—an unsuccessful ploy to thwart passage of what became the 1957 Civil Rights Act. Today, you don't have to do anything so labor-intensive. Simply indicating one's *intent* to filibuster is enough to prevent the Senate from invoking cloture—that is, cutting off debate and proceeding with a vote. Given how sharply and fiercely partisan politics are today, it's near impossible to move forward on most types of bills that don't fall within exceptions to the filibuster rule.

Filibuster reform requires only a simple majority vote of the senators. It was high on the agenda of most Democrats at the start of the Biden presidency. Initially with a 50-50 Senate, and Vice President Kamala Harris available to cast tiebreaking votes, a decision to end the filibuster would have allowed the Biden administration to proceed with, among other things, important voting rights measures, criminal justice reform, Supreme Court reform, and abortion rights legislation. Yet at least two Democrats remained steadfastly opposed. The Senate thus remains a roach motel for all but the most urgent or uncontroversial federal legislation. Bills check in, but they never leave.

The Electoral College

Even if Congress will not, or cannot, pass new legislation to combat Vigilante Democracy, the president and the fleet of federal executive agencies can draw on already enacted laws to limit a great many authoritarian excesses. But, alas, winning the presidency is hardly a straightforward democratic exercise, either.

In 2020, Democratic strategists estimated that for Joe Biden to have even odds of winning the presidency, he'd have to capture 52 percent of the vote.[35] As David Shor, a data analyst, explains, that's because the Electoral College—the body that actually selects our president—has a fairly skewed partisan bias. The directional skewing changes over time. In 2012, Democrats had a slight partisan advantage. But now, because an important segment of white midwestern voters without college degrees have left the Democratic Party and embraced MAGA Republicanism, the Electoral College will likely favor Republicans for the foreseeable future.

Lest you consider the partisan biases to be negligible—i.e., 52 percent doesn't seem *too hard* to reach—*Vox*'s Ian Millhiser is here to tell us otherwise. As he recounts, Biden's 4.5 percent national popular vote victory in 2020 was the second largest in the past twenty years. Even with that impressive vote lead, "if a total of 43,000 Biden voters had stayed home in the states of Georgia, Arizona, and Wisconsin, Trump would have won a second term."[36]

Little surprise, then, that Democratic strategists and pundits who, understandably, prioritize winning hesitate to advocate for certain civil rights that don't play well among certain white voters. Matt Yglesias asserts that Democrats should tread carefully when opposing such things like Don't Say Gay or bans on transgender student participation in athletics.[37] Ruy Teixeira has even suggested that the Democrats tone down their fury over *Dobbs* lest they alienate suburban white women.[38] James Carville has urged Democrats to abandon "faculty lounge" politics and steer clear of "metropolitan, overeducated arrogance." He says, "The only way Democrats can hold power is to build on their coalition, and that will have to include more rural white voters from across the country."[39]

While we too recognize the importance of beating back candidates hostile to democracy, we worry about the concessions. By conceding too much ground to the religious Right, we run the risk of capitulating to Vigilante Democracy.

The Judicial Backstop

We think we've said more than enough to dissuade folks from assuming we can vote our way out of the current morass. But even if there is some Democratic breakthrough, the federal courts (and many state courts) remain bastions of reactionary jurisprudence. If recent history is any guide, federal and state laws are apt to be struck down or may be gutted by courts that insist on carving out exemptions for right-wing

Christians who feel morally compelled to reject vaccines or deny services to LGBTQ+ individuals or families. For those laws that survive constitutional scrutiny, federal agencies' ability to administer them is likely to be called into question. Over just the past couple of years, the Supreme Court has denied federal agencies the authority to implement key provisions of signature pieces of legislation, all of which were signed into law by Republican presidents: the 1970 Clean Air Act, the 1972 Clean Water Act, the 2003 Higher Education Relief Opportunities for Students Act, and a 2020 Covid relief act.

Here, too, there is no likely short- or medium-term solution. A much-cited study by a pair of Princeton political scientists predicts that Republican-appointed justices are likely to control the Supreme Court at least until the 2050s.[40] Another study, by a group of law professors and political scientists, estimates that the Court will remain in Republican hands at least through 2065.[41] Empirical projections as to state courts are hard to come by. But we do know this: The partisan divide among state supreme court justices right now is significant, if not jaw-dropping.

STATE SUPREME COURT JUDGES BY PARTY AFFILIATION (REPUBLICAN-DEMOCRATIC, AS OF AUGUST 2023)[42]
Arkansas 7-0
Florida 7-0
Idaho 5-0
Indiana 5-0
Louisiana 5-1 (1 no party affiliation)
Mississippi 7-2
Missouri 4-3
South Carolina 3-0 (2 no party affiliation)
Texas 9-0
Tennessee 4-1

Justice Alito's suggestion that folks just exercise political power, then, presents a manifestly inadequate response to surging vigilantism. Joe Biden is, for sure, right. Organizing, fundraising, voting, lobbying, and taking to the streets—all this remains crucial. But if Vigilante Democracy is to be contained, and to be contained here and now, more is needed.

"Divide and Inflame"

Why Corporations Won't Save Us

Vigilantism is bad for business. Yet while states have unleashed vigilantes on abortion providers, teachers, Black Americans, LGBTQ+ people, and their allies, corporations have remained awfully quiet. Corporate lobbyists haven't descended on state capitols to resist vigilante-empowering bills. The airwaves haven't been jammed with ads urging voters to call their lawmakers and governor to demand that they call off the vigilantes. The U.S. Chamber of Commerce's powerhouse litigation shop hasn't raced to courthouses across the range of red states with briefs explaining how legalized vigilantism is terrible for the American economy.

OLD ALLIANCES DIE HARD

The Powell Memo, which we discussed earlier, provided a template for corporate activism to protect the American free enterprise system from radicals.[1] Today's radicals are, of course, extremists on the far right.

But corporate America's army of think tanks, lobbying teams, lawyers, and ultra-wealthy benefactors aren't free to fight *those* extremists. That's because big business long ago joined forces with religious and social traditionalists to counteract what both perceived as the liberal takeover of America's schools, universities, courts, and government agencies. The terms of their alliance were straightforward: Pro-business Republicans would fund candidates, provide organizational power, and support think tanks such as the Heritage Foundation, the Manhattan Institute, and the Claremont Institute that trumpeted unrestrained capitalism and social conservativism. For their contributions, they would get to dictate the party's economic policy. The religious and social traditionalists would contribute by mobilizing voters, whom they appealed to via scare tactics about an America that lost touch with its moral grounding and via promises that the traditionalists would lead the Republican Party's social agenda on abortion and school prayer.[2]

Understanding this alliance—*we do economics, you do morals*—provides some context for corporate America's tepid response to state-supported vigilantism. And make no mistake: The old marriage between country club Republicans and the religious Right has proven its worth, time and again. Our current right-wing Supreme Court; tax policies that prevent the federal government from funding a welfare state; protections for "freedom of contract" and restrictions on government regulation that allow corporations to write the law they're governed by—all of these wins and more owe a debt to the business-religious alliance that has regularly delivered Congress, the White House, state legislatures, and governorships to right-wing politicians. Given all that we just said, why on earth would we expect businesses to align with folks on the left who, when they're not resisting vigilantism, are clamoring for more government spending, more progressive taxation, and greater labor and environmental protections?

Our answer is simple. The old business-religious alliance has outlived its utility. The world today is far different from the one in which that alliance was forged. And it's changed in ways that actually pit the interests of business leaders against those who want nothing more than to aggressively enforce America's traditional hierarchies of race, wealth, gender, and class.

Back when Powell typed out his memorandum, much of America's wealth, purchasing power, and human capital was concentrated within the straight, white Christian, male cohort. Women were a far smaller and more marginal segment of the workforce. Black Americans, still reeling from historic patterns of racial subordination and ongoing racism, were likewise peripheral players in the marketplace. LGBTQ+ persons—stigmatized and forced to live in the closet, precluded from entering certain professions, and subject to criminal prosecution for intimate relationships—were all but invisible in the American political economy. All of these things meant that whatever reactionary social policies the religious Right was peddling imposed few, if any, costs on America's business elites.

While there are real, lingering barriers to education and employment, pay equality, job promotion, and wealth-building, today's marketplace is considerably more inclusive, cosmopolitan, and diverse. Many firms welcome and actively recruit racial minorities, women, and LGBTQ+ persons and help advance them into leadership positions. These firms understand that a disproportionate percentage of the nation's academic talent, entrepreneurial energy, artistic creativity, and purchasing power resides in highly progressive enclaves on both the East and West Coasts. As countless executives have explained, investors, partners, and customers are all looking to do business with companies that not only "look" diverse, but that also have the diversity of background and experience to be effective, sensitive, and innovative players in the global marketplace.[3]

Purchasing power, too, has changed drastically. Many more women today are either financially independent or equal financial decision-makers (within domestic partnerships) than was true when Powell wrote his memo in 1971. Many more racial minorities have far larger earning power and greater disposable income. For these reasons, if no other, they command greater respect in the marketplace.

Moreover, corporations' pursuit of shareholder value maximization—the idea that the only proper aim of corporate activity is generating profits for shareholders—is not the monolithic force it was back in the early 1970s. Recently, some firms have even come to question the anti-tax, anti-regulatory policies they've lobbied and litigated for;

they now wonder whether those policies harm society, and with it, the firms' long-term profitability. This doesn't mean that corporations aren't interested in making money. It does mean, however, that they know their customers and employees care about the environment, social justice, and income inequality; as a result, executives are pivoting to align corporate policies with customers' and employees' demands. Whether it's big businesses' support for the Paris Climate Pact, their commitment to diversity and equity in hiring and promotion decisions, or their embrace of corporate social responsibility, firms have signaled that they at least care about how they present themselves to constituencies who genuinely value those things.

THE VIGILANTE RIGHT COMES FOR CORPORATE AMERICA

Given what we just described, today's Republican alliance seems increasingly untenable. Not only do business elites have reason to bristle at right-wing social policies but the religious Right has reason to see "woke" corporate policies as unforgivable. These changed circumstances should, we think, lend themselves to a clean divorce and subsequent realignment. But, for now, at least, the jilted party—that is, the Christian nationalists—won't make things easy.

Just ask Mickey Mouse.

Though officially headquartered in Burbank, California, the Walt Disney Corporation is very much a Florida institution. Ranked forty-eighth on the latest Fortune 500 list (and sixth in *Fortune*'s survey of the "World's Most Admired Companies"), Disney is both Florida's economic juggernaut and cultural touchstone. Disney World boasts four iconic theme parks, two water parks, a sports complex, thirty-some hotels and spas, a wedding pavilion, and multiple eighteen-hole golf courses, shopping plazas, and restaurants. Despite Central Florida's blistering heat and punishingly long hurricane season, Disney World is always listed among the most visited destinations in the world.

Disney's reach is certainly global; but its magic is felt nowhere as acutely as in and around the Florida statehouse some 250 miles away from Cinderella's Castle. It's been this way ever since Walt Disney began scouting locations to build an East Coast complement to California's Disneyland. In 1967, the Florida legislature gifted Disney the modest-sounding Reedy Creek Improvement District, quasi-privatizing over twenty-five thousand acres of Florida land and authorizing Disney to exercise regulatory dominion over it. (For comparison's sake, the twenty-five-thousand-acre Reedy Creek is roughly the size of the Bronx—and nearly twice the size of Manhattan.[4]) In the years and decades that have followed, successive governors and legislatures remained unflaggingly attentive to the whims and wishes of the state's biggest revenue generator.[5] As recently as 2021, Disney secured for itself a categorical exemption from a highly coercive effort by the state to control the editorial decisions of media companies. Lest there be any doubt as to Disney's singular heft, the legislature tacked on an amendment ensuring the regulations did not apply to media companies that just so happened to own a theme park![6] And in that same session, Florida gave Disney a $578 million tax credit, underwriting more than half of the company's promised outlay to relocate a large number of its employees from California to Orlando.[7]

All of this makes Disney's response to the spread of legal vigilantism even more shocking. When Florida's Don't Say Gay law was introduced in early 2022, Floridians targeted by the law were optimistic that Disney would leverage its enormous influence to quash it. The law, you'll recall, prohibits classroom "instruction" relating to gender identity or sexual orientation. Its vague, overbroad prohibitions and vigilante-powered enforcement scheme risk exposing teachers who so much as acknowledge LGBTQ+ identities to disciplinary proceedings, the loss of employment, and monetary damages.[8] Disney, of course, has a diverse, inclusive, and cosmopolitan customer base and attracts and recruits highly educated, creative talent from around the world. The company employs large cohorts of executives and employees in Southern California and in New York—locations where LGBTQ+-friendly policies are culturally and legally de rigueur. Moreover, some eighty-two thousand Disney employees live and work in Florida. They and their families would be directly affected by Don't Say Gay. The company thus had strong reasons to resist a bill that aimed to push LGBTQ+ students and teachers back into the closet, and to create an educational environment that many creative types, straight or queer, would find especially insular and oppressive.

But despite clamoring from within the company, across Florida, and across the nation by those yearning for someone to step up and confront the state's smugly authoritarian governor, the company's response clocked in somewhere between anemic and perfunctory. Then-CEO Bob Chapek told a group of LGBTQ+ employees that Disney wouldn't be making a public statement, because speaking up would "divide and inflame" the situation, whatever that meant. Even state legislators, accustomed to Disney lobbyists always getting their way, were surprised at Disney's failure to flex its muscle on this issue.[9]

Even after Ron DeSantis signed Don't Say Gay into law, Disney remained quiet for several days. Only after employees went public in expressing their frustration and disappointment with the company did Disney respond. Don't Say Gay, the company announced, "should never have been passed and should never have been signed into law." Chapek reportedly placed a quiet call to DeSantis, underscoring the company's disapproval. Disney also announced it was suspending all political donations in Florida.[10] Given that MAGA Republicans were already in control of both the governor's mansion and the statehouse and that it generally takes more money to unseat an elected official than for an incumbent to win reelection, a suspension of *all* funds would have the clear and predictable effect of only further entrenching the right-wing status quo.

A governor who passed a law noxious to the biggest employer and revenue driver in the state might have considered himself lucky that all that firm did was issue a mildly critical statement. Such a governor might have taken the win and moved on. But not DeSantis. Outraged by even that spiritless rebuke, the Florida governor came out swinging. In a press conference at the state capitol, he accused Disney of "cross[ing] the line" and vowed, "We're going to make sure we're fighting back when people are threatening our parents and threatening our kids." DeSantis also took to social media and cable news to trash Disney, lambasting the firm as a woke outfit run by "California corporate executives."[11] Disney, DeSantis baselessly charged, was attacking parental rights, threatening the people of Florida, and pushing "transgenderism" in kindergarten classrooms.[12]

Other right-wing politicians and pundits soon joined in the attacks on Disney—all over, mind you, a milquetoast, almost begrudging statement and a private call to DeSantis! Ted Cruz warned that any firm that opposed Don't Say Gay might well peddle porn to preschoolers.[13] Colorado's Lauren Boebert introduced a House bill to override long-standing federal regulations establishing no-fly zones over Disney theme parks.[14] Josh Hawley threatened to shorten the duration of federal copyright protections, introducing a bill tailored to injure Disney (and only Disney).[15] The *Daily Wire*, Ben Shapiro's right-wing media outfit, promised to invest $100 million to develop content for families distressed by what the " 'woke' Walt Disney Company" produces.[16]

But that was nothing compared to what the state lawmakers had in the works. DeSantis's allies in the Florida legislature stripped Disney of many of its long-held special privileges, foremost among them governance of the Reedy Creek Improvement District.[17] In fact, Reedy Creek had long been saving Florida taxpayers considerable sums of money. Economists and tax lawyers estimate that punishing Disney by dissolving Reedy Creek may result in Florida taxpayers having to absorb over $1 billion in Disney debt.[18]

Both Disney's token opposition to Don't Say Gay and the furious counterattack it provoked capture the rocky dissolution of the

Republican corporate-cultural alliance, signal who won, and reveal why the culture warriors came out on top. Disney has a long history of playing politics and playing it well. Provided corporate political advocacy didn't conflict with Christian nationalists' vision of society, that activism was just fine. Indeed, Florida politicos no doubt welcomed opportunities to wheel and deal with a company so vital to the Sunshine State. But Disney's venturing ever so slightly into progressive *cultural* politics—on issues broadly popular with the company's employees, customers, and a majority of Americans—was a bridge too far. And as Disney learned, the penalty for challenging a vindictive governor backed by MAGA supermajorities in both legislative houses was swift and unsparing.[21]

Disney is far from the only corporation whose business interests seemingly conflict with core components of the MAGA agenda. Legislation in some two dozen states authorizes gun owners to bring weapons onto corporate property, prioritizing the rights of militant culture warriors over the rights of commercial property owners.[22] In Texas, guns may be carried everywhere unless property owners affirmatively prohibit them after complying with onerous notice requirements.[23]

Then there are policies that limit corporate autonomy when it comes to matters of recruitment and training. Florida's "Stop WOKE" Act (whose legality is currently being challenged on First Amendment grounds) empowers workers to sue employers for mandating training that "espouses, promotes, advances, inculcates, or compels" understandings relating to, among other things, systemic racism, restorative justice (including affirmative action), and implicit bias.[24]

Journeying back to Texas, most associate S.B. 8 with anti-abortion vigilantes surveilling and prosecuting medical professionals. But the statute is designed to sweep far more broadly. Its sponsors and drafters insist that S.B. 8 reaches employers who provide financial assistance to employees seeking abortions, in-kind benefits (including health insurance), or even nothing more than time off from work for employees or their covered family members to travel and receive the care they need.[25] Who would possibly know this information? Disgruntled employees in HR and payroll, subordinates with an axe to grind against a supervisor, and coworkers seeking any advantage over rivals for a potential promotion.

As of 2024, two additional bills impinging on employer-employee relations are pending before the Texas legislature. One designates any company officer who facilitates travel for an employee seeking an abortion to be violating a "fiduciary duty to the company"—allowing shareholders or other "aggrieved person[s]" to sue for damages. A second bill strips any business that assists an employee seeking an abortion (by, among other things, providing financial assistance for the procedure or for travel to a clinic) of otherwise applicable state tax incentives.[26]

It gets worse. Responding to right-wingers' paranoia over being "censored" on platforms where they long for clout, both Florida and Texas have recently enacted laws prohibiting private social media companies from engaging in content moderation based on political viewpoints. (And both allow state residents to sue.[27]) These laws brazenly interfere with business autonomy, and do so in a way that's surely going to force private firms to publish right-wing hate speech, dangerous conspiracy theories, and pro-fascist propaganda—all of which is not only bad for democracy but also bad for business, as that content pushes would-be users off the platforms. In essence, the two biggest stars in the MAGA constellation are telling private platforms they're obligated to amplify virulently antidemocratic speech, the very type of state interference in corporate decision-making that Lewis Powell feared from the political Left.

AND CORPORATE AMERICA TURNS
TO HALF MEASURES

Given the undeniable vulnerability of not only women across red America but also transgender kids in Tennessee, Black teachers in Florida, and election workers in Georgia, one might hope that corporate executives—armed with money and lobbyists and capable of offering services and products even vigilantes rely on—would put these MAGA bullies in their place. It would be nice if the corporate executives, investors, and board members stepped up because it's the right thing to do. But a realignment is also warranted for dollars-and-cents reasons. If only to maximize their profits and ensure *their liberty*, corporations should ally themselves with the victims of vigilantism and advocates for democratic equality.

But whereas the religious Right is quick to turn on their old alliance partners, the business elites seem unwilling to respond in kind.

Instead, they're turning to half measures. They're quietly working around repressive laws and shielding employees and customers from certain vigilante attacks.

These half measures aren't only incomplete. They're also making things worse.

Health, Dental, 401(k) . . . and Vigilante Insurance?

Let's start with corporate support for employees in states with abortion bans, some of which are enforced through vigilante schemes like S.B. 8. After *Dobbs*, Citigroup, Yelp, Uber, Amazon, Lyft, Tesla, Bumble, Levi Strauss, Starbucks, Salesforce, Hewlett Packard, Disney, and J.P. Morgan, among others, promised to cover the expenses of employees and family members forced to travel out of state to obtain reproductive healthcare.[28] Some firms have gone further. When S.B. 8 first came into effect, Lyft and Uber announced they'd indemnify drivers targeted by vigilante lawsuits simply for driving a pregnant person to an abortion clinic. "We wanted to raise our hand and say, this is not right to pit citizens against citizens," said Lyft's president, who stated that the company would fund "100% of legal fees" for drivers targeted by the Texas law.[29]

Firms' responses to anti-CRT or anti-LGBTQ+ statutes have been far weaker. But the U.S. Air Force—an organization considered "woke" only in the most febrile of Christian nationalist fever dreams—has taken impressive (albeit exceptional) steps. The air force has offered not only to provide service members and their families with medical and legal help in states restricting LGBTQ+ rights; it has also promised to relocate families to safer states—that is, non-vigilante jurisdictions.[30]

These efforts are, let's be clear, hardly heroic. Corporations want good press and happy stakeholders, so they help a few employees here and there against one, maybe two, prongs of the January 7 Project. Meanwhile, the firms can maintain good relations with the Christian nationalists running vigilante jurisdictions. Here's the deal: The firms don't butt heads with the vigilantes (or threaten to move their operations out of the vigilante jurisdictions). In turn, the firms continue to enjoy the benefits of low taxes and lax regulations that are staples of most MAGA political communities.

This arrangement hurts several constituencies. Even those ostensibly directly supported by their firms still run tremendous risks. For instance, Lyft may cover 100 percent of drivers' legal fees, but being named a defendant in a civil lawsuit will still wreak havoc on someone's access to credit and require them to take time off to appear in court—something we venture that few employed in the hardscrabble gig economy can afford. The burdens on individuals who are forced to cross state lines to obtain access to reproductive healthcare are even greater. We should not treat an emotionally and physically fraught trip to an "abortion sanctuary" as if it were a corporate perk, let alone a fun-filled weekend getaway.[31]

Furthermore, work-arounds help only a relatively privileged subset of vigilante targets. Traveling to an out-of-state clinic might be an option for people with uncomplicated pregnancies and whose personal circumstances allow them to take time to, say, fly from San Antonio to Chicago or Philadelphia. The situation is different for people like Anna Zargarian, who must travel for urgently needed medical care; for those with considerable child- or eldercare responsibilities; for undocumented persons, given that train, bus, and airport terminals are policed by immigration officials; for those on parole who may not be allowed to leave the state; and for those who live with an abusive relative or partner.[32]

Outside of the abortion context, the idea of traveling to safe-haven jurisdictions is a cruel joke. The transgender kids whose parents work for Levi Strauss or Hewlett Packard in jurisdictions that penalize LGBTQ+-inclusivity may be able to secure out-of-state gender-affirming medical care. But they can't be ferried out of state every time they have a track meet, or anytime they need to use a restroom during school hours. And, by our reckoning, no major firm or, again, federal employer has done much of anything to promote the safety or enrich the education of the children of employees who reside in communities subject to book bans and whitewashed lesson plans.

Most important, while some corporate measures provide a modicum of support to select targets of vigilantism, those measures will, we fear, ultimately make it more difficult for coalitions of advocates to secure the repeal of pernicious legislation (or otherwise end pernicious practices). When firms help to insulate their employees from vigilantism, they are implicitly accepting that others in the state, including some of their customers, will continue to be targeted and harmed. In acting to protect, say, employees' access to reproductive healthcare, the firms are reducing solidarity across targeted populations and thus lessening the pressure employers and their employees feel to agitate for reform.

The Dangers of Privatizing and Parceling Out
Anti-Vigilante Countermeasures

Fighting vigilantism is going to require solidarity among *all* the groups the January 7 Project targets. If the Right's embrace of vigilantism is a comprehensive and concerted strategy, that strategy's vulnerability lies in the fact that it sweeps so far, so fast. One of the reasons Jim Crow was wildly effective and durable was that southern politicos primarily singled out Black Americans, who made up only around 10 percent of the national population (and a disproportionately small segment of most workforces and customer bases). Those plagued by Jim Crow needed white allies from up north and out west—and lots of them. But northern and West Coast whites weren't particularly affected. Southern Black Americans didn't wield much political, cultural, or economic power. So long as southern Black men, women, and children were the only ones targeted, the rest of the nation could turn a blind eye to pervasive, harrowing, institutionalized racism.[33]

In contrast to Jim Crow's targeting of Black Americans, today's vigilante regimes threaten more than half the U.S. population. If the targeted groups stand tall together, the alliance of women, Black and brown Americans, and LGBTQ+ persons (plus doctors, nurses, teachers, and coaches imperiled by vigilantism) will have numerical strength. This alliance will also have considerable political and economic power, certainly leagues more than those terrorized by Jim Crow segregationists could wield. But employers, ostensibly well-meaning in their efforts to mitigate the effects of vigilantism, run the risk of diluting and dividing otherwise strong, would-be coalitions.

As far as corporate protections extend, a good number of pregnant persons may be safeguarded, but very few transgender kids (and quite possibly no teachers) will be covered. What's more, the dilutions and divisions are not just between groups but also between socioeconomic classes within the same group. Pregnant persons who work for Citicorp or J.P. Morgan in Texas may be okay, but those who work the floor at a Dollar General, wait tables at a neighborhood bar and grill, or manage sales at some midsize shipping company are unlikely to have employers who will pay for out-of-state abortions. And it is quite plausible that those who work for Citicorp as opposed to Dollar General are also disproportionately better educated, enjoy more flexible schedules (to lobby, organize, volunteer on campaigns), have more resources to influence the highly commercialized "marketplace" of political persuasion and debate, and are more likely to be mobile and able to "vote with their feet" by transferring to a safer state if all else fails.

What's more, employers who are able to at least moderately protect their workers will have fewer reasons to exercise their most forceful option: to relocate their operations elsewhere. It hardly needs saying that firms threaten to relocate all the time; the quest for more favorable tax and regulatory environments is precisely what has driven national and multinational corporations from California (as well as from the relatively highly unionized Rust Belt) to places like Texas, Alabama, Tennessee, and Florida. If firms located in red states can't recruit or retain personnel fearful of the suppression of reproductive rights, those owners and executives might lobby the states to ease up on the vigilantism or else expect a business exodus. That's a powerful cudgel but one major corporations haven't shown a willingness to use against vigilantism. It's simply cheaper and easier to, say, privately underwrite the costs of out-of-state abortions for employees and their partners (most of whom will never need abortions). So this appears to be how firms make peace with their employees and state governments, accepting that they may struggle to recruit and retain (unprotected) Black and LGBTQ+ workers.

We've already seen examples of this sort. In 2021, Tesla announced it was moving from California to Texas. According to CEO Elon Musk, California's public health protections were intolerably "fascist."[34] The electric car maker now concentrates many of its business lines in red states to take advantage of low taxes, lax regulations, and cheaper (and less unionized) labor.[35] Hewlett Packard left right around the time Tesla left, as did Oracle. They, too, relocated to Texas.[36]

These firms have promised to support the reproductive rights of their employees. Assuming they remain true to their word, their work-arounds for individuals seeking reproductive healthcare create exactly the political dynamics we fear. Tesla, Oracle, and HP moved to a state knowing full well that MAGA and MAGA-friendly officials were firmly in control of all three branches of government. They did so to maximize profits. And then, they drew headlines (and accolades) when, after the *Dobbs* ruling, they announced they'd privately insure employees' abortion costs, including travel and time for those needing to venture out of state.

NO MERCY

Someone else drew headlines (and accolades), too. Governor Greg Abbott was lauded for luring companies to his state notwithstanding that jurisdiction's open hostility to democratic equality.

Given that "business friendly" Texas benefits from the arrival of corporate newcomers, one might think that state officials would give firms latitude to quietly flout Christian nationalist dogma. Not unlike the arrangements in some of the authoritarian states hugging the Persian Gulf, where Western business and luxury travelers are exempt from following those states' strict social codes, Texas conceivably could allow firms to help their employees access gender-affirming care and reproductive health services—and also keep state inspectors monitoring school curricula and library books some distance from such progressive enclaves as Austin.

But Vigilante Democracy doesn't allow states to soft-pedal enforcement of their laws. Because it has empowered vigilantes, Texas cannot give any assurances to firms. As long as aggrieved culture warriors are ready and willing to enforce the state's authoritarian mandates, there's only so much that government officials can do. Perhaps, though, this is a moot point. MAGA politicians, so far, seem prepared to harass firms that try to protect employees' and customers' autonomy. Even more surprising, right-wing think tanks that corporate America has long funded are likewise siding with MAGA politicians.

Of late, Manhattan and Heritage have called for heightened state control over industries, or have otherwise sought to vest governments with greater authority over the business decisions of private firms and corporations.[37] The sharp-elbowed American Legislative Exchange Council, another Powell-inspired organization that once was characterized as a "dating agency for Republican state legislators and big corporations,"[38] is suddenly rallying support for laws that restrict firms' liberty to decide which companies to partner with (and which ones to avoid).[39] Meanwhile, right-wing pundits churn out sensationalist accounts with titles such as *The Dictatorship of Woke Capital* and *Woke, Inc.* (the latter written by onetime 2024 GOP presidential aspirant Vivek Ramaswamy).

Vehement and highly politicized hostility to public health precautions during the Covid pandemic led governors to override decisions of individual business owners (including healthcare providers) to require masking. At the height of the health crisis, Ron DeSantis went so far as to take on cruise lines, insisting that the struggling industry ignore—that is, *defy*—then–federal regulations requiring bans on unvaccinated passengers or else find ports of call out of state.[40] And as if he weren't content to wage war against Mickey Mouse, the Little Mermaid, and Florida's cruise-tourism industry, DeSantis went after our national pastime, too—specifically targeting baseball's Tampa Bay Rays. Upon learning that Rays ownership donated a mere $50,000 to gun violence prevention organizations (and penned a single anti-gun violence tweet)—*on the heels of the horrific school shooting in*

Uvalde, Texas—the Florida governor pulled back an already promised $35 million in state funds.[41]

Increasingly, MAGA politicians such as DeSantis, Ted Cruz, and Josh Hawley are denouncing business elites as woke, globalist, and anti-American.[42] These politicos and the judges they've installed on the federal bench seek to shame, discipline, and sue corporations and even the conservative law firms that advise them[43] for—as federal judge James Ho has claimed—"threatening to subvert American democracy."[44]

WAITING FOR THE CORPORATIONS

The vigilante agenda enjoys nothing like majority support—and its proponents hardly command the lion's share of American purchasing power. Yet the zealotry of MAGA partisans allows the movement to punch above its weight, not just in the political arena but in the marketplace. The Christian nationalists threaten boycotts and lawsuits, and they stir hysteria about companies being woke or corrupting the morals of the young. Their relentless threats of violence against medical providers who offer gender-affirming care have led to repeated lockdowns of healthcare facilities, causing chaos and endangering the lives of, among others, babies in neonatal intensive care units.[45]

Moreover, firms' obligation to report quarterly results—and pressure on management to deliver short-term wins even at the expense of long-term profitability—make it harder for corporations to take on vigilantism.[46] Boycotts against firms that elevate LGBTQ+ voices, expression of outrage over corporations' supposed sexualization of children, claims that firms are "discriminating" against conservatives, and other varieties of culture war activism can have an immediate effect. When right-wing influencers launched a campaign against Anheuser-Busch over an Instagram ad that featured a trans influencer, Bud Light sales dropped 23 percent.[47] A smear campaign against

Target, claiming that the company was marketing trans-inclusive clothing to minors, triggered a series of bomb threats.[48] In the long run, these campaigns might fizzle out. Given enough time, companies like Disney could bury even someone as powerful as Ron DeSantis. But the firms simply don't have the time—because their shareholders simply don't have the patience. And so executives react immediately and cave to right-wing pressure.

We're left with a good deal of corporate waffling that satisfies no one: neither the right-wingers who insist on absolute loyalty to Christian nationalist dogma, nor liberals and progressives who have come to see gestures in favor of civil rights and democratic equality as mere virtue signaling. But make no mistake: Just because no one is satisfied doesn't mean there are no winners. The winners are the vigilantes. They know that threats work—the bigger the threat, the better.

Meanwhile, another vicious circle keeps spinning—the urge to quickly forgive and forget. Following the January 6 insurrection, firms including Blue Cross Blue Shield, Marriott, Dow, Pfizer, Mastercard, and Airbnb all pledged that they would halt donations to the so-called Sedition Caucus, the 147 senators and House members who had voted against certifying the 2020 presidential election. But well before the 2022 midterms, more than 70 percent of the pledge signatories had reopened their checkbooks. An investigation by good-government watchdog CREW found that 1,345 corporate and industry group PACs gave $50.5 million to the campaigns or leadership PACs of members of the Sedition Caucus.[49] More broadly than the January 6 context, firms continue to finance political candidates whose agendas are at odds with the donors' stated corporate values. Consider the telecommunications giant AT&T. Human Rights Campaign, a blue-chip LGBTQ+ advocacy group with a sterling record, awarded the telecommunications giant a perfect 100 percent score on its Equality Index. But the index measures only workplace conditions without accounting for firms' broader political activity. That's a good thing for AT&T, which between 2020 and 2022 donated $244,050 to state officeholders supporting anti-transgender laws.[50]

Where's this leave us? Corporations are not likely to be a powerful political counterweight to Vigilante Democracy. Making matters worse, corporate measures to buffer employees, customers, and others from some aspects of legal vigilantism's effects, while perhaps well intentioned, may perversely make the long-term fight against Vigilante Democracy more difficult to win.

So we're left to ask: If corporations with their economic clout won't save us, who can?

CHAPTER **12**

More Like 1850 Than 1950:
The International Community Won't Save the Day

It is not Russia that threatens the United States so
much as Mississippi.

An Appeal to the World, NAACP (October 23, 1947)

The way they are treating my people in the South, the
[U.S.] government can go to hell.

*Louis Armstrong, explaining why he canceled a State
Department–sponsored trip to the Soviet Union (September 17, 1957)*[1]

In February 1946, the U.S. Embassy in Moscow was buzzing. World War II had ended just months earlier. Now, practically overnight, wartime allies had turned into postwar rivals, if not outright antagonists. George Kennan, America's chargé d'affaires, wired Washington what became widely known as the Long Telegram. In it, the man whom *Foreign Policy* would later call "the most influential diplomat of the twentieth century"[2] stressed the need for the United States to remain vigilant to the threat posed by the Soviets—militarily, diplomatically, and even as a matter of domestic politics. Kennan warned against concerted campaigns to "disrupt national self-confidence . . . increase social and industrial unrest, [and] stimulate all forms of disunity." Those harboring "grievances," he added, "whether economic

or racial, will be urged to seek redress not in mediation and compromise, but in defiant violent struggle for destruction of other elements
of society."³

During the months and years that followed, diplomatic cables re-
layed to Foggy Bottom stressed how the ongoing subordination of Black
Americans imperiled the United States' standing around the world.
Another missive from Moscow explained that "the Soviet press ham-
mers away unceasingly on such things as 'lynch law,' segregation, racial
discrimination, deprivation of political rights, etc." In China, which
had not yet been "lost" to communism, embassy staff quoted a Shang-
hai periodical pointing to Jim Crow as evidence of America's moral
bankruptcy. "If the United States wants to 'lead' the world, it must
have a kind of moral superiority in addition to military superiority."
Similar unease was being expressed from places such as Greece, a country that very easily could have also been "lost." American diplomats
there mentioned that even pro-Western journalists were commenting
on the "deplorable situation" in the American South.

Government officials in the United States got the message loud and
clear. They understood that the United States' standing on the world
stage was being compromised. International disapprobation gave them
both the incentive and leverage to take on white supremacists (as well as
the politicians and judges who gave the segregationists a free pass). The
alternative to taking on Jim Crow, the diplomats explained, was that
the United States would continue to be (justly) derided in the United
Nations and the Soviet sphere as a sham democracy. At a time when the
United States and the USSR were competing throughout Asia, Africa,
and Latin America for military allies and economic partners—and when
the United States was poised to institute a "peacetime" draft in response
to the Soviet threat—the overseas critiques cut deep.⁴

Harry Truman famously issued an executive order directing the integration of the armed services. His and Dwight Eisenhower's Justice
Departments intervened regularly in court proceedings, reminding judges
that "the United States has been embarrassed in the conduct of foreign

relations by acts of discrimination taking place in this country,"[5] and that "if the imprimatur of constitutionality should be put on such a denial of equality, one would expect the foes of democracy to exploit such an action for their own purposes."[6] In turn, the Supreme Court's unanimous decision in *Brown v. Board of Education* "gave the U.S. government the counter to Soviet propaganda it had been looking for" and "had the kind of effect on international opinion that the government had hoped for."[7] Later, John F. Kennedy—whose staff listed progress "in the fields of civil rights and education" among its foreign policy imperatives—earned praise around the world for ordering federal marshals to ensure James Meredith could enroll at the University of Mississippi.[8] Then, in championing what would eventually become the Civil Rights Act of 1964, Kennedy argued, "We preach freedom around the world, and we mean it . . . but are we to say to the world . . . that this is the land of the free except for the Negroes; that we have no second-class citizens except Negroes?"[9]

THE IMPORTANCE OF INTEREST CONVERGENCE

As the late legal scholar Derrick Bell argued, the convergence of interests—specifically, global statecraft and domestic civil rights— offers perhaps the most powerful explanation for why American elites were finally willing and able to clamp down on Jim Crow.[10] Diplomatic embarrassment, military vulnerability, and the possible closure of foreign markets to U.S. business interests demanded swift and decisive action at home.

Unfortunately, there had been no such interest-convergence a century earlier, as the abomination that was slavery led us into the Civil War. Western European nations, which at that time were themselves presiding over sprawling colonial empires and actively subjugating and exploiting Black and brown populations across the globe, were too morally compromised to criticize America's racial caste system. Those nations were also tethered financially to American slavocracy, reliant on cheap American cotton and thus the perpetuation of the South's plantation economy. What's more, imperial powers such as France, Spain, and Britain, long frustrated by American enforcement of the Monroe Doctrine, saw that a bloody, costly, all-consuming Civil War might be an opportunity to be more aggressive and adventurous in the Western Hemisphere. So, far from chiding President James Buchanan's reluctance to use federal power to counter secessionist stirrings, decrying the *Dred Scott* decision in 1857, or denouncing the Confederacy, those nations maintained a position of neutrality that, more often than not, buoyed the southern rebellion.

But even if our peer nations had been outraged by the enslavement of millions in the United States, it is not clear that American elites would have cared. Surely the Court that decided *Dred Scott* would not have been moved by claims that a constitutional jurisprudence of white supremacy was damaging to our reputation abroad. The United States was not looking to lead on the world stage. And ending chattel slavery would not have helped America's balance of trade.

Alarmingly, things today look and feel a lot more like 1850 than 1950. That holds two lessons for the fight against state-sponsored vigilantism and the broader assault on inclusive, multiracial democracy. First, the world is not going to apply the type of geostrategic pressure that might stir Americans to summon our better angels once again. And, second, even if foreign nations were to take a strong stand against the civil rights retrenchment taking place in the United States right now, a large and influential component of the American governing class would be unmoved. If anything, many MAGA Republicans would wear such international disapprobation as a badge of honor.

COMPROMISED ALLIES

Right now, some of our closest and most trusted allies in Europe are far from democratic bulwarks. They are adopting, or facing strong domestic pressure to adopt, American-style right-wing politics.[11] For this reason, they are in no position to lecture, chide, or shame the United States.

France, for example, has had two successive *hold-your-breath* national elections. In both instances, a centrist, Emmanuel Macron, fended off serious challenges from his far-right rival, Marine Le Pen. Le Pen is the daughter of Jean-Marie Le Pen, the fringe National Front leader who espoused ugly xenophobic and antisemitic views well before those sentiments came back into vogue.[12] Knowing that the younger Le Pen has found favor with a sizeable percentage of the French electorate, Macron and his government have regularly tacked to the right—so much so that the French political establishment has co-opted aspects of the culture war that MAGA partisans are fighting in the United States.

As reported by a research fellow at the French National Centre for Scientific Research, mainstream French officials have denounced imported American "woke[ness]" as a "risk to French values and identity." Incredibly, Macron's education minister from 2017 to 2022 blamed the rise of Trump on American progressives moving too far to the left. As this minister sees things, it was anger against American diversity, equity, and inclusivity initiatives that swept Donald Trump into office. "France and its youth must escape" a similar fate, he urged.[13]

Though that minister has been replaced,[14] the rest of the Macron government continues to lean to the right. For example, a major December 2023 immigration law, which the nation's finance minister says "protected the French" and critics call the "most regressive bill" in forty years, was hailed by the French Right as "incontestably inspired by Marine Le Pen."[15] Importantly, Macron's prime minister (and de facto successor), Gabriel Attal, has been among those pushing the government to "move right on immigration." In his inaugural parliamentary speech as prime minister, Attal insisted that France should "refuse [to allow] our identity to be diluted or dissolved"—a statement that the *New York Times*' Roger Cohen characterized as a "scarcely subtle" appeal to Le Pen supporters.[16]

In the United Kingdom, Tories have occupied 10 Downing Street since 2010, during which time the Conservative Party (like the U.S. Republican Party) has veered further and further to the right. In 2016, a yes vote on the referendum to leave the European Union set in motion the UK's tumultuous Brexit. Economically and culturally impoverishing, Brexit was, in the words of former prime minister Gordon Brown, selfishly nationalist, insular, and bleak.[17] This shift away from the nation's liberal internationalist history became even more pronounced in 2019, when the uncannily Trumpy Boris Johnson became prime minister.

Johnson's cabinet was "unequivocally against" critical race theory and sought to restrict the definition of racism to the "explicit invocation of skin color."[18] During a debate marking Black History Month, one Tory minister insisted that the government did "not want teachers to teach their white pupils about white privilege" and that any instructor teaching "elements of critical race theory . . . is breaking the law." Meanwhile, Johnson's culture secretary threatened to pull funding from British museums that took down statues of controversial historical figures. Said one *Guardian* essayist, the government was "importing Trump's culture war" and transplanting the American Right's "moral panic into the UK."[19]

When it comes to LGBTQ+ issues, the Rishi Sunak–led government (which succeeded Johnson's) fostered a toxic transphobia that in some respects outstripped what we're encountering in America. It's "common sense," the prime minister insisted in an October 2023 speech, that "a man is a man and a woman is a woman."[20] Consistent with Sunak's remarks, the UK government required parental notification for children who wish to go by another name, use different pronouns, or wear a different-gendered uniform.[21]

And, as in red state America, the culture wars have been prosecuted through efforts to distort democracy. In 2022, the British Parliament passed the Elections Act—a bill some expressly characterized as "U.S. Republican-style 'voter suppression'" that entailed stringent ID requirements, curtailments on mail-in voting, and the politicization of a previously independent election commission.[22] Baroness Natalie Bennett, a leading member of the Green Party, described the law as borrowing from "the American right's playbook."[23] As of this writing, Labour is well-positioned to retake Parliament, aided in part by a far-right challenge to Sunak. Leading this challenge is the bombastic Nigel Farage, a Euroskeptic and Trump ally whom the *Wall Street Journal* says is "on a mission to destroy the ruling Conservative Party and rebuild it in his own populist image."[24]

Turning to Italy, in 2022, voters elected Giorgia Meloni, a far-right politician who once served as a youth foot soldier in the neo-fascist party she now leads. Meloni's rhetoric and policies are very much in line with those of American Christian nationalists—pro-"natural family," anti-immigrant, anti-abortion, anti-LGBTQ+, anti–civil servant, and anti–international financiers (seemingly an indirect but barely veiled snipe at Jews).[25] One of her government's first major policy initiatives was to limit parental rights for same-sex couples.[26] And though Meloni is herself pro-Ukraine, she leads a governing coalition that's far less committed to international cooperation and mutual security arrangements.[27]

Far-right politics in Germany are becoming increasingly militant, and popular. In 2022, some Alternative for Germany (AfD) party activists, who embrace QAnon conspiracies and in some respects bear similarities to those in the sovereign citizen movement here in America, attempted to forcibly oust the chancellor and his government. They aimed to install a "new Teutonic monarchy."[28] Despite, or perhaps because of, AfD member involvement in this would-be coup, and increased media coverage of the party's extremist ideology, AfD continues to surge in national polls. As of February 2024, the government was debating whether to ban the party that calls for, among other things, the deportation of millions of migrants and "unassimilated citizens."[29]

And, last, the European Union itself is poised to move considerably further to the right as analysts suspect that "nationalist right and far right [parties] could pick up nearly a quarter of seats in the

European Parliament" in the 2024 elections. And though a more centrist government can be formed without the participation of far-right representatives, "there's still a significant chance that the far right will, *for the first time*, be able to influence Europe's policy agenda [and] . . . threaten the EU's sacred values on rule of law and human rights, and block or even overturn major green and climate laws."[30]

BETWEEN A ROCK AND A HARD PLACE

One might think, or at least hope, that our friends in East Asia would be better positioned to nudge and challenge us. They have just as much, if not more, to lose were the United States to become irretrievably illiberal and isolationist.

Given China's ever-growing military and economic power, its East Asian neighbors benefit tremendously from strategic relationships with a democratic and cosmopolitan United States—that is to say, a United States that *isn't* so self-absorbed by domestic conflict, so nativist as, or so invested in its own authoritarian projects that its leaders find more in common with China's Xi Jinping, or even North Korea's Kim Jong-un, than with the leaders of Taiwan, South Korea, and Japan.

The Pacific Rim democracies all struggled during the Trump presidency and, at least quietly, fear a second act by Trump. As president, Trump mused that it might not be in America's interest to provide military support to those nations.[31] He even publicly suggested that South Korea and Japan ought to consider developing their own nuclear weapons.[32] Behind the scenes, things sounded even more dire. In his book *Chaos Under Heaven: Trump, Xi, and the Battle for the Twenty-First Century*, Josh Rogin recounts how "Trump's attitude towards Taiwan would vacillate between indifference and disrespect." Rogin depicts Trump as extremely anxious to maintain good relations with Xi. Showing his affinity for the Chinese strongman, Trump once snapped at his national security advisor John Bolton, a staunch Taiwan supporter, "I never want to hear from you about Taiwan, Hong Kong, or the Uyghurs."[33] Trump's own secretary of defense wrote that Trump complained regularly about the South Koreans and "pressed multiple times for us to withdraw U.S. forces" from the peninsula.[34]

Surely, our East Asian allies are rooting hard for the United States to regain its democratic footing and recommit to liberal projects at home and abroad. But they simply can't risk incurring the wrath of the already vengeful Trump. Reports out of Japan have the Japanese government already making quiet overtures to the Trump camp, undoubtedly "a preemptive move to stave off a potential 'nightmare' scenario for Tokyo."[35] And calls abound in Seoul for the Yoon Suk Yeol government to do the same.[36]

But it's arguably even worse than just remaining silent. Perhaps Japan, South Korea, and Taiwan (not to mention Germany) have no choice but to, per Trump's suggestion, become more militaristic in outlook[37]—and, if so, they may turn to right-wing politicians to lead that transformation.[38] A major part of our arrangements with postwar Germany and Japan is that we guarantee their security. We do so, of course, precisely so those nations don't, once again, feel any need or compulsion to revert to imperialist or fascist politics.

Alternatively, perhaps the East Asian nations fall under the sway of Beijing, while the likes of Ukraine and Poland succumb to the same fate vis-à-vis Moscow. MAGA Republicans have consistently downplayed Russian aggression and have attempted to thwart efforts by Congress and the Biden administration to support Ukraine.[39] On multiple occasions between 2017 and 2021, Trump reportedly contemplated withdrawing from NATO.[40] Retired admiral James G. Stavridis, the former supreme allied commander, declared that American withdrawal from what arguably is the most powerful and successful alliance in world history would be "a geopolitical mistake of epic proportion."[41] Trump has repeatedly intimated his fondness for Vladimir Putin, whom he has referred to as "savvy," "smart," and a "genius."[42] Close observers have described Trump as having a "school-boy crush on Putin."[43] As recently as February 2024, Trump announced that he'd be fine with Russia doing "whatever the hell they want" to any NATO nation not deemed (by Trump, of course) to be living up to its collective-defense obligations.[44]

Absent steadfast U.S. support, Ukraine would be swallowed whole by Russia. Alternatively, Russia would oust Volodymyr Zelensky—a move Trump, still embittered at the Ukrainian president's unwitting involvement in the first Trump impeachment, might well welcome[45]—in favor of yet another mini-dictator loyal to Moscow, akin to the arrangement Putin has in place with Alexander Lukashenko of Belarus.[46]

All these possibilities are bad for the United States. Cataclysmic shifts in geopolitics of these sorts would surely reach even the most barricaded of American borders, prompting the United States to react impulsively in ways sure to further destabilize nations and markets alike.

CHAOS, NOT CONQUEST

We've come a long way since the early years of the Cold War, when the Soviets and China were actively competing against the West, wooing would-be allies by emphasizing the egalitarianism that they claimed was hardwired into their brands of Communism. Our enemies and rivals no longer try to win global beauty pageants. Instead, they're fanning the flames of American discord and democratic decay—and taking full advantage of the MAGA-engineered tumult, violence, and corruption that's already hamstringing the United States militarily, diplomatically, and economically.

As political analysts Lee Drutman and Sean McFate recently

argued, Trump and his surrogates merely causing chaos—that is, even if they lose elections but remain politically relevant, reckless, and obstreperous—serves as a "victory party for Russia and China." These analysts insist that Moscow and Beijing's "objective is not to destroy the U.S. outright but to rupture it internally so it becomes a first-world country without first-world power, like Italy."[47]

There is thus plenty of method to Putin's madness. Investing in American decline is smart politics. He prized a Trump presidency so much that he endeavored to interfere in the 2016 and 2020 elections on the Republicans' behalf. Even in the 2022 races, which the U.S. director of national intelligence confirmed Putin sought to influence,[48] the Kremlin was hoping for MAGA victories.

We doubt that even Putin could have predicted that Trump would invite Russia to attack NATO allies. But he surely expected (and rightly so) that GOP sway in Congress would not only dampen support for Ukraine but also impede efforts by Biden and the Democrats in Congress to mitigate red state repressive policies. Why would Putin care about the latter? The same reason MAGA politicians in the United States support vigilantism: to undermine democratic equality in America and thus perpetuate right-wing control by Christian nationalists who are antidemocratic, nativist, and isolationist.[49] As usual, Steve Bannon lays MAGA priorities bare: "I don't give a shit about Ukraine—what I give a shit about is the invasion of America's southern border."[50]

Likewise, even though Trump often talks tough about China, countless reports point to Beijing wanting or having reason to wish for MAGA political success.[51] From China's vantage point, one *Foreign Policy* columnist explains, "a Trump win in November [2024] could very well look like a tempting opportunity to benefit from the chaos, the divisions, and the hit to U.S. prestige that it would unleash."[52] A Democratic victory, by contrast, would further stabilize the international community and make it that much harder for China to pull other nations into its orbit on the premise "that Washington is not a reliable partner."[53]

No doubt Russia and China relish the infusion of MAGA politics into American foreign policy and are very happy to fill any void left by a United States that retreats from its international commitments. At a March 2023 summit between Putin and Xi, the two proudly announced that they are prepared "to stand guard over the world order."[54]

SHAMELESS

At the end of the day, it's quite possible that the international reaction to Vigilante Democracy is in important respects beside the point. Even if our allies and rivals were to speak out against the United States' democratic decay and embrace of legal vigilantism, their words would likely fall on deaf ears. International pressure mattered in the mid-twentieth century because America's two major political parties were deeply invested in constructing a stable postwar order and protecting the United States' reputation as a nation that respected fundamental rights and the rule of law. Those still clinging to Jim Crow politics were, by contrast, regional, provincial actors. For sure, some held key positions in Congress because of their seniority. But Jim Crow's staunchest supporters were figures such as Arkansas governor Orval Faubus and Bull Connor, the commissioner of public safety for Birmingham, Alabama, who had no place on the national stage.

The dominant players in today's MAGA Right are far closer in outlook to these provincial figures than they are to internationalists like Harry Truman or Dwight D. Eisenhower. But their political prominence is unmistakable. Obviously, there's Donald Trump and his shadow cabinet of culture warriors. Christian nationalists also serve as governors, legislators, and state supreme court judges in Florida, Texas, Tennessee, Indiana, Missouri, Louisiana, and Ohio; hold senior leadership positions in the U.S. House of Representatives;

MORE LIKE 1850 THAN 1950

occupy some of the most powerful federal judgeships in the nation; and helm national, if not global, media outlets and think tanks. It's simply too hard—and, as we said, too dangerous—to try to shame or close ranks on this large and well-positioned contingent of power brokers.

In fact, it's more likely than not that MAGA partisans would draw strength from such foreign criticism. Central to their political ideology is a deep distrust of international commitments and transnational ("globalist") partnerships. They are thus apt to welcome the opportunity to stand apart from our closest allies whom they unjustly view as parasitic and a threat to U.S. sovereignty.

Mentioning the likely inefficacy of any campaign to nudge or shame the United States may seem academic in light of the fact that, as we've just argued, no such campaign exists. But we nonetheless think it's worth noting, if for no other reason than to underscore how precarious the state of American democracy really is, and how creative we're going to have to be in combating Vigilante Democracy and regaining our liberal footing.

CHAPTER 13

"A World Where . . . Texas Is at War with California"

The Blue State Counterstrike

L ittle fanfare surrounds most midterm elections, particularly in reliably blue states like California. The contests in 2018 were no different. To no one's surprise, sizeable majorities sent Dianne Feinstein back to the U.S. Senate and selected Gavin Newsom to succeed Jerry Brown as governor. But neither California's senior senator nor its telegenic new chief executive outpaced Proposition 12, one of the handful of ballot initiatives presented to the state's voters.[1] Sixty-three percent of Californians supported a ban on the in-state sale of pork, veal, and eggs produced from animals that were not raised humanely.[2]

As it happens, very few pig farming facilities around the country met California's stringent new standards for non-cruel confinement. (Cruel confinement includes conditions that prevent pigs from "lying down, standing up, fully extending [their] limbs or turning around freely.") This left pig farmers with a choice: forgo the large, lucrative California market, or comply with Prop 12's requirements.

FIGHTING VIGILANTES WITH . . . PIGS?

Prop 12 is, of course, about far more than animal rights—and far more than the profit margins of America's pig farmers. And that's why the successful ballot initiative sent shock waves throughout state capitals, corporate boardrooms, and the upper echelons of the U.S. Department of Justice. Quickly, clusters of farming consortia, wide-ranging trade associations including the National Association of Manufacturers, and twenty-six of the reddest states in the Union lawyered up. Along with the U.S. solicitor general, they recognized Prop 12 for what it was: a disruptive, destabilizing effort by a powerful, progressive state to fill a regulatory void left by a federal government unwilling or unable to act forcefully. By endorsing Prop 12 and leveraging its vast size and customer base, California had used a hybrid market-regulatory approach to effectively (and unilaterally) raise the nation's regulatory standards. Given the terms and tenor of this legal battle, it was hardly shocking when fourteen of the nation's bluest states plus the District of Columbia rushed to California's defense.

What *was* surprising, however, was that in the inevitable legal battle over Prop 12, California prevailed. Writing for the Supreme Court, Justice Neil Gorsuch reaffirmed states' general authority to promulgate wide-ranging regulations, including those that have the practical effect of controlling commerce across the nation.[3]

California and its blue state allies played a version of what legal scholars call "constitutional hardball"[4]—and won. As the justices acknowledged in *National Pork Producers Council v. Ross*, the blue state coalition won far more than the right to prohibit the in-state sale of cruelly rendered pork products. They won the right to use these hybrid market-regulatory instruments to protect their citizens, reward socially conscious businesses, and nudge firms and states across the country to adopt any number of progressive policies.

We see the victory as something even more significant. As *Ross* makes clear, blue states possess a powerful weapon useful in confronting Vigilante Democracy, counteracting its effects, and ultimately helping restore safety, security, and prosperity to the United States writ large. For varied reasons, some sensible and others disgraceful, there is scant history of progressive states individually or collectively using legislation, regulation, and their citizens' economic clout to attack white supremacy or Christian nationalism at its roots. Had we that history, it is possible slavery would have ended sooner, Reconstruction would have lasted longer, and the likes of Greg Abbott and Glenn Youngkin would, today, be regarded as provincial cranks rather than drivers of national policy.

But, as *Ross* highlights, blue states have real power to support democracy, civil rights, and the rule of law. The challenge is how to do so. How do we leap from regulating literal pigpens to policing metaphorical ones—and, by doing so, reestablish our footing as a democratic country committed to civil rights and equal protection? It's not that big of a jump. But before we suggest a strategy, we need to address a threshold question. Blue state governors and legislators have plenty of homegrown problems. Why should they stick their necks out, open up their wallets, and expend significant political capital fighting repressive policies that are being enacted in red states?

IT IS NOT THEIR FIGHT

There's a strong argument for blue states to devote considerable resources to striking back at red state vigilantism because it's the right thing to do. But we're also realistic. So let's just concede that moral obligations are unlikely to dictate blue state politics and policy.

All the same, there are also powerful instrumental reasons for blue states to counterattack red state vigilantism—and to strike with force and urgency. Blue states should do so to protect the economic, democratic, and legal interests of their own residents; to preserve the vibrancy and autonomy of their civic and commercial institutions; and, ultimately, to lay the groundwork for a more democratic allocation of power in Washington, where red states currently wield disproportionate influence, far more than ought to be the case given that many more people live in progressive states than in MAGA states (and also given that blue America possesses the lion's share of the nation's economic heft).

Most important, and as we've shown in the preceding three chapters, blue states should do this *because no one else will.*

The Crushing Externalities of Red State Vigilantism

When states have lax environmental standards, the effects are felt acutely by their neighbors. Most appreciate that these spillover effects—what economists and lawyers call *externalities*—must be addressed. But so should the spillover effects of state-supported vigilantism. Ideas, money, lawsuits, people, and guns traverse state lines, too. And, right now, the vigilantism that's spilling out of red states is just as toxic as any petrochemical.

Red states that deploy vigilantes to go to war with corporations, to coarsen and debase their public schools and colleges, and to create unhealthy or unsafe school, work, and living conditions for residents are already seeing drops in wellness measures and outflows of educated professionals.[5] People pushed further into the shadows of civic, scholastic, and economic life will work less, earn less, and thus pay less in state and federal taxes. They'll also require more welfare services, many of which are funded through federal entitlement programs.

Who's going to pay for the red state shortfall in federal tax revenues? And who's going to pay (more) to finance the federal welfare programs that victims of vigilantism are increasingly going to need to rely on? In many cases, it'll be the blue states.

Even before the rise of today's state-sponsored vigilantism, blue America tended to subsidize federal spending in red America through tax-and-transfer programs. Relying on estimates from the nonpartisan Rockefeller Institute, Paul Krugman notes that "if you look at how the federal budget affects U.S. regions, there's a consistent pattern in which conservative states that preach the importance of self-reliance are in fact heavily subsidized by liberal states, especially in the Northeast."[6] Although it's far from a perfect measure, consider a simple tally (likewise drawn from Rockefeller data) of net receipts and distributions per capita. In 2021, of the ten states that sent the *most* money per person to the federal government, nine were blue states.[7] The sole red state was Wyoming; given that it has the lowest population of the fifty states, Wyoming's contributions were hardly doing much to offset the red-blue imbalance, let alone to keep the Treasury afloat. Conversely, of the thirteen states that sent the least money per person to the federal government that year, only one (New Mexico) was blue.[8] Meanwhile, the continued debasement of red America's civic and economic infrastructure—as evidenced by reports of a "brain drain" of doctors, teachers, and university students; library closures; and spending cuts at public colleges—will only increase the blue states' relative tax contributions.

There are other costs, too. Jurisdictions providing sanctuary to besieged red state individuals and families are, of course, having to shoulder the attendant financial burdens. In 2022, the first wave of abortion refugees came from Texas, which had deployed vigilantes to shut down access to clinics and hospitals that provided reproductive healthcare. In response, California committed $20 million to support individuals seeking access to abortion clinics. New Mexico, no doubt expecting a surge of Texans, quickly allocated $10 million to build a new reproductive health clinic not too far from El Paso. The city of Chicago gave $500,000 in funding to local nonprofits to support their efforts to facilitate abortion access. New Jersey allocated $6 million across over twenty women's health clinics in anticipation of out-of-state demand,[9] while New York established a $35 million fund for in-state abortion providers.[10] These are big states, and Chicago is a large city. The amounts first earmarked were quite modest—and insufficient. Researchers at the Guttmacher Institute believe the number of people traveling to California to seek safe, secure abortions will rise quickly and precipitously, with the annual out-of-state patient load climbing from 46,000 to as high as 1.4 million.[11] And a recent UCLA study estimates that another 1,000 people per month will travel to Illinois.[12] So, as long as red states continue to enact more aggressive abortion restrictions—*and empower vigilante enforcers*—safe-haven measures are going to need to be extended and expanded.

Then there are the costs of absorbing political refugees—just as there are when we admit asylum seekers from overseas (or when, as has become trendy, red state governors transfer migrants arriving in Florida and Texas to Massachusetts and California[13]). We classify *domestic* political refugees as those compelled to leave their jobs, relatives, and friends behind because they are queer teachers, have transgender children enrolled in public school, want to teach—or want their children to learn—actual American history and engage with Black and LGBTQ+ literature, or simply don't want their political activities suppressed. Families are already fleeing, and there are countless more planning (and saving) for their own exoduses. Many journeying to blue states will encounter difficulties. They may not have jobs lined up; they may lack social and familial networks to aid with childcare and provide insurance against food, housing, or transportation insecurity; and their children may struggle academically and psychologically.

But the externalities are not limited to supporting refugees arriving from out of state. When government officials and party leaders foment vigilantism, they endanger blue state citizens, businesses, and government operations. In 2020, Trump issued a Twitter call to "LIBERATE MICHIGAN."[14] Just weeks later, waves of armed vigilantes rallied on the grounds of the state capitol in Lansing to intimidate lawmakers voting on key public health and education matters. The "liberators" showed up with not only guns but also nooses, Confederate flags, and provocative signs. On days when the protesters entered the statehouse and menaced state police, several state representatives reportedly were forced to don bulletproof vests.

Similar campaigns of intimidation and violence have played out on smaller but no less consequential stages as threats to public health officials, school boards, and organizers of LGBTQ+ rallies have spilled over from red bastions like Florida, Texas, and Ohio into California, Michigan, Colorado, and Minnesota. It doesn't take thousands or even hundreds of MAGA culture warriors, whether out-of-state agitators or locals, to disrupt life in blue America. Nor does it require the communities attracting MAGA-led campaigns to be especially, or even remotely, welcoming of the MAGA agitators or their messages. Even in solidly blue counties (like Los Angeles County or Bernalillo County, New Mexico), where contingents of police and sheriff's deputies have expressed allyship with the Far Right, just a few aggressive MAGA foot soldiers can disrupt if not destroy civic life.

Businesses, doctors, pharmacists, and lawyers are imperiled, too. Thanks to red states weaponizing commonplace "long-arm" statutes and using them to target charitable organizations, medical facilities, mail-order pharmacies, and everyday activists in blue states, Americans around the country are at risk from vigilante lawsuits.[15] Fearing they'd be sued under S.B. 8, nonprofits that support low-income pregnant persons seeking abortions scaled back their outreach. The National Abortion Federation, headquartered in Washington, D.C., reportedly stopped funding abortion services in red states and has been wary about even providing red state residents with information and travel grants, lest the organization be ensnared in vigilante suits. As the federation's CEO said, continuing services to red state residents "would put our entire operation at risk, ultimately leaving hundreds of thousands without access to care."[16]

The federation may seem to be unduly cautious. But consider what it's up against. In one federal court filing, MAGA lawyer and S.B. 8 architect Jonathan Mitchell likened donors who helped finance abortions to hit men and sponsors of terrorism. Elaborating, Mitchell told the *Washington Post* that the objective was to bully out-of-state donors into compliance: "It's not clear whether the courts would ultimately allow an antiabortion state to prosecute abortion funders in these situations, but they can't take the risk."[17]

Laying the Foundation for a Democratic Recalibration

Some may insist that blue states that engage in counterstrikes are hastening or intensifying the splintering of the United States. A version of this argument appeared in the U.S. Justice Department's lawyering before the Supreme Court in the Prop 12 case. Joining the interests aligned against California's animal rights initiative, Deputy Solicitor General Edwin Kneedler insisted Prop 12 "fails to respect the autonomy of California's sister states." The California law "invites conflict and retaliation and threatens the balkanization of the national economic union."[18]

Kneedler was being a good advocate, trying to win a case and protect what he doubtless thought was in his client's—that is, the United States'—interests. But anyone thinking about how this case fits into the particular moment should realize the greater danger of further disarming and disempowering blue states. We've already documented how red states are in open war with the rest of the nation. We've also traced how the federal government has done woefully little to prevent surging vigilantism in red America, let alone its effects on blue states. When one looks beyond the narrow scope of a particular case—as Justice Department lawyers necessarily must do—the shortsightedness of the government's position is unmistakable. Admonishing California for striking back at the likes of Texas, Tennessee, and Florida is a bit like criticizing the United States for declaring war on Japan after the bombing of Pearl Harbor. It's technically true that America's war declaration further fomented world conflict and splintered the international order. But c'mon.

Kneedler wasn't alone. Justice Elena Kagan also seemed troubled by what Prop 12 might stir up. She wondered whether "we want to live in a world where . . . you know, Texas is at war with California, and California at war with Texas?"[19] Just as we would suggest to Kneedler that his Justice Department has let us down, we'd say substantially the same thing to Kagan and the Court she sits on. The justices could have halted enforcement of S.B. 8, depriving the January 7 Project of a potent weapon rather than validating it. The Court could have done more to respect reasonable, democratically enacted gun control laws and, in doing so, reduced the likelihood and lethality of political violence.[20] The Court could have affirmed long-standing protections for reproductive autonomy, but the justices instead invited states to ban abortion and force pregnant people to carry pregnancies to term.[21] And the Court could have preserved the right of LGBTQ+ families and interracial families to engage in commerce without fear of discrimination or denial of service; instead, it's endorsed religious fundamentalists' claims that, in having to serve all customers, *they* are being discriminated against.[22] Of course, Kagan was in the minority in all of these cases. Our critique of Kagan isn't keyed to how she voted. Rather, we think she misjudged where we're at as a nation. Kagan should have better appreciated that, in part thanks to her own Court's rulings, Texas was *already* at war with California and that, in various ways, the Court had been emboldening red state culture warriors. The dystopian contest she feared was underway all around her.

CONFRONTATION, NOT COMITY

Blue states cannot watch from the sidelines as red state vigilantism reaches far beyond red state borders. Given these intrusions into jurisdictions dominated by Democrats, anything short of confrontation would be tantamount to an affirmative policy of appeasement.

Many, understandably, summon a specific mental image when they hear the term appeasement: British prime minister Neville Chamberlain's assertion that the 1938 agreement he reached with the Nazis in Munich would guarantee "peace for our time." But we need not look overseas for vivid examples. Northern appeasement was on full display in both the Declaration of Independence and the Constitution itself. In the decades that followed, northern appeasement legitimated, perpetuated, and extended slavery—causing damage and chaos so severe that it could be remedied only through the Civil War. Northern appeasement also enabled the premature political and legal abandonment of

Reconstruction and the ensuing century of Jim Crow, the consequences of which we're living with to this day.

Progressive states should not make the same mistake again. The need to be confrontational now ought to be apparent. It's a necessary precursor to forging a more stable, more democratic, and more lasting national reconciliation.

Blue States Need to Show Red States They Can Play Hardball

State-supported vigilantism is hardly the only source of blue-red tension. The same politicians, lawyers, and policy shops that are working overtime to legitimize vigilantism are impeding democracy (and, likely, Democratic votes) by suppressing voting. And they're interfering with federal regulatory policies in ways that are both brutal and disruptive to blue state governance.

But here's the thing. Red state politicos aren't the only ones who should be playing for the long term—blue state officials should, too. A muscular response in this context—that is, a strike against Vigilante Democracy—will strengthen the position of blue America across the full range of conflicts. Blue states can show that they aren't constitutional pushovers; they can develop the tools and infrastructure to advance their vision of American democracy; and they may well end up bruising red states enough that the architects of today's vigilante regimes think twice before attempting to assert dominance over the entire United States.

An Eventual National Reconciliation Cannot, Once Again, Vest Disproportionate Power in the Hands of an Antidemocratic Minority Faction

There's an even longer-term payoff. We remain optimistic that, eventually, there will be a moment when Americans of all stripes are able to come back together and start governing collaboratively and constructively. And we're hopeful that a powerful blue state response today will hasten its arrival. Equally important, if we're able to come together again, it will be good for all parties and persons to know that liberals and progressives (rather than just those on the right) can and will play hardball. Whatever negotiated settlement may be achieved that would allow us to return to the business of democratic governance without key stakeholders resorting to political sabotage and outright violence, it will have to include recognition that some of our principal legislative institutions and electoral systems are insufficiently democratic—and that those democratic deficiencies are contributing to a root cause of our current, sustained period of civic decay and civil rights retrenchment. Assuming we arrive at this moment of reconciliation, the blue states will need to show that they're returning to the table from a position of strength.

BLUEPRINT FOR THE FIGHT

We're accustomed to blue states being disempowered in the American political system because of the Constitution's antidemocratic features. Those features stymie progressive solutions to urgent social problems and, as we suggested, are proven, powerful accelerants of today's rightward lurch. But as the Prop 12 story reveals, power can be asserted by commingling regulatory and economic tools.[23] And when it comes to those hybrid tools, blue states have tremendous advantages over their red rivals.

We conclude this book with a plan for blue state counterstrikes, one that relies on combinations of legal, political, cultural, regulatory, and economic tools to protect blue state residents and push back against the scourge of legal vigilantism. These tools advance six key objectives—*our Six Rs.*[24]

Ramparts: Erecting Firewalls to Stop Vigilantism's Spread

"Put your own oxygen mask on before assisting others." These are good instructions for passengers on commercial flights. And they're good instructions for blue state officials embarking on their own journey. Simply stated, if blue states don't first safeguard their own politics—and people—against vigilantism, they can hardly be expected to fight vigilantism elsewhere.

Our focus here is on healthcare rights, equality for LGBTQ+

persons, and a commitment to ensuring public schools remain safe havens for inclusive scholastics and athletics as well as for social growth and self-esteem. All of these are prime targets of America's Christian nationalists.

MODEL BLUE STATE LAW 1:
THE RIGHT TO REPRODUCTIVE HEALTHCARE

The state shall not deny, interfere with, or sanction private interference with an individual's reproductive freedom in their most intimate decisions, including their fundamental rights to abortion services, fertility treatments, and contraceptives.

MODEL BLUE STATE LAW 2:
EQUAL RIGHTS AND DIGNITY FOR FAMILY UNIONS

The state recognizes the full and equal rights of couples, regardless of the parties' gender identities or sexual orientations, to marry; the state recognizes the full and equal rights of individuals, regardless of their gender identity or sexual orientation, to birth, foster, adopt, or otherwise raise children.

MODEL BLUE STATE LAW 3:
HEALTHCARE EQUALITY AND AUTONOMY

The state recognizes the right of parents or legal guardians, in consultation with medical professionals, to secure age-appropriate gender-affirming care for their minor children.

MODEL BLUE STATE LAW 4:
EQUALITY AND INCLUSIVITY IN PUBLIC EDUCATION

All public schools shall recognize the equal rights and dignity of all students, teachers, staff, and coaches. All curricular and extracurricular programming must respect and take reasonable steps to ensure equality, inclusivity, and dignity.

MODEL BLUE STATE LAW 5:
LIBRARIES AS LEARNING BEACONS

All public libraries hereby adopt the American Library Association's Bill of Rights, including the requirement that "materials should not be proscribed or removed because of partisan or doctrinal disapproval."

MODEL BLUE STATE LAW 6:
PROTECTING LGBTQ+ STUDENTS

All public schools shall respect and preserve the privacy of students by not disclosing any information that may reveal any student's sexual orientation or gender identity to others—including parents, guardians, or school staff—unless a student authorizes such disclosure or there is a compelling medical or scholastic need.

MODEL BLUE STATE LAW 7:
PROTECTING GOVERNMENT OFFICIALS FROM HARASSING OR THREATENING BEHAVIOR

Notwithstanding any other state transparency law or regulation, government employees have the right to shield personal or personally identifying information from the public upon a credible showing or expectation that such information has resulted or would result in online or in-person threats, harassment, or violence.

MODEL BLUE STATE LAW 8:
PRIVATE RIGHTS TO PROTECT CIVIL RIGHTS

The state hereby eliminates qualified immunity for state, county, or municipal personnel proven to have deprived any person of or facilitated the deprivation of any person's civil or political rights. Officials sued for any such violations shall be personally liable for the total judgment. The agency or entity employing said officials shall be liable for any amount of the total judgment the officials cannot themselves pay.

Refuge: Providing Safe Havens for Those Credibly Threatened or Endangered

Next, there's the urgent matter of accommodating red state refugees. There are people in need of reproductive healthcare, almost all of whom can rather quickly return to their lives in red America. But there are also individuals and families threatened or marginalized in civic spaces, in their workplaces, in their schools, or even when attempting to use public bathrooms. Those folks require more permanent solutions. No different from any other family contemplating an out-of-state move, those seeking relief from repressive red state policies may struggle to raise funds, find new jobs, sell their old homes, and say goodbye to friends and family, particularly elderly members.

Blue states need to facilitate these painful, often daunting relocations, as well as provide a sanctuary to those seeking healthcare. Assistance may well be a moral imperative but it's also a strategic opportunity. The short-term expenses and inconveniences will, quite likely, be outweighed by the contributions refugees make in the years to come.

As we did in the last section, we propose model state laws to support red state refugees.

MODEL BLUE STATE LAW 9:
EDUCATION ASSISTANCE

The state shall provide tuition, housing, and nutritional assistance for young adults who leave other states, are accepted at a state public college or university, and can show both financial need and that their race, gender identity, sexual orientation, religion, or present health needs or conditions have or will put them at risk for state-sponsored or state-countenanced discrimination and subordination in their home state.

MODEL BLUE STATE LAW 10:
RELOCATION ASSISTANCE

The state shall supply transitional housing, childcare, transportation, and nutritional assistance for any individual or family seeking to relocate, provided they can show both financial need and that their (or at least one member of their immediate family's) race, gender identity, sexual orientation, religion, or present health needs or conditions have or will put them at risk for state-sponsored or state-countenanced discrimination and subordination in their home state.

We don't need to wade into the weeds to specify the amount of support, the length of support, and the criteria for determining eligibility. We do, though, want to note that the United States—and some states and localities—have all sorts of support programs for displaced persons, ranging from those affected by natural disasters, to those whose service as government witnesses imperils their lives, to those international migrants who seek asylum on the grounds of political, religious, or LGBTQ+ oppression.

Is it unfair to draw a strong comparison between those feeling compelled to leave Mississippi and those escaping from, say, Syria or Venezuela? For sure, and we're not doing that. Nor do we need to. But let's be equally careful not to minimize or ignore the harms experienced by some Americans right here in the United States *just because things are much, much worse overseas.* Perhaps of even greater weight, an argument could be made that New Yorkers, Marylanders, and Washingtonians owe a greater duty to imperiled fellow Americans than to imperiled foreigners—and, most certainly, will have an easier time accommodating them. All of these points weigh in favor of acting quickly and comprehensively to facilitate the integration of red state refugees.

Reinforcement: Supporting Work on the Ground to Fight Vigilantism
Our third cluster of safeguards recognizes that much good work can and desperately needs to be done in red states.

Again, parallels to international migration patterns are hard to ignore. One of the most effective strategies in addressing refugee crises is working to improve conditions back home. With that in mind, efforts to provide stability and security in red America likewise ought to be considered.

MODEL BLUE STATE LAW 11:
JOURNALISM BEACHHEADS

The state shall fund state colleges, universities, and independent student newspapers for the purpose of establishing investigative journalism bureaus in states that fail to respect civil rights recognized in this state, staffed by faculty, postgraduate journalism fellows, and current students who may receive academic credit for semester-long externships.

Given what targets of legal vigilantism must endure, a proposal to fund what we call journalism beachheads may seem underwhelming. We concede it's hardly a cure-all. But it does respond to a key driver of democratic decline in the United States. According to a 2022 study by Northwestern's Medill School of Journalism, news "deserts"—regions bereft of credible local newspapers—are swallowing up greater and greater swaths of American terrain. Not surprisingly, the deserts are concentrated in red states, mainly those in the old Confederacy, but also in the Mountain West. Counties that have become newspaper deserts tend to be poorer, older, and less well educated. And, as the Medill study explains: "The loss of local journalism has been accompanied by the malignant spread of misinformation and disinformation, political polarization, eroding trust in media, and a yawning digital and economic divide among citizens. In communities without a credible source of local news, voter participation declines, corruption in both government and business increases, and local residents end up paying more in taxes and at checkout."[25]

In light of this alarming trend—and the fact that the few thriving for-profit newspapers concentrate most of their reporting on national and international topics[26]—blue states should use their university infrastructure to set up "bureaus" in areas most in need of bold and well-resourced investigative reporting. At first blush, it may seem strange for the University of Maryland's *Diamondback* or the University of Illinois's *Daily Illini* to have regional bureaus in Jackson, Mississippi, or Montgomery, Alabama. But why? Students spend semesters all over the world. Studying art in Europe is still a possibility. We're just saying that they can also learn a lot by doing some good reporting on municipal corruption, school board bigotry, and voter suppression.[27]

MODEL BLUE STATE LAW 12:
ANTI-VIGILANTE LEGAL CLINICS

The state shall provide funds to law schools for the purpose of establishing anti-vigilante legal clinics. These clinics will be staffed by professional attorneys and postgraduate fellows strategically placed around the nation in areas of need. They shall defend those who are the victims of vigilantism, including vigilantism supported by a state, and shall initiate affirmative litigation on behalf of clients alleging deprivations of their civil or political rights. In furtherance of the schools' academic missions, currently enrolled students and full-time faculty shall be afforded opportunities to support the clinics' work.

There is a legal advocacy analogue to our journalism proposal. Law schools in red states are operating under tremendous financial and political pressure. Governors DeSantis and Abbott, among others, are trying to stamp out classes and programs that seek to protect or elevate women, people of color, and members of the LGBTQ+ community. Law school clinics, across red and blue America, perform vital services. They advance reform initiatives and represent those without the resources to hire private attorneys. So, in the same spirit of our proposal for schools and school newspapers to set up regional journalism bureaus, we call on blue states to establish or fortify clinics aimed at protecting those endangered by Vigilante Democracy.

To be clear, in neither the journalism nor the legal advocacy context are we aiming to disparage the hard work of local red state activists, including student activists. And we're well aware of the problems associated with "liberals" swooping in to save the day. Yet let's be clear about our choices in this moment and the difficulty of getting local institutional actors to step up and preserve American democracy and civil rights. We simply understand how strapped the locals are by political, financial, and legal conditions and, at the same time, we recognize that blue states can extend themselves in ways that are beneficial to all parties involved.

Retaliation: Apply Pressure through Economic Sanctions

If California were a nation, it would be the fifth-largest economy in the world.[28] New York isn't that far behind, clocking in at eleventh.[29] Across the board, blue state economic clout is impressive. According to 2022 data, the most economically powerful blue states, which we've been referencing time and again, had around twice the per capita GDP of many red states. Texas does fine, but is a middling fifteenth out of fifty-one (counting Washington, D.C.) and lags behind almost all of the large and influential blue states. Florida weighs in at thirty-nine.[30]

Of course, it's true that states like New York, Massachusetts, and California have long been among the most affluent. In the late 1950s and early 1960s, those states were economically influential; and the old Confederacy states—then, as now, the cradle of legal vigilantism—were just as laggard as they are today. Yet there's a key difference. The economically powerful states weren't surefire progressive strongholds in the 1950s or early 1960s. They didn't vote for Adlai Stevenson in 1952 or 1956; and, even in 1960, California and Washington sided with Richard Nixon over John Kennedy. As political junkies no doubt recall, Nixon nearly won Illinois, too.

We mention this to say that the states we'd have deemed economic powerhouses during the heyday of the civil rights movement were not the ones clamoring for progressive political or legal reform.

(Obviously, it was even worse during the days of slavery. However morally outraged northerners were over the continuation and expansion of slavery in the United States, the economics of that monstrous arrangement were advantageous to many in the North.) But now, the most economically powerful and affluent of states are also the most politically progressive. In a nation as fixated on wealth and commerce as the United States, that ought to matter.

Democratic Investing

States, counties, and cities have massive securities portfolios. The CalPERS system for public employees of the Golden State has slightly more than $452 billion in assets.[31] The New York State Common Retirement Pension Fund holds more than $246 billion,[32] and the California State Teachers' pension's assets total close to $318 billion.[33] When these funds buy or sell securities, the market takes due notice.

Already many blue state, county, and city investment funds have restrictions of various sorts. California funds have divested from firms or projects tied to tobacco, firearms, private prisons, and fossil fuels.[34] Connecticut prohibits pension holdings in firms that manufacture civilian firearms.[35] Illinois prohibits investments in for-profit firms that assist the feds in segregating and sheltering migrant children.[36] Maine has divested from private prisons and fossil fuel companies.[37] Minnesota has divested from some fossil fuel (specifically, thermal coal–producing)[38] and tobacco firms.[39] New York's largest pension has a mandate to transition its entire portfolio to net zero greenhouse gas emissions by 2040,[40] while New York City prohibits buying or holding securities in fossil fuel companies, private prisons, or firearms dealers.[41] (To be sure, red states do this as well, in the reverse direction. There is, for instance, a nineteen-state alliance led by Florida in which state pension managers are directed to ignore environmental, social, and governance ["ESG"] impacts when evaluating investment vehicles and to instead focus only on maximizing investment returns.[42])

Clearly, and notwithstanding Justice Kagan's assumptions to the contrary, the economic war between red and blue America is well underway. With that in mind, blue states ought to use their economic power to deter state-supported vigilantism.

MODEL BLUE STATE LAW 13:
RESPONSIBLE GOVERNMENT INVESTING

All state, county, and municipal pensions and related public investment vehicles shall cease investing in firms that engage in discriminatory practices anywhere in the United States. These investment vehicles must, within six months of this act's passage, divest themselves from any and all institutions that continue to engage in discriminatory practices anywhere in the United States. For purposes of this provision, discriminatory practices include any and all that would be illegal were they to occur in this state, pursuant to this state's constitution and civil rights code. They further include practices that (a) interfere or attempt to interfere with any exercise of a right protected in this state pursuant to this state's civil rights code; or (b) fail to provide reasonable protections to employees whose rights, as recognized by this state pursuant to this state's civil rights code, are threatened or violated.

Democratic Procurement

Another economic hammer that blue states wield is their purchasing, or procurement, power. Procurement most often penetrates the public's consciousness when evidence surfaces of graft, waste, or delay—think Halliburton during the occupation of Iraq or Boston's decades-long "Big Dig" project. But when we step back from the sensationalist headlines and focus only on the fact that government contracting occurs in massive numbers every day and everywhere in America, we ought to appreciate that smart, sensible procurement can be an important and user-friendly lever for advancing civil rights.

MODEL BLUE STATE LAW 14:
RESPONSIBLE GOVERNMENT PROCUREMENT

This state or any office, department, or subdivision of the state, including counties and cities, may enter into contracts only with firms, organizations, or entities that do not engage in discriminatory practices anywhere in the United States. For purposes of this provision, discriminatory practices include any and all practices that would be illegal were they to occur in this state. They further include practices that (a) interfere or attempt to interfere with any exercise of a right recognized by this state and protected pursuant to this state's civil rights code; or (b) fail to provide reasonable protections to employees whose rights, as recognized by this state pursuant to this state's civil rights code, are threatened or violated.

What we're prescribing here is anything but new or radical. Long before Congress passed the 1964 Civil Rights Act—legislation delayed, with deadly consequences, thanks in no small part to the undemocratic nature of the U.S. Senate—the federal government advanced the cause through its commercial heft. In June 1941, Franklin Roosevelt signed Executive Order 8802, which prohibited discrimination "based on race, color, creed, and national origin" among government contractors and federal agencies involved in defense readiness. Roosevelt expanded this nondiscrimination imperative two years later, when he made Executive Order 8802 applicable to all government contractors regardless of their involvement in defense planning or production.[43] Given how heavily Washington spent on government contractors during this crucial surge in the war effort, the requirement that *anyone* doing business with the feds comply with Roosevelt's antidiscrimination policy had drastic effects on the American political and cultural landscape.

Again, the template exists, the precedent is powerful, and the cause just. What's more, as we've seen, red states such as Texas are already using their procurement power to prohibit state and local agencies from contracting with businesses that discriminate against the firearms industry or fossil fuel companies.[44] It's only sensible for blue states to build on what FDR set out to do in the 1940s and counter what Texas is doing right now. Blue states should refuse to do business with companies that themselves take advantage of their relationships with vigilante governments, defined to include those who sanction or support antidemocratic or Christian nationalist acts of violence and repression, to engage in discriminatory behavior. At the very least, such measures would force firms—including those discussed in Chapter 11 and especially those that decamped to red states during those states' embrace of Vigilante Democracy—to internalize the full costs of their enabling vigilantism.

MODEL BLUE STATE LAW 15:
RESPONSIBLE COMMERCE

No business operating in whole or in part in this state shall sell or lease products that are designed, manufactured, assembled, or transported by entities that engage in discriminatory practices anywhere in the United States. For purposes of this provision, discriminatory practices include any and all practices that would be illegal under state civil rights law were they to occur in this state. They further include practices that (a) interfere or attempt to interfere with any exercise of a right recognized by this state and protected pursuant to this state's civil rights code; or (b) fail to provide reasonable protections to employees whose rights, as recognized by this state pursuant to this state's civil rights code, are threatened or violated.

This is a biggie. Recall once again Prop 12. With an aim to push regulatory reform throughout the nation, the law (and the Court's blessing of said law) serves as a powerful precedent. The likes of New York, Illinois, Massachusetts, Minnesota, Michigan, and California could, in effect, force firms to make a hard choice: forgo access to these big lucrative markets or distance themselves from states and firms that fall tragically short on civil rights and civil liberties.

As we've emphasized throughout this chapter, the alignment of market power and progressive politics is key here. It takes economies as big as California's and New York's and legislatures as reliably Democratic as those in Sacramento and Albany to initiate and effectuate change. In a perfect world, the red states would simply refrain from promoting legal vigilantism or the feds would prohibit it. But because we're far from that world, leaning on firms makes sense. Ultimately, firms won't want to give up either California and New York *or* Texas and Florida—so they just may muscle the Texas and Florida legislatures, getting those bodies to walk back their vicious policies of terror. Ensuring the end of legal vigilantism would be the only way those firms could resume doing business efficiently everywhere.

Resistance

Courthouse vigilantism right now is devastatingly punitive and potentially wildly lucrative. It threatens to bankrupt teachers, schools, and medical practitioners. And, even assuming the courthouse vigilantes ultimately lose the cases that they bring, the targets of those suits will nonetheless have been required to expend tremendous sums of money and devote considerable time to defending themselves. Blue states can, and should, disrupt this dynamic. They can do so by making courthouse vigilantism sufficiently costly that many would-be vigilantes are deterred from getting into the game at all.

The first order of business is to protect the free flow of people within the United States, especially when they are forced to travel from red to blue states to receive reproductive or gender-affirming care. We've long understood travel of this sort to be something the Constitution guarantees. But it's quite possible that those who secure medical services in Illinois or New Jersey will be slapped with lawsuits upon returning to their red state homes—and the federal courts won't step in to put an end to such nonsense. Assuming the absence of adequate federal safeguards—a safe bet after the Court permitted S.B. 8 to go into effect—blue states should enact laws that punish the vigilantes who interfere with interstate travel:

MODEL BLUE STATE LAW 16:
PROTECTING INTERSTATE TRAVEL

It shall be unlawful for any person or government, in any state, to restrict, sanction, hold liable, discriminate against, or otherwise disadvantage any individual traveling to this state to exercise a right or privilege this state recognizes. Any person may bring suit to ensure compliance with this section. A person injured by a violation of this section is entitled to injunctive and declaratory relief and damages of at least $10,000/violation from any person who violates this section, any person who aids or abets a violation of this section, or any person who intends to violate this section.

The next task is to protect blue state residents targeted by courthouse vigilantes for providing services, funding, and support to individuals in red states. To deter such extra-jurisdictional suits—essentially legal parlor tricks that have the potentially devastating effect of nationalizing MAGA laws passed by far-right state legislatures—blue states can enact "clawback" laws. If carefully drafted, these laws could effectively neutralize extra-jurisdictional vigilante suits.

MODEL BLUE STATE LAW 17:
CLAWBACK PROTECTION

When a judgment is entered against any person in any state in which liability is premised on activities that are protected in this state pursuant to this state's civil rights code, the person against whom the judgment is entered may recover three times the amount of the judgment, plus costs and attorney's fees, from the party that initiated the original suit, their attorney(s), and any person that provided material support to the plaintiff or plaintiff's attorney in connection with the original lawsuit. In an action seeking damages under this section, it shall not be a defense that the out-of-state action was authorized by another state's law.

Reorientation

All things being equal, strong and cohesive domestic commercial and cultural ties are unquestionably beneficial. Most would likely say that, today, those ties are even more important, lest we risk losing large swaths of America to right-wing extremists. We take the converse approach in part because we see no such risk. We're already losing large swaths of America to right-wing extremists.

So, instead, we advocate for blue states to disengage from and reorient away from red states as much as practicable. It's in the long-term strategic interests of the targets of vigilantism, and it's in the long-term strategic interests of those hoping to ensure Vigilante Democracy never surfaces again.

Consider calls by Trump bedfellows Ted Cruz and Marjorie Taylor Greene for red states to secede. (In fairness, the senator from Texas said he's "not there yet." But he's close, and when he's ready, he wants to "take NASA, take the military, take the oil" with him.[45]) Consider, too, Florida senator Rick Scott's announcement in 2023 that those who believe in "big government" aren't welcome in his home state of Florida, even just for a quick vacation.[46] It's easy to discount such talk as political grandstanding. But the January 7 Project converts shocking, divisive, and violent rhetoric into political and legal strategies of harassment, subordination, and debasement. Niceties aside, it's time for blue states to recognize that red states are not reliably safe or attractive partners. And as red America loses homegrown talent, repels would-be talent, continues to sabotage their public secondary schools, colleges, and universities, and legislates policies of xenophobia and isolationism,[47] these states will only become less valuable collaborators.

In earlier times, any type of distancing or disengagement by blue states would leave those blue states isolated. But no longer. Today, thanks to technological advances, globalized markets, and cosmopolitan individuals, civic organizations, and industries, blue America can readily find any number of willing overseas partners.

MODEL BLUE STATE LAW 18:
TRANSNATIONAL PARTNERSHIPS

The governor and other state officials are directed to forge or strengthen transnational understandings and agreements that prioritize cultural, educational, economic, democratic, and public health ties. Those understandings and agreements may be with nations, coalitions of nations, or subnational regions (such as specific Canadian provinces and Mexican states).

Here, too, we're not suggesting anything especially radical. Blue states have long taken advantage of the post-WWII globalization trends. New York, Chicago, and West Coast media, legal, banking, and consulting firms are far more likely to have clients (and offices) in Sydney, Paris, Tokyo, and Buenos Aires than in Birmingham, Bismarck, Charleston, or Little Rock. California, Washington, New York, and other blue states have entered into important environmental and trade partnerships with other nations. And blue state universities and blue state cities have sizeable and sophisticated offices of international affairs to further connect those cultural and economic hubs to the larger world.

We're hardly alone in emphasizing this moment as being an opportune one for American states to play an uncharacteristically large role in foreign affairs.[48] The federal dysfunction we've addressed time and again has compromised our transnational trade, security, and diplomatic efforts; and any such shortfalls are particularly unnerving at a time when other long-standing members of the liberal democratic family of nations are struggling to fend off right-wing insurgencies of their own. So blue states stepping up now constitutes yet another win-win. Building up blue state ties to the world makes our progressive communities less dependent on problematic and potentially dangerous domestic partnerships. These ties fortify blue states' leadership at home and internationally, which will become even more important if and when red America decides it wants to constructively reengage with the rest of the country. And these ties elevate blue state policy preferences, perhaps to such heights that they become the de facto position of the United States, certainly to an extent that isn't true when bipartisan compromise is a necessary feature of ordinary foreign affairs conducted by the president and Congress.

MODEL BLUE STATE LAW 19:

COORDINATION, CONSISTENCY, AND COST-SHARING

Whenever feasible and practicable, the governor, in conjunction with the state legislature, shall endeavor to enter into interstate understandings, agreements, and compacts with like-minded states to achieve greater efficiencies in designing, implementing, and financing initiatives that cannot or will not be undertaken by the federal government in a timely fashion.

One of the big downsides associated with the splintering of the nation is that we lose tremendous opportunities to share costs, coordinate policies, standardize civil rights laws (especially insofar as demands are placed on firms to comply with multiple blue states' civil rights codes), and ensure consistency and ease of administration and enforcement. With this in mind, the blue states that constitute this anti-vigilante coalition should collaborate as much as practicable. Creating agreements to jointly design, implement, and finance the blue state counterstrike will certainly require some up-front haggling and negotiating. But those initial costs will pay big dividends in the form of a united front of states big, medium, and small jointly opposed to Vigilante Democracy.

The strategies and tactics we prescribe by way of conclusion don't weigh lightly on our shoulders. They challenge many of our long-held political and legal commitments, not to mention our social, cultural, and psychic attachments to the indivisibility of the United States, its shared goals, and its collective strengths.

But, we ask, again, what's the alternative? How is the federal government helping right now? When will federal officials, including Supreme Court justices, take responsibility for accelerating the erosion of American democracy? When will corporations, for economic or principled reasons, stand up to bullies and mobs? When will our overseas allies give us the tough love we need?

The minute those things happen—and we hope it comes soon— these suggestions (and this book) can be put aside. We welcome that moment, though even then we'd urge you not to discard this copy or dismiss our account of America's latest experiment with state-supported vigilantism. We've been down this road before.

Acknowledgments

I n the spring of 2021, a colleague in Nashville sought our advice on how the local chapter of the ACLU could challenge a new Tennessee law that banned transgender schoolkids from accessing bathrooms that matched their gender identities. Bathroom bans were, sadly, nothing new. Some years earlier, North Carolina had adopted a similar measure only to rescind it after receiving extraordinary pushback from the White House, corporate America, the NCAA, and ordinary North Carolinians. The new Tennessee measure put a ghastly twist on the earlier bans: It enlisted *private parties* to monitor schools' compliance, commence legal proceedings, and punish trans kids and their allies. Students, parents, teachers, and school employees had the right under the law to sue for "emotional harm" caused by the mere presence of a trans student.

Thus began a whirlwind effort to document and understand the American Right's embrace of state-supported vigilantism in the months and years after the failed coup of January 6, 2021. Our efforts were aided immensely by the journalists and public interest lawyers who have done critical work documenting state policies supporting vigilantism and explaining those policies' deleterious effects on targeted communities. And, of course, *their* efforts were aided by the resilient victims of America's resurgent vigilantism.

For sharing their painful stories, those individuals and families have our deepest admiration and thanks.

We owe further debts of gratitude to our (respective) law school deans—Rutgers's Johanna Bond and Rose Cuison-Villazor, and UCLA's Russell Korobkin, Jennifer Mnookin, and Michael Waterstone—and to an array of friends and colleagues. For feedback on drafts and for discussions that have helped us better understand the vigilante project, we thank Carlos Ball, William Boyd, Steve Burbank, Jake Charles, Jessica Clarke, Kim Clausing, Zach Clopton, Cathren Cohen, Blake Emerson, Tara Leigh Grove, Rick Hasen, Aziz Huq, Olati Johnson, Maggie Lemos, Doug Lichtman, Dave Marcus, Darrell Miller, Doug NeJaime, Luke Norris, Jim Pfander, Joanna Schwartz, Miriam Seifter, Liz Sepper, Clyde Spillenger, Dan Urman, Lindsay Wiley, Diego Zambrano, Adam Zimmerman, and Eric Zolt. Anju Gupta was an invaluable source of insight on matters large and small and read the entire manuscript with a lawyer's eye for detail. We extend additional appreciation to the participants at workshops hosted by Rutgers Law School, UCLA School of Law, and Vanderbilt Law School; to the students enrolled in Duke Law School's Colloquium on Civil Rights History, Enforcement, and Policy; and to our colleagues who attended the Seventh Annual Civil Procedure Workshop.

Invaluable research support was provided by our bicoastal team of students—Rutgers's Anusha Das and Saturday Zammit, along with UCLA's Lauren Brown, Andrea Capone, Meghan Gehan, Joshua Hickman-Kramer, Emmet Hollingshead, and Amanda Wade—as well as UCLA's crack librarians, notably Kevin Gerson, Caitlin Hunter, and Lynn McClelland.

We are grateful to the editors at the *Cornell Law Review* and *Pepperdine Law Review*, where some of the ideas presented in this volume first appeared. Julia Cheiffetz, formerly the publisher at One Signal, believed in our book from the outset. William Patrick lent us his keen eyes, steady pen, encyclopedic knowledge, and moral compass. The Atria/One Signal team, including Libby McGuire, Nick Ciani, Hannah Frankel, and Abby Mohr, masterfully navigated the journey from first draft to finished volume. Throughout it all, our agent, Carolyn Savarese, gave us sage advice and tireless support as she served as this book's first and still-fiercest champion.

Last but hardly least, we recognize that our book interfered with family outings, dinners, playdates, and birthday parties. David thanks his family and friends for their patience and understanding as the project consumed weeks, months, and years. Jon extends his gratitude and love to his mom and dad, as well as to Toni, Blaine, and his twin mensches, Izzy and Sammy.

Notes

INTRODUCTION: "YOU JUST HAVE TO IMPOSE YOUR WILL"

1. Written Statement of Harry A. Dunn, Hearing Before the Select Committee to Investigate the January 6th Attack on the United States Capitol, U.S. House of Representatives (January 27, 2021), https://www.congress.gov/117/meeting/house/113969/witnesses/HHRG-117-IJ00-Wstate-DunnO-20210727.pdf.

2. Bannon released two broadcasts on January 5, 2021. Transcripts are contained in the supporting materials to the Final Report of the Select Committee to Investigate the January 6th Attack, H.Rep. No. 117-66 (2022).

3. Barack Obama, Keynote Address at the 2004 Democratic National Convention, July 24, 2004, https://www.presidency.ucsb.edu/documents/keynote-address-the-2004-democratic-national-convention.

4. J. Lester Feder, "This Is How Steve Bannon Sees the Entire World," *BuzzFeed*, November 16, 2016, https://www.buzzfeednews.com/article/lesterfeder/this-is-how-steve-bannon-sees-the-entire-world.

5. Zack Beauchamp, "Sen. Mike Lee's Tweets Against 'Democracy,' Explained," *Vox*, October 8, 2020, https://www.vox.com/policy-and-politics/21507713/mike-lee-democracy-republic-trump-2020.

6. Quoted texts reprinted from "Texts Show Utah Sen. Lee's Early Work to Overturn Election," Associated Press, April 15, 2022, https://apnews.com/article/capitol-siege-2022-midterm-elections-mark-meadows-utah-mike-lee-bcd25f8edaa18f6419ef275a8229e868.

CHAPTER 1: "WE NEED SOMETHING FROM STATE LEGISLATURES TO MAKE THIS LEGITIMATE"

1. Jonathan Obert, *The Six-Shooter State: Public and Private Violence in American Politics* (2018). See also, e.g., Jon D. Michaels, "Deputizing Homeland Security," *Texas Law Review* 88 (2010): 1435; Robert C. Ellickson, *Order Without Law: How Neighbors Settle Disputes* (2009); Lee Johnston, "What Is Vigilantism?," *British Journal of Criminology* 36 (1996): 220. For the argument that vigilantism should be defined by its extralegal character, see, e.g., Regina Bateson, "The Politics of Vigilantism," *Comparative Political Studies* 54 (2020): 923.

2. Jordain Carney, "Schumer Says He Was Targeted on Jan. 6 for His Religion," *The Hill*, January 6, 2022, https://thehill.com/homenews /senate/588571-schumer-says-he-was-targeted-on-jan-6-for-his-religion/; Holmes Lybrand, "Jan. 6 Rioter Who Said She Wanted to Shoot Nancy Pelosi Sentenced to 60 Days Behind Bars," CNN, July 21, 2022, https:// www.cnn.com/2022/07/21/politics/rioter-pelosi-bancroft/index.html.

3. Eric L. McDaniel, Irfan Nooruddin, Allyson F. Shortle, *The Everyday Crusade: Christian Nationalism in American Politics* (2022).

4. Charles Blow, "Trump's Army of Angry White Men," *New York Times*, October 25, 2020, https://www.nytimes.com/2020/10/25/opinion /trump-white-men-election.html.

5. See, e.g., Jeffrey S. Solochek, "School Book Challenges Hijacked by 'Bad Actors,' DeSantis Says," *Tampa Bay Times*, February 16, 2024, https://www.tampabay.com/news/education/2024/02/16/school-book -challenges-hijacked-by-bad-actors-desantis-says/.

6. See, e.g., Amelia Abraham, " 'It's Been a Total Witch-Hunt. It Takes Its Toll': The LGBTQ+ Families Fleeing Red States," *Guardian*, June 6, 2023, https://www.theguardian.com/world/2023/jun/06 /lgbtq-rights-trans-gay-texas-florida-north-carolina; Shefali Luthra, " 'We're Not Going to Win That Fight': Bans on Abortion and Gender-Affirming Care Are Driving Doctors from Texas," *The 19th*, June 21, 2023, https://19thnews.org/2023/06/abortion-gender -affirming-care-bans-doctors-leaving-texas/.

CHAPTER 2: "ABSCONDED"

1. This account is drawn from Lindsay M. Chervinsky, "The Remarkable Story of Ona Judge," White House Historical Association, October 21, 2019, https://www.whitehousehistory.org/the-remarkable-story-of-ona-judge;

"Ona Judge," Washington Library Center for Digital History, https://www
.mountvernon.org/library/digitalhistory/digital-encyclopedia/article/ona
-judge/ [Mount Vernon History]; Erica Armstrong Dunbar, *Never Caught:
The Washingtons' Relentless Pursuit of Their Runaway Slave, Ona Judge* (2017).

2. "Ona Judge."
3. Chervinsky, "Remarkable Story."
4. Ibid.
5. Phil McCombs, "The Vigilante Mystique," *Washington Post*, January 17,
   1985, https://www.washingtonpost.com/archive/lifestyle/1985/01/17
   /the-vigilante-mystique/c1887806-d4f6-4032-a5a0-a569fb19b227/.
6. Within the voluminous writing on racial backlash, Ta-Nehisi Coates's
   2017 essay stands out for its identification of the central dynamics of
   Trump-era politics. Ta-Nehisi Coates, "The First White President,"
   Atlantic, October 15, 2017, https://www.theatlantic.com/magazine
   /archive/2017/10/the-first-white-president-ta-nehisi-coates/537909/.
   For further discussions, see, e.g., Nathan P. Kalmoe and Lilliana Mason,
   *Radical American Partisanship: Mapping Violent Hostility, Its Causes, and
   the Consequences for Democracy* (2022); Justin Gest, *Majority Minority*
   (2020); Jonathan M. Metzl, *Dying of Whiteness: How the Politics of Racial
   Resentment Is Killing America's Heartland* (2019).
7. For histories of the clause that we have drawn on, see, e.g., Andrew
   Delbanco, *The War Before the War: Fugitive Slaves and the Struggle for
   America's Soul from the Revolution to the Civil War* (2018); Steven Lubet,
   Fugitive Justice: Runaways, Rescuers, and Slavery on Trial (2010); Paul
   Finkelman, "The Kidnapping of John Davis and the Adoption of the
   Fugitive Slave Law of 1793," *Journal of Southern History* 56 (1990): 397; Dan
   Farbman, "Resistance Lawyering," *California Law Review* 107 (2019): 1877.
8. John Hope Franklin and Loren Schweninger, *Runaway Slaves: Rebels on
   the Plantation* (2000), Chapter 7.
9. For the Langdon family's stance on slavery, see Dunbar, *Never Caught:
   The Washingtons' Relentless Pursuit*, 132–35, 165–67.
10. Act of February 12, 1793, ch. 7, 1 Stat. 302.
11. Ibid. section 4.

CHAPTER 3: "WE ARE THE OPPRESSED"

1. Elaine Frantz Parsons, "Midnight Rangers: Costume and Performance
   in the Reconstruction-Era Ku Klux Klan," *Journal of American History*
   92 (2005): 811, 816.

2. Enforcement Act of 1870, ch. 114, 16 Stat. 140; Enforcement Act of February 1871, ch. 99, 16 Stat. 433; Enforcement Act of April 1871, ch. 22, 17 Stat. 13.

3. For a leading history, see Eric Foner, *Reconstruction Updated Edition: America's Unfinished Revolution, 1863–1877* (2014).

4. U.S. Constitution, amend. 14, section 1.

5. *Slaughter-House Cases*, 83 U.S. 36 (1873).

6. Ibid. at 96 (Field, J., dissenting).

7. *United States vs. Cruikshank*, 92 U.S. 542 (1876).

8. Foner, *Reconstruction Updated*, 531.

9. Obert, *The Six-Shooter State*, 150; Allen W. Trelease, *The Ku Klux Klan Conspiracy and Southern Reconstruction* (1971), xlii.

10. *Civil Rights Cases*, 109 U.S. 3 (1883).

11. Trelease, *The Ku Klux Klan Conspiracy*, xliii.

12. Ibid.

13. On the rise of the second KKK and its campaigns of violence, see, e.g., Linda Gordon, *The Second Coming of the KKK: The Ku Klux Klan of the 1920s and the American Political Tradition* (2017); Nancy K. MacLean, *Behind the Mask of Chivalry: The Making of the Second Ku Klux Klan* (1994); Wyn Craig Wade, *The Fiery Cross: The Ku Klux Klan in America* (1987); C. Vann Woodward, *Origins of the New South, 1877–1913* (1951).

14. For a pathbreaking recent exploration of these dynamics, drawing on archival accounts of murders in the Jim Crow South, see Margaret A. Burnham, *By Hands Now Known: Jim Crow's Legal Executioners* (2022). See also, e.g., Amy Louise Wood, *Lynching and Spectacle: Witnessing Racial Violence in America, 1890–1940* (2009); Leon F. Litwack, *Trouble in Mind: Black Southerners in the Age of Jim Crow* (1998); Woodward, *Origins of the New South*.

15. Adolph L. Reed, Jr., *The South: Jim Crow and Its Afterlives* (2022), 29.

16. In focusing on Jim Crow's mechanisms of racial terror and oppression, we in no way mean to downplay the importance and vitality of Black resistance to the Jim Crow order. For recent work exploring the dynamics of Black resistance, see Dylan C. Penningroth, *Before the Movement: The Hidden History of Black Civil Rights* (2023); Myisha S. Eatmon, *Public Wrongs, Private Rights: African Americans, Private Law, and White Violence during Jim Crow* (unpublished doctoral dissertation, 2020), available at https://arch.library.northwestern.edu/concern

/generic_works/7s75dc619?locale=en. For a classic account of legal movement-making in the run-up to *Brown v. Board of Education*, see Richard Kluger, *Simple Justice: The History of* Brown v. Board of Education *and Black America's Struggle for Equality* (2011).

17. On media coverage of the civil rights movement and the white backlash it provoked, see, e.g., Omar Wasow, "Agenda Seeding: How 1960s Black Protests Moved Elites, Public Opinion and Voting," *American Political Science Review* 114 (2020): 638; Aniko Bodroghkozy, *Equal Time: Television and the Civil Rights Movement* (2012); Sasha Torres, *Black, White, and in Color: Television and Black Civil Rights* (2008). For a broader history of the movement, see Taylor Branch, *Parting the Waters: America in the King Years 1954–63* (2007). On the international dimensions of the movement, see Mary L. Dudziak, *Cold War Civil Rights* (2000).

18. See *Katzenbach v. Morgan*, 384 U.S. 641 (1966); *Heart of Atlanta Motel, Inc. v. United States*, 379 U.S. 241 (1964); *Katzenbach v. McClung*, 349 U.S. 294 (1964); *Jones v. Alfred H. Mayer Co.*, 392 U.S. 409 (1968).

19. Avidit Acharya, Matthew Blackwell, and Maya Sen, *Deep Roots: How Slavery Still Shapes Southern Politics* (2018), 194 tbl 8.2.

20. Brookings Institution, Vital Statistics on Congress, https://www.brookings.edu/wp-content/uploads/2021/02/Chpt-1.pdf.

21. Bernard Grofman and Lisa Handley, "The Impact of the Voting Rights Act on Black Representation in Southern State Legislatures," *Legislative Studies Quarterly* 16 (1991): 111.

22. U.S. Census Bureau, "Black High School Attainment Nearly on Par with National Average," June 10, 2020, https://www.census.gov/library/stories/2020/06/black-high-school-attainment-nearly-on-par-with-national-average.html.

23. For accounts of the realignment in party politics that transpired in the aftermath of the Civil Rights Act, see, e.g., Kevin M. Kruse and Julian E. Zelizer, *Fault Lines: A History of the United States Since 1974* (2019); Sam Rosenfeld, *The Polarizers: Postwar Architects of Our Partisan Era* (2018); Matt Grossmann and David A. Hopkins, *Asymmetric Politics: Ideological Republicans and Group Interest Democrats* (2016); Matthew Levendusky, *The Partisan Sort: How Liberals Became Democrats and Conservatives Became Republicans* (2009).

24. House Minority Leader Richard Gephardt reportedly observed, "Politics is a substitute for violence." See UVA Miller Center, Richard Gephardt Oral History, https://millercenter.org/the-presidency/presidential

-oral-histories/richard-gephardt-oral-history. For an effort to formally model the relationship between elections and violence, see S. P. Harish and Andrew T. Little, "The Political Violence Cycle," *American Political Science Review* III (2017): 237.

25. We take the basic facts of the Goetz case from *People v. Goetz*, 68 N.Y.2d 96 (1986). For works collecting additional reporting, see, e.g., Richard Maxwell Brown, *No Duty to Retreat: Violence and Values in American History and Society* (1991); George P. Fletcher, *A Crime of Self-Defense: Bernhard Goetz and the Law on Trial* (1988).

26. 68 N.Y.2d at 102.

27. Pia Beumer, "Bernhard Goetz and the Roots of Kyle Rittenhouse's Celebrity on the Right," *Washington Post*, June 15, 2022, https://www .washingtonpost.com/outlook/2022/06/15/bernhard-goetz-roots-kyle -rittenhouses-celebrity-right/.

28. Steven V. Roberts, "D'Amato and Doonesbury," *New York Times*, February 7, 1985, https://www.nytimes.com/1985/02/07/us/d-amato -and-doonesbury.html.

29. "A Majority of Americans Support Subway Vigilante Bernhard Goetz," UPI, March 3, 1985, https://www.upi.com/Archives/1985/03/03 /A-majority-of-Americans-support-subway-vigilante-Bernhard-Goetz /9249478674000/.

30. Bob Kappstatter, "The Story of Bernhard Goetz, the Subway Vigilante," *New York Daily News*, August 14, 2017, https://www .nydailynews.com/2017/08/14/the-story-of-bernhard-goetz-the -subway-vigilante/.

31. Quoted in Jonathan Markovitz, *Legacies of Lynching: Racial Violence and Memory* (2004), 74.

32. Phil McCombs, "The Vigilante Mystique," *Washington Post*, January 17, 1985, https://www.washingtonpost.com/archive/lifestyle/1985/01/17 /the-vigilante-mystique/c1887806-d4f6-4032-a5a0-a569fb19b227/.

33. The President's News Conference, January 9, 1985, https://www .reaganlibrary.gov/archives/speech/presidents-news-conference-21.

34. For some writing by one of us on the post-9/11 transformations in the U.S. security state, see Jon D. Michaels, *Constitutional Coup* (2017); Jon D. Michaels, "Separation of Powers and Centripetal Forces: Implications for the Institutional Design and Constitutionality of Our National Security State," *University of Chicago Law Review* 83 (2016): 199; Jon D. Michaels,

"Deputizing Homeland Security," *Texas Law Review* 88 (2010): 1435; Jon D. Michaels, "All the President's Spies: Private-Public Intelligence Gathering in the War on Terror," *California Law Review* 96 (2008): 901.

35. The following two paragraphs follow David Neiwert, *And Hell Followed with Her: Crossing the Dark Side of the American Border* (2013), and Rick Perlstein, "The Minutemen and the Mainstream Media," *Nation*, April 3, 2013, https://www.thenation.com/article/archive /minutemen-and-mainstream-media/.

36. Neiwert, *And Hell Followed*, 75; Perlstein, *The Minutemen*.

37. Ibid.

38. David Lane, Southern Poverty Law Center, https://www.splcenter.org /fighting-hate/extremist-files/individual/david-lane.

39. David Holthouse, "Minutemen, Other Anti-Immigrant Militia Groups Stake Out Arizona Border," *Intelligence Report*, June 27, 2005, https://www.splcenter.org/fighting-hate/intelligence-report/2005 /minutemen-other-anti-immigrant-militia-groups-stake-out-arizona -border.

40. Heidi Beirich, "Nativist Movement Collapses Amid Infighting," Intelligence Report, March 1, 2012, https://www.splcenter.org/fighting -hate/intelligence-report/2012/nativist-movement-collapses-amid -infighting.

41. Dan Glaister, "Schwarzenegger Backs Minutemen," *Guardian*, May 1, 2005, https://www.theguardian.com/world/2005/may/02/usa.mexico (spelling Americanized).

42. Solomon Moore, "Immigration Official Praises Citizen Patrols," *Los Angeles Times*, July 21, 2005, https://www.latimes.com/archives/la-xpm -2005-jul-21-me-patrol21-story.html.

43. "Minutemen Group to Watch NM-Mexico Border for Illegal Aliens," Associated Press, June 10, 2005.

44. Ibid.

45. Michael Leahy, "Crossing the Line," *Washington Post*, March 19, 2006, https://www.washingtonpost.com/archive/lifestyle/magazine/2006/03 /19/crossing-the-line/705a016f-1433-4820-8940-a2a6de273a4a/.

46. John Pomfret and Sonya Geis, "Schwarzenegger Tries New Script; California Governor Reaches Out to Democrats, Independents," *Washington Post*, May 28, 2006, https://www.washingtonpost.com /archive/politics/2006/05/28/schwarzenegger-tries-new-script

-span-classbankheadgovernor-reaches-out-to-democratsspan/0263e812
-5a24-4914-acb9-4e8feadbc2da/.

47. Our description of the Flores murders is based on David Neiwert, "The Minutemen's Demise," *Type Investigations*, July 23, 2012, https://www.typeinvestigations.org/investigation/2012/07/23/minutemens-demise/.

48. Ibid.

49. Associated Press, "Arpaio to Militias: Beware or Be Shot," *Politico*, August 20, 2013, available at https://www.politico.com/story/2013/08/arizona-sheriff-joe-arpaio-militias-095732.

50. See, e.g., Minutemen Project, http://baesic.net/minutemanproject/.

CHAPTER 4: "THE WAY THINGS OUGHT TO BE"

1. Our history of the rise of right-wing media relies heavily on Brian Rosenwald, *Talk Radio's America: How an Industry Took Over a Political Party That Took Over the United States* (2019); Nicole Hemmer, *Messengers of the Right: Conservative Media and the Transformation of American Politics* (2016); Matt Grossmann and David A. Hopkins, *Asymmetric Politics: Ideological Republicans and Group Interest Democrats* (2016), 14.

2. Adam Serwer, *The Cruelty Is the Point: The Past, Present, and Future of Trump's America* (2021).

3. Talmon Joseph Smith, "Rush Limbaugh in His Own Words," *New York Times*, February 17, 2021, https://www.nytimes.com/2020/02/07/sunday-review/rush-limbaugh-trump-medal.html; Kevin Robillard, "Rush: Obama 'Hates this Country,'" *Politico*, July 16, 2012, https://www.politico.com/story/2012/07/rush-obama-hates-this-country-078553.

4. "Arizona Patrol Ordered to Stand Down," *The Rush Limbaugh Show*, May 13, 2005, https://www.rushlimbaugh.com/daily/2005/05/13/arizona_border_patrol_ordered_to_stand_down/.

5. "Minutemen to Protest Lax Border Enforcement," *The Rush Limbaugh Show*, March 16, 2005, https://www.rushlimbaugh.com/daily/2005/03/16/minutemen_to_protest_lax_border_enforcement/.

6. "Shocker: NBC News Doctors a Tape!" *The Rush Limbaugh Show*, April 2, 2012, https://live-rush-limbaugh.pantheonsite.io/daily/2012/04/02/shocker_nbc_news_doctors_a_tape/.

7. "Rush Limbaugh: 'Well, Where Are All the People With Guns' to 'Push Back' Against the Left?," Media Matters, June 15, 2020, https://www.mediamatters.org/rush-limbaugh/rush-limbaugh-well-where-are-all-people-guns-push-back-against-left-0.

8. Nick Niedzwiadek, "Trump Urges 'Special' Capitol Rioters to 'Go Home Now,'" *Politico*, January 6, 2021, https://www.politico.com/news /2021/01/06/trump-addresses-capitol-rioters-455607.

9. Tweet by @GoAngelo, January 7, 2021, https://x.com/GoAngelo/status /1347267821710024705?s=20.

10. Gabriel Sherman, *The Loudest Voice in the Room: How the Brilliant, Bombastic Roger Ailes Built Fox News—and Divided a Country* (2014).

11. Anna Altman, "Matt Gertz Tracks How Fox News Manipulates Trump," *Columbia Journalism Review*, Februrary 13, 2019, https://www .cjr.org/politics/matt-gertz-trump-tweets.php; Carlos Maza, "The Trump–Fox & Friends Feedback Loop, Explained," *Vox*, February 9, 2018, https://www.vox.com/2018/2/9/16997022/strikethrough-trump -fox-friends-feedback-loop-explained-tweet.

12. Ryan J. Reilly, "Infowars Host Owen Shroyer Sentenced to 60 Days in Jan. 6 Case," NBC News, September 12, 2023, https://www.nbcnews .com/politics/justice-department/infowars-host-owen-shroyer -sentenced-jan-6-case-rcna104378.

13. Timothy Bella, "Alex Jones Is 'Holding Firearms' for Jan. 6 Participants, Bankruptcy Docs Show," *Washington Post*, February 16, 2023, https:// www.washingtonpost.com/nation/2023/02/16/alex-jones-holding -firearms-jan-6-rioters/.

14. "Joe Rogan Says It's a 'Fact' That Jan. 6 Was a False Flag, Cites Ray Epps," Yahoo, July 31, 2023, https://www.yahoo.com/entertainment /joe-rogan-says-fact-jan-180044649.html.

15. See Daniel Ziblatt, *Conservative Parties and the Birth of Democracy* (2017).

16. Jeremy W. Peters, *Insurgency: How Republicans Lost Their Party and Got Everything They Wanted* (2022), 14.

17. Ron Eyerman, *The Making of White American Identity* (2022), 192.

18. Brian Montopoli, "Tea Party Supporters: Who They Are and What They Believe," CBS News, December 14, 2012, https://www.cbsnews .com/news/tea-party-supporters-who-they-are-and-what-they-believe/.

19. Kate Zernike, "NAACP Report Raises Concerns About Racism Within Tea Party Groups," *New York Times*, October 20, 2010, https://www .nytimes.com/2010/10/21/us/politics/21naacp.html.

20. David Hoffman, "Reagan to Invoke '11th Commandment,'" *Washington Post*, July 12, 1987, https://www.washingtonpost.com /archive/politics/1987/07/12/reagan-to-invoke-11th-commandment /105a89fa-cf1e-4f1b-b48a-2d704caf9590/.

21. For histories of post–Tea Party governance crises, see, e.g., Rachel M. Blum, *How the Tea Party Captured the GOP: Insurgent Factions in American Politics* (2020); David L. Noll, "Administrative Sabotage," *Michigan Law Review* 120 (2022): 753; Joseph Fishkin and David E. Pozen, "Asymmetric Constitutional Hardball," *Columbia Law Review* 118 (2018): 915; Jacob D. Charles, "The Debt Limit and the Constitution: How the Fourteenth Amendment Forbids Fiscal Obstructionism," *Duke Law Journal* 62 (2013): 1227.

22. Thomas B. Edsall, "The Embodiment of White Christian Nationalism in a Tailored Suit," *New York Times*, November 1, 2023, https://www.nytimes.com/2023/11/01/opinion/mike-johnson-christian-nationalism-speaker.html.

23. For scholarly efforts to understand this surge of populist sentiment, see, e.g., David Goodhart, *The Road to Somewhere: The Populist Revolt and the Future of Politics* (2020); Pippa Norris and Ronald Inglehart, *Cultural Backlash: Trump, Brexit, and Authoritarian Populism* (2019); Frances E. Lee, "Populism and the American Party System: Opportunities and Constraints," *Perspectives on Politics* 18 (2019): 370; Rachel J. Kramer, *The Politics of Resentment: Rural Consciousness in Wisconsin and the Rise of Scott Walker* (2016).

24. Philip Bump, "Donald Trump Reverses Course on Paying Legal Fees for Man Who Attacked Protester. But Could He Do It?," *Washington Post*, March 15, 2016, https://www.washingtonpost.com/news/the-fix/wp/2016/03/10/trump-once-said-he-would-pay-legal-fees-for-people-who-beat-up-protesters-now-that-its-happened-can-he/.

25. The refusal to abide by, and eagerness to buck, the unwritten norms of democratic play is a focus of much of the literature on democratic decline. See, e.g., Steven Levitsky and Daniel Ziblatt, *How Democracies Die* (2018).

26. Steve Benen, "Trump Reportedly Told Tribal Leaders to Ignore Federal Laws," MSNBC, November 6, 2017, https://www.msnbc.com/rachel-maddow-show/trump-reportedly-told-tribal-leaders-ignore-federal-laws-msna1035451.

CHAPTER 5: "AN INSTITUTIONALIZATION OF THE HECKLER'S VETO"

1. Patrick Wilson, "Youngkins Received 95% Tax Cut Due to Conservation Status of Their Horse Farm," *Richmond Times Dispatch*, July 21, 2021, https://richmond.com/news/state-and-regional

/youngkins-received-95-tax-cut-due-to-conservation-status-of
-their-horse-farm/article_a54e290b-0879-5ed9-bfcd-486ee9e394eb
.html#tracking-source=home-top-story.

2. Jessica Flint, "Where Washington, D.C.'s Elites Sleep," *Wall Street
Journal*, April 13, 2019, https://www.wsj.com/articles/where
-washington-d-cs-elites-sleep-11554992950.

3. Jeremy W. Peters, "Glenn Youngkin Was a Traditional Republican.
Then He Became a Culture Warrior," *New York Times*, October 29,
2021, https://www.nytimes.com/2021/10/29/us/politics/glenn
-youngkin-virginia-governors-race.html.

4. Giacomo Tognini, "Virginia's New Governor Glenn Youngkin Is One
of the Nation's Richest Politicians," *Forbes*, November 3, 2021, https://
www.forbes.com/sites/giacomotognini/2021/11/03/virginias-new
-governor-glenn-youngkin-is-one-of-the-nations-richest-politicians
/?sh=644f9d2670fd.

5. *Plyler v. Doe*, 457 U.S. 202 (1982); *University of California Regents v. Bakke*,
438 U.S. 265 (1978).

6. Lewis F. Powell, Jr., *Attack on American Free Enterprise System*, August
1971, available at https://scholarlycommons.law.wlu.edu/powellmemo/.

7. Ibid., 24.

8. Ibid., 8.

9. Sol Stern, "Think Tank in the Tank," *Democracy*, July 7, 2020, https://
democracyjournal.org/arguments/think-tank-in-the-tank/.

10. *Project 2025: Mandate for Leadership*, Heritage Foundation 481 (2023),
https://thf_media.s3.amazonaws.com/project2025/2025
_MandateForLeadership_FULL.pdf.

11. David Corn, "How Right-Wing Groups Are Plotting to Implement
Trump's Authoritarianism," *Mother Jones*, September 14, 2023, https://
www.motherjones.com/politics/2023/09/heritage-foundation-project
-2025-trump-authoritarianism-our-land/.

12. Hannah Natanson, "Parental Say in Schools, Resonant in Va.
Governor's Race, Bound for GOP National Playbook," *Washington Post*,
November 3, 2021, https://www.washingtonpost.com/local/education
/parent-control-schools-republican-virginia/2021/11/03/313e8a68
-3cc3-11ec-a493-51b0252dea0c_story.html; Aaron Zitner and Douglas
Belkin, "Youngkin's Election Win in Virginia Offers Playbook for
Republicans: Parents' Rights," *Wall Street Journal*, November 5, 2021,
https://www.wsj.com/articles/in-education-battles-republicans

-see-a-winning-campaign-issue-11636109260?st=t4frd75u95ly68u&refli
nk=desktopwebshare_permalink.

13. Omar Abdel-Baqui and Jennifer Calfas, "New Virginia Hotline Lets
Parents Report 'Divisive Teaching Practices,'" *Wall Street Journal*,
January 26, 2022, https://www.wsj.com/articles/new-virginia-hotline
-lets-parents-report-divisive-teaching-practices-11643236044; Hannah
Natanson, "Va. Parents File Lawsuit, Schools Vow Resistance Against
Youngkin's Order Making Masks Optional," *Washington Post*, January 18,
2022, https://www.washingtonpost.com/education/2022/01/18/virginia
-schools-youngkin-masks/.

14. Alex Seitz-Wald, "In Virginia, Republicans See Education, Curriculum
Fears as a Path to Victory," NBC News, October 17, 2021, https://www
.nbcnews.com/politics/elections/virginia-republicans-see-education
-curriculum-fears-path-victory-n1281676; Jake Lahut, "'An Anti-Woke
Rebellion': GOP Takes Victory Lap After Virginia Governor's Race
That Retook Suburbs Biden Had Carried," *Business Insider*, November 3,
2021, https://www.businessinsider.com/virginia-governor-race-critical
-race-theory-republican-talking-point-messaging-2021-11.

15. Executive Order Number Two (2022) and Order of Public Health
Emergency One, https://www.governor.virginia.gov/media
/governorvirginiagov/governor-of-virginia/pdf/74---eo/74---eo/EO-2
---School-Mask-Mandate-Executive-Order-Exception.pdf.

16. See Virginia Code sections 22.1–254.1.

17. See, e.g., Latoya Hill and Samantha Artiga, "COVID-19 Cases and
Deaths by Race/Ethnicity: Current Data and Changes Over Time,"
Kaiser Family Foundation, August 22, 2022, https://www.kff.org
/racial-equity-and-health-policy/issue-brief/covid-19-cases-and-deaths
-by-race-ethnicity-current-data-and-changes-over-time/; A. K.
Ghosh et al., "Association Between Overcrowded Households,
Multigenerational Households, and COVID-19: A Cohort Study,
2021," Public Health 273 (2021); Gregorio A. Millet et al., "Assessing
Differential Impacts of COVID-19 on Black Communities," *Annals of
Epidemiology* 47 (2020): 37.

18. *Meyer v. Nebraska*, 262 U.S. 390 (1923).

19. *Pierce v. Society of Sisters*, 268 U.S. 510, 535 (1925).

20. *Mozert v. Hawkins Cnty. Bd. of Educ.*, 827 F.2d 1058, 1069 (6th Cir. 1987).

21. *Brown v. Hot, Sexy & Safer Prods., Inc.*, 68 F.3d 525, 533 (1st Cir. 1995),

abrogated on other grounds, *County of Sacramento v. Lewis*, 523 U.S. 833 (1998).

22. Melody Alemansour et al., "Sex Education in Schools," *Georgetown Journal of Gender and Law* 20, 467 (2019).

23. Jamelle Bouie, "What the Republican Push for 'Parents' Rights' Is Really About," *New York Times*, March 28, 2023, https://www.nytimes .com/2023/03/28/opinion/parents-rights-republicans-florida.html.

24. H.B. 1447 (In. 2023).

25. See, e.g., Casey Smith, "Tensions Rise at Indiana Statehouse Over Bill Targeting 'Harmful' Library Materials for Minors," *Indiana Capital Chronicle*, February 16, 2023, https://indianacapitalchronicle.com /2023/02/16/tensions-rise-at-indiana-statehouse-over-bill-targeting -harmful-library-materials-for-minors/; Kristin Bien, "Educators, Librarians Could Face Criminal Prosecution and a Level 6 Felony Over Controversial Books," WSBT, October 4, 2023, https://wsbt.com/news /operation-education/educators-librarians-criminal-prosecution-level -6-felony-controversial-books-teachers-transparent-state-law-obscene -harmful-minors-ban-library-indiana.

26. Lee V. Gaines, "Bill to Ban 'Bad' Books, Strip Protections from Teachers, Librarians Passes Indiana Senate," *Chalkbeat Indiana*, March 1, 2023, https://www.chalkbeat.org/indiana/2023/3/1/23620174/book-ban -prosecution-criminalize-teachers-librarians-schools-indiana-senate -harmful-materials/.

27. H.B. 1447 (In. 2023).

28. H.B. 1557 (Fl. 2022).

29. H.B. 1069 (Fl. 2023).

30. Ibid., section 5.

31. Ibid.

32. David Brooks, "Why People Are Fleeing Blue Cities for Red States," *New York Times*, April 13, 2023, https://www.nytimes.com/2023/04/13 /opinion/sun-belt-migration.html.

33. S.B. 2247, 111th Gen. Ass. (Tenn. 2021).

34. Marta W. Aldrich, "After Book Burning Comment, Tennessee Lawmakers Vote to Let State Veto Library Materials," *Chalkbeat Tennessee*, April 28, 2022, https://www.chalkbeat.org/tennessee/2022 /4/28/23047535/book-ban-tennessee-textbook-commission-legislation -age-appropriate/.

35. Blaise Gainey, "Tennessee Librarians, School Boards Could Face Criminal Penalties If 'Obscene' Books Wind Up in Schools," WKU, March 9, 2022, https://www.wkyufm.org/2022-03-09/tennessee-librarians-school-boards-could-face-criminal-penalties-if-obscene-books-wind-up-in-schools.

36. Claire Woodcock, "It Only Takes One Parent to Get All the Graphic Novels Removed from a School Library," *Vice*, November 23, 2022, https://www.vice.com/en/article/g5vnqb/it-only-takes-one-parent-to-get-all-the-graphic-novels-removed-from-a-school-library.

37. S.B. 1470 (Ok. 2022), https://legiscan.com/OK/text/SB1470/id/2484266.

38. H.B. 1467 (Fl. 2022), https://www.flsenate.gov/Session/Bill/2022/1467/BillText/er/PDF.

39. Hannah Natanson, "Hide Your Books to Avoid Felony Charges, Fla. Schools Tell Teachers," *Washington Post*, January 31, 2023, https://www.washingtonpost.com/education/2023/01/31/florida-hide-books-stop-woke-manatee-county-duval-county-desantis/.

40. Hannah Natanson, "Objection to Sexual, LGBTQ Content Propels Spike in Book Challenges," *Washington Post*, May 23, 2023, https://www.washingtonpost.com/education/2023/05/23/lgbtq-book-ban-challengers/.

41. "Banned in the USA: State Laws Supercharge Book Suppression in Schools," PEN America, April 20, 2023, https://pen.org/report/banned-in-the-usa-state-laws-supercharge-book-suppression-in-schools/; "Florida Book Bans Are No Hoax: Here Are the Facts," PEN America, March 10, 2023, https://pen.org/florida-book-bans-not-a-hoax/; "Duval Schools Rejected These 34 Books Under Florida's New Laws," *Jax Today*, March 23, 2023, https://jaxtoday.org/2023/03/28/explore-duval-schools-rejected-these-34-books-under-floridas-new-laws/.

42. Hannah Natanson, "Half of Challenged Books Return to Schools. LGBTQ Books Are Banned Most," *Washington Post*, December 23, 2023, https://www.washingtonpost.com/education/2023/12/23/school-book-challenges-shelves-lgbtq-authors/.

43. See, e.g., Jamie Stengle, "Texas County Roiled by Book Ban Considered Closing Libraries," Associated Press, April 13, 2023, https://apnews.com/article/texas-library-banned-books-73f17143237d57784efd2746d292ab68; Kelly Weill, "Book Banners Are Now Trying to Close Public Libraries," *Daily Beast*, April 14, 2023, https://www.thedailybeast.com/book-banners-are-now-trying-to-close

-public-libraries; Domingo Ramirez, Jr., "Fort Worth Libraries Reopen Tuesday after Bomb Threats Forced Closures," *Fort Worth Star-Telegram*, September 20, 2022, https://www.star-telegram.com/news/local/crime/article266059931.html; Ethan Illers, "Metro Police Investigating 'Non-location-specific Bomb Threat' Emailed to Nashville Public Library," WKRN News, September 22, 2022, https://www.wkrn.com/news/local-news/nashville/nashville-public-library-locations-closed-due-to-operational-issue/; Fabiola Cineas, "The Rising Republican Movement to Defund Public Libraries," *Vox*, May 8, 2023, https://www.vox.com/politics/2023/5/5/23711417/republicans-want-to-defund-public-libraries-book-bans.

44. Joanna Kakissis, "In Trump, Hungary's Viktor Orbán Has a Rare Ally in the Oval Office," NPR, May 13, 2019, https://www.npr.org/2019/05/13/722620996/in-trump-hungarys-viktor-Orbán-has-a-rare-ally-in-the-oval-office.

45. Shaun Walker and Flora Garamvolgyi, "Viktor Orbán Sparks Outrage with Attack on 'Race Mixing' in Europe," *Guardian*, July 24, 2022; Jennifer Rankin, "Hungary Is No Longer a Full Democracy, Says European Parliament," *Guardian*, September 15, 2022, https://www.theguardian.com/world/2022/sep/15/hungary-is-no-longer-a-full-democracy-says-european-parliament.

46. *Report of a Special Committee: Political Interference and Academic Freedom in Florida's Public Higher Education System*, American Association of University Professors (December 2023), https://www.aaup.org/report/report-special-committee-political-interference-and-academic-freedom-florida%E2%80%99s-public-higher.

47. Lewis F. Powell, Jr., "A Lawyer Looks at Civil Disobedience," *Washington and Lee Law Review* 23 (1966): 205.

48. See, e.g., Leah M. Litman, "Disparate Discrimination," *Michigan Law Review* 121 (2022): 1; Jenny Samuels, "Religious Exemptions Are Becoming the Rule," *Harvard Law Review* (blog), April 6, 2023, https://harvardlawreview.org/blog/2023/04/religious-exemptions-are-becoming-the-rule/.

49. *Greer v. Spock*, 424 U.S. 828, 843–44 (1976) (Powell, J., concurring) (quoting in part from Thomas I. Emerson, *The System of Freedom of Expression* (1970), 57).

50. 475 U.S. 503 (1986).

51. Ibid. at 507.

52. Steve Vladeck, "Texas Judge's Covid Mandate Ruling Exposes Federal 'Judge-Shopping Problem,'" MSNBC, January 11, 2022, https://www.msnbc.com/opinion/texas-judge-s-covid-mandate -ruling-exposes-federal-judge-shopping-n1287324; Tierney Sneed, "Why Texas Is a Legal Graveyard for Biden Policies," CNN, March 3, 2022, https://www.cnn.com/2022/03/03/politics/texas-biden-court -losses-paxton-bush/index.html.

53. Emma Platoff, "By Gutting Obamacare, Judge Reed O'Connor Handed Texas a Win. It Wasn't the First Time," *Texas Tribune*, December 19, 2018, https://www.texastribune.org/2018/12/19/reed-oconnor-federal -judge-texas-obamacare-forum-shopping-ken-paxton/; Erin Doherty, "How a Federal Judge in Texas Became an Obamacare Boogeyman," *Axios*, April 12, 2023, https://www.axios.com/2023/04/12/obamacare -judge-reed-oconnor-preventive-care-aca.

54. Julian Mark and Taylor Telford, "Federal Judge Orders Minority- Business Agency Opened to All Races," *Washington Post*, March 6, 2024, https://www.washingtonpost.com/business/2024/03/06/minority -business-programs-racial-disadvantage-unconstitutional/. Danielle Douglas-Gabriel, "Federal Judge in Texas Strikes Down Biden's Student Loan Forgiveness Plan," *Washington Post*, November 11, 2022, https:// www.washingtonpost.com/education/2022/11/10/student-loan -forgiveness-texas-lawsuit/; Roxanna Asgarian, "Texas Drops Fight to Prevent 18-To-20-Year-Olds from Carrying Handguns in Public," *Texas Tribune*, December 21, 2022, https://www.texastribune.org/2022/12/21 /texas-handguns-unconstitutional-public-carry/.

55. *U.S. Navy SEALs 1-26 v. Biden*, 578 F. Supp. 3d 822 (N.D. Tex. 2022).

56. Ian Millhiser, "The Trumpiest Court in America," *Vox*, December 27, 2022, https://www.vox.com/policy-and-politics/2022/12/27/23496264/supreme -court-fifth-circuit-trump-court-immigration-housing-sexual-harrassment.

57. *U.S. Navy Seals 1-26 v. Biden*, 27 F.4th 336 (5th Cir. 2022).

58. *Austin v. U.S. Navy Seals 1-26*, 142 S. Ct. 1301, 1302 (2022) (Alito, J., dissenting).

CHAPTER 6: "YOU'RE JUST GONNA HAVE YOUR F-CKING LIFE DESTROYED"

1. Our description of Anna Zargarian's story is taken from the pleadings and supporting declarations in *Zurawski v. State of Texas*, No. D-1-GN-23-000968 (Travis County, Texas 353rd Judicial District),

and a March 7, 2023, press conference organized by the Center for Reproductive Rights, available at https://tinyurl.com/2t35acp9.

2. Michael Tchirikov et al., "Mid-Trimester Preterm Premature Rupture of Membranes (PPROM): Etiology, Diagnosis, Classification, International Recommendations of Treatment Options and Outcome," *Journal of Perinatal Medicine* 46 (2018): 465, https://doi.org/10.1515/jpm-2017-0027.

3. Center for Reproductive Rights press conference.

4. Ibid.

5. Ibid.

6. 597 U.S. 215 (2022).

7. The statute is codified at Tex. Health & Safety Code section 171.201-212. We do not use its official title, the "Texas Heartbeat Act," because it is medically inaccurate. See Bethany Irvine, "Why 'Heartbeat Bill' Is a Misleading Name for Texas' Near-Total Abortion Ban," *Texas Tribune*, September 2, 2021, https://www.texastribune.org/2021/09/02/texas-abortion-heartbeat-bill/.

8. The day *Dobbs* was decided, ninety elected prosecutors "commit[ted] to exercis[ing] our well-settled discretion and refrain from prosecuting those who seek, provide, or support abortions." Among the signatories were prosecutors from cities and counties in deep-red states. "Joint Statement from Elected Prosecutors," Fair and Just Prosecution, June 24, 2022, https://fairandjustprosecution.org/wp-content/uploads/2022/06/FJP-Post-Dobbs-Abortion-Joint-Statement.pdf.

9. Charlotte Huff, "In Texas, Abortion Laws Inhibit Care for Miscarriages," NPR, May 10, 2022, https://www.npr.org/sections/health-shots/2022/05/10/1097734167/in-texas-abortion-laws-inhibit-care-for-miscarriages.

10. See Plaintiff's Original Petition, *Silva v. Noyola*, NO. 23-CV-0375 (District Court, Galveston County).

11. Tessa Stuart, "Texan Suing Ex's BFFs Over Abortion Allegedy Promised to Drop Lawsuit for Sex," *Rolling Stone*, October 4, 2023, https://www.rollingstone.com/politics/politics-news/texan-suing-abortion-promised-drop-lawsuit-sex-1234839569/.

12. Professor Joanna Grossman summed up the purpose and effect of the suit in asking: "Who is going to want to help a friend find an abortion if there is some chance that their text messages are going to end up in the news? And maybe they're going to get sued . . . and it's going to get dropped eventually, but in the meantime, they will have been

terrified." Dahlia Lithwick and Mark Joseph Stern, "Sued for Offering Friendship," *Slate*, March 15, 2023, https://slate.com/news-and-politics /2023/03/texas-lawsuit-suing-friends-explained.html (https://perma.cc /6YFU-GETD).

13. For an extended analysis of these issues, see Melissa Murray and Katherine Shaw, "Dobbs and Democracy," *Harvard Law Review* 137 (2024): 729.

14. "U.S. Same-Sex Marriage Support Holds at 71% High," Gallup, June 5, 2023, https://news.gallup.com/poll/506636/sex-marriage-support -holds-high.aspx.

15. Pub. L. No. 117-228.

16. We document this in greater detail in Jon D. Michaels and David L. Noll, "Vigilante Federalism," *Cornell Law Review* 108 (2023).

17. Russell Berman, "The Last of the Establishment Republicans," *Atlantic*, April 3, 2022, https://www.theatlantic.com/politics/archive/2022/04 /how-ohio-governor-mike-dewine-survived-trump/629450/.

18. "Ohio Bans Gender-Affirming Care and Restricts Transgender Athletes Despite GOP Governor's Veto," Associated Press, January 24, 2024, https://apnews.com/article/transgender-care-ohio-bans-veto-override -4877522111308e8c2c6cb1fef212ba0f.

19. Tenn. Code. Ann. section 49-2-805.

20. Christy Mallory et al., "Legal Penalties for Physicians Providing Gender-Affirming Care," *Journal of the American Medical Associaton* (June 6, 2023).

21. H.B. 1, 113th Gen. Ass. (Tenn. 2023).

22. Henry Seaton, "I'm a Trans Tennessean. This New Law Will Hurt So Many of Us," CNN, March 14, 2023, https://www.cnn.com/2023/03 /14/opinions/anti-transgender-legislation-tennessee-seaton-ctrp/index .html (compiling studies).

23. Our account here owes a debt to Jennifer Berkshire, who writes regularly for the *Nation* and hosts the *Have You Heard* podcast. Her reporting is collected in two indispensable volumes coauthored with Jack Schneider, *A Wolf at the Schoolhouse Door: The Dismantling of Public Education and the Future of School* (forthcoming 2024), and *A Wolf at the Schoolhouse Door* (2020).

24. For an accessible recent introduction to the central questions CRT engages, see Victor Ray, *On Critical Race Theory: Why It Matters and Why You Should Care* (2022). As Ray observes, practitioners of CRT "have intense disputes over disciplinary, methodological, and epistemological

issues." Kimberlé Crenshaw, the academic credited with first identifying
CRT, "even claims the framework is a 'verb' because it is a broadly
adaptable attempt to explain how racism is produced and maintained."

25. Josh Dawsey and Jeff Stein, "White House Directs Federal Agencies
to Cancel Race-Related Training Sessions It Calls 'Un-American
propaganda,'" *Washington Post*, September 4, 2020, https://www
.washingtonpost.com/politics/2020/09/04/white-house-racial
-sensitivity-training/.

26. Ibid.

27. See, e.g., James R. Copland, "How to Regulate Critical Race Theory
in Schools: A Primer and Model Legislation," Manhattan Institute,
August 26, 2021, https://www.manhattan-institute.org/copland-critical
-race-theory-model-legislation [https://perma.cc/VZS9-T57A];
"Protecting K–12 Students from Discrimination," Heritage Foundation,
June 18, 2021, https://www.heritage.org/article/protecting-k-12-students
-discrimination [https://perma.cc/DG4Z-25KX]. See generally Sarah
Schwartz, "Who's Really Driving Critical Race Theory Legislation? An
Investigation," *Education Week*, July 19, 2021, https://www.edweek.org
/policy-politics/whos-really-driving-critical-race-theory-legislation-an
-investigation/2021/07 [https://perma.cc/X35X-CSS6].

28. Jeremy C. Young and Jonathan Friedman, "America's Censored
Classrooms," PEN America, August 17, 2022, https://pen.org/report
/americas-censored-classrooms/.

29. Fl. Stat. section 760.10 (2022).

30. See, e.g., Jeannie Suk Gersen, "The Conservative Who Wants to
Bring Down the Supreme Court," *New Yorker*, January 5, 2023,
https://www.newyorker.com/news/annals-of-inquiry/the
-conservative-who-wants-to-bring-down-the-supreme-court
(https://perma.cc/D8A3-Z9WE) (quoting a statement by S.B. 8
attorney Jonathan Mitchell to the effect that "there never were
going to be vigilantes and bounty hunters under the S.B. 8 regime,"
because "the whole point" was that abortion providers would
comply with the law to not risk being sued"); *N. Texas Equal Access
Fund v. Am. First Legal Found.*, No. CV 22-0728 (ABJ), 2023 WL
7002675, at *9 (D.D.C. Oct. 24, 2023) (quoting an argument by an
attorney for the America First Legal Foundation to the effect that
the organization "is not filing lawsuits 'because abortion has been

completely outlawed in Texas after *Dobbs.* So no one is violating SB-8. There are no more abortion providers who are providing abortion services in the state of Texas. SB-8 only applies to abortions performed by a Texas-licensed physician'").

31. Bryan Hughes, "The Texas Abortion Law Is Unconventional Because It Had to Be," *Wall Street Journal,* September 12, 2021, https://www.wsj .com/articles/texas-abortion-law-unconventional-lawsuit-pro-life-roe -v-wade-heartbeat-six-weeks-11631471508.

32. For analyses of these dynamics, see, e.g., Danielle Keats Citron, "Intimate Privacy in a Post-Roe World," *Florida Law Review* 75 (2023): 1033; Aziz Z. Huq and Rebecca Wexler, "Digital Privacy for Reproductive Choice in the Post-Roe Era," *N.Y.U. Law Review* 98 (2023): 555.

33. For the economic theory of foot voting, see, e.g., Charles Tiebout, "A Pure Theory of Local Expenditures," *Journal of Political Economy* 64 (1956): 516. For sources speculating that foot voting is an adequate response to courthouse vigilantism, see Michaels and Noll, "Vigilante Federalism," 1260 n.315.

34. Center for Reproductive Rights press conference, March 7, 2023.

35. For a classic articulation of the factors that influence prosecutorial discretion, see *Heckler v. Chaney,* 470 U.S. 821, 831 (1985): "The agency must not only assess whether a violation has occurred, but whether agency resources are best spent on this violation or another, whether the agency is likely to succeed if it acts, whether the particular enforcement action requested best fits the agency's overall policies, and, indeed, whether the agency has enough resources to undertake the action at all. An agency generally cannot act against each technical violation of the statute it is charged with enforcing."

CHAPTER 7: "YOU CAN RUN THEM OVER. DESANTIS SAID SO!"

1. "The American Presidency Project, 1976 Election Results," https:// www.presidency.ucsb.edu/statistics/elections/1976.

2. Angie Maxwell and Todd Shields, *The Long Southern Strategy: How Chasing White Voters in the South Changed American Politics* (2019); James L. Sundquist, *Dynamics of the Party System: Alignment and Realignment of Political Parties in the United States* (rev. ed. 2011).

3. For contemporaneous reports, see, e.g., Douglas E. Kneeland, "Reagan Campaigns at Mississippi Fair," *New York Times,* August 4,

1980, A11; Lou Cannon, "Reagan Campaigning from County Fair to Urban League," *Washington Post*, August 5, 1980, https://www .washingtonpost.com/archive/politics/1980/08/04/reagan -campaigning-from-county-fair-to-urband-league/f4aa5726-a0e6 -4206-8239-cb3b4bff5ac9/?itid=sr_4.

4. Bruce Watson, *Freedom Summer: The Savage Season of 1964 That Made Mississippi Burn and Made America a Democracy* (2010), Chapter 4.

5. Ibid.; Ben Chaney, "Schwerner, Chaney, and Goodman: The Struggle for Justice," *Human Rights* 27 (2000): 3.

6. Pub. L. No. 88-352, 78 Stat. 241 (1964).

7. Pub. L. No. 89-110, 79 Stat. 437 (1965).

8. Bob Herbert, "Righting Reagan's Wrongs?," *New York Times*, November 13, 2007.

9. Ibid.

10. "The Klan and the Campaign," *Christian Science Monitor*, August 26, 1980, https://www.csmonitor.com/1980/0826/082608.html; "Reagan Spurns Klan Support," *New York Times*, May 2, 1984, D26, https://www .nytimes.com/1984/05/02/us/reagan-spurns-klan-support.html.

11. "Jeb Bush: 'Stand Your Ground' Doesn't Cover Teen's Death," WFTV, March 24, 2012, https://www.wftv.com/news/jeb-bush-stand-your -ground-doesnt-cover-teens-deat/287881704/.

12. Elliot C. McLaughlin et al., "George Zimmerman Sues Trayvon Martin's Parents and Others for More than $100 Million," CNN, December 5, 2019, https://www.cnn.com/2019/12/04/us/george -zimmerman-lawsuit-trayvon-martin-mother/index.html.

13. "Gun That Killed Trayvon Martin 'Makes $250,000 for Zimmerman,'" BBC, May 22, 2016, https://www.bbc.com/news/world-us-canada -36354206.

14. McKay Coppins, *Romney: A Reckoning* (2023).

15. Oliver Laughland, "Donald Trump and the Central Park Five: The Racially Charged Rise of a Demagogue," *Guardian*, February 17, 2016, https://www.theguardian.com/us-news/2016/feb/17/central-park-five -donald-trump-jogger-rape-case-new-york.

16. Jan Ransom, "Trump Will Not Apologize for Calling for Death Penalty over Central Park Five," *New York Times*, June 18, 2019, https://www .nytimes.com/2019/06/18/nyregion/central-park-five-trump.html. The quoted language is from the original advertisement, which the *Times* republished in conjunction with Ransom's 2019 article.

17. Dara Lind, "The Problem with Violence at Trump Rallies Starts with Trump Himself," *Vox*, March 13, 2016, https://www.vox.com/2016/3 /11/11202540/trump-violent; email from Professor Glenn Reynolds to the College of Law Community, University of Tennessee College of Law, September 27, 2016, https://law.utk.edu/2016/09/27/reynolds-email/.

18. Ed Mazza, "USA Today Columnist Urges Motorists to 'Run Down' Protesters on North Carolina Highway," *HuffPost*, September 22, 2016, https://www.huffpost.com/entry/glenn-reynolds-instapundit-protesters _n_57e37445e4b0e80b1ba06a85.

19. Our account of the Fields murder draws on reporting including Jonah Engel Bromwich and Alan Blinder, "What We Know About James Alex Fields, Driver Charged in Charlottesville Killing," *New York Times*, August 13, 2017, https://www.nytimes.com/2017/08 /13/us/james-alex-fields-charlottesville-driver-.html; "Neo-Nazi Sympathizer James Alex Fields Jr., Faces Jury Over Deadly Actions, Decision at 'Unite The Right,' " Southern Poverty Law Center, November 26, 2018, https://www.splcenter.org/hatewatch/2018 /11/26/neo-nazi-sympathizer-james-alex-fields-jr-faces-jury -over-deadly-actions-decision-unite; Kristine Philips, " 'Moments of Terror': Survivors Describe Chaos at Charlottesville Rally," *Washington Post*, December 3, 2018, https://www.washingtonpost .com/local/public-safety/moments-of-terror-survivors-describe -chaos-at-charlottesville-rally/2018/12/03/9cc87898-f711-11e8-863c -9e2f864d47e7_story.html.

20. Justin Wm. Moyer and Lindsey Bever, "Vanguard America, a White Supremacist Group, Denies Charlottesville Ramming Suspect Was a Member," *Washington Post*, August 15, 2017, https://www .washingtonpost.com/local/vanguard-america-a-white-supremacist -group-denies-charlottesville-attacker-was-a-member/2017/08/15 /2ec897c6-810e-11e7-8072-73e1718c524d_story.html.

21. "Crash Suspect's Ex-Teacher Says He Idolized Hitler, Nazism," Associated Press, August 13, 2017, https://apnews.com/article /93d3cba12d134836ae243af285b27eaf.

22. "Events Surrounding White Nationalist Rally in Virginia Turn Fatal," NPR, August 12, 2017, https://www.npr.org/sections/thetwo-way/2017 /08/12/542982015/home-to-university-of-virginia-prepares-for-violence-at -white-nationalist-rally.

23. "Trump Condemns 'Hatred, Bigotry and Violence on Many Sides' in Charlottesville," CNN, August 13, 2017, https://www.cnn.com/2017/08/12/politics/trump-statement-alt-right-protests/index.html.

24. Jenna Johnson and John Wagner, "Trump Condemns Charlottesville Violence but Doesn't Single Out White Nationalists," *Washington Post*, August 12, 2017, https://www.washingtonpost.com/politics/trump-condemns-charlottesville-violence-but-doesnt-single-out-white-nationalists/2017/08/12/933a86d6-7fa3-11e7-9d08-b79f191668ed_story.html.

25. Statement by President Trump, August 14, 2017, https://trumpwhitehouse.archives.gov/briefings-statements/statement-president-trump/.

26. "Trump Says Both Sides to Blame Amid Charlottesville Backlash," CNN, August 16, 2017, https://www.cnn.com/2017/08/15/politics/trump-charlottesville-delay/index.html.

27. "Sessions Defends Trump's Comments on Charlottesville, Says Car Ramming Fits Definition of Domestic Terror," ABC News, August 14, 2017, https://abcnews.go.com/Politics/trumps-attorney-general-evil-charlottesville-car-ramming-fits/story?id=49202191.

28. Joe Heim et al., "Man Accused of Driving into Crowd at Charlottesville 'Unite the Right' Rally Charged with Federal Hate Crimes," *Washington Post*, June 27, 2018.

29. Mitch Smith, "James Fields Sentenced to Life in Prison for Death of Heather Heyer in Charlottesville," *New York Times*, June 28, 2019, https://www.nytimes.com/2019/06/28/us/james-fields-sentencing.html.

30. "From Debate Stage, Trump Declines to Denounce White Supremacy," NPR, September 30, 2020, https://www.npr.org/2020/09/30/918483794/from-debate-stage-trump-declines-to-denounce-white-supremacy.

31. Ben Collins and Brandy Zadrozny, "Proud Boys Celebrate After Trump's Debate Callout," NBC News, September 29, 2020, https://www.nbcnews.com/tech/tech-news/proud-boys-celebrate-after-trump-s-debate-call-out-n1241512.

32. Ibid.

33. "Attorney General William P. Barr's Statement on Riots and Domestic Terrorism," May 31, 2020, https://www.justice.gov/opa/pr/attorney-general-william-p-barrs-statement-riots-and-domestic-terrorism.

34. "Rush Limbaugh: 'Well, Where Are All the People with Guns' to 'Push Back' Against the Left?," Media Matters, June 15, 2020, https://www

.mediamatters.org/rush-limbaugh/rush-limbaugh-well-where-are-all
-people-guns-push-back-against-left-0.

35. Kyle Cheney, "Proud Boys Sedition Trial Shows Group Keying Off
Trump Comments," *Politico*, February 9, 2023, https://www.politico
.com/news/2023/02/09/proud-boys-sedition-trial-trump-00082067.

36. "VA Governor on Charlottesville: Militias Had 'Better' Guns Than
Police," Military.com, August 15, 2017, https://www.military.com
/daily-news/2017/08/15/va-governor-charlottesville-militias-better
-guns-than-police.html.

37. Jacob D. Charles, "Securing Gun Rights by Statute: The Right to
Keep and Bear Arms Outside the Constitution," *Michigan Law Review*
581 (2022).

38. *New York State Rifle & Pistol Assn, Inc. v. Bruen*, 142 S. Ct. 2111,
2128 (2022).

39. 37 A.L.R. Fed. 696 (2023 update).

40. For an insightful analysis of the effects of this on public participation in
the democratic process, see Joseph Blocher and Reva B. Siegel, "When
Guns Threaten the Public Sphere: A New Account of Public Safety
Under *Heller*," *Northwestern University Law Review* 116 (2021): 139.

41. "What Are 'Stand Your Ground Laws'?," Brady Center, https://www
.bradyunited.org/fact-sheets/what-are-stand-your-ground-laws.

42. "The Effects of Stand-Your-Ground Laws," Rand, updated January 10,
2023, https://www.rand.org/research/gun-policy/analysis/stand-your
-ground.html.

43. See, e.g., Nathan P. Kalmoe and Lilliana Mason, *Radical American
Partisanship: Mapping Violent Hostility, Its Causes, and the Consequences for
Democracy* (2022), Chapter 5.

44. Mike German, "The FBI Warned for Years That Police Are Cozy
with the Far Right. Is No One Listening?," *Guardian*, August 28, 2020,
https://www.theguardian.com/commentisfree/2020/aug/28/fbi-far
-right-white-supremacists-police.

45. Confronting Violent White Supremacy (Part IV): White Supremacy in
Blue: The Infiltration of Local Police Departments, Hearing Before the
Subcomm. on Civil Rights and Civil Liberties, 116th Cong., 2d Sess.,
September 29, 2020.

46. Hassan Kanu, "Prevalence of White Supremacists in Law Enforcement
Demands Drastic Change," Reuters, May 12, 2022, https://www

.reuters.com/legal/government/prevalence-white-supremacists-law
-enforcement-demands-drastic-change-2022-05-12/. See also Julia Harte
and Alexandra Ulmer, "U.S. Police Trainers with Far-Right Ties Are
Teaching Hundreds of Cops," Reuters, May 6, 2022, https://www
.reuters.com/investigates/special-report/usa-police-extremism/.

47. Peter Stone, "Rightwing Sheriffs' Groups Ramp Up Drive to Monitor
US Midterm Elections," *Guardian*, August 17, 2022, https://www
.theguardian.com/us-news/2022/aug/17/rightwing-sheriffs-trump
-midterm-elections-voting-arizona.

48. Emily M. Farris and Miyra R. Holman, "Sheriffs, Right-Wing
Extremism, and the Limits of U.S. Federalism During a Crisis," *Social
Science Quarterly* 104 (2023): 59.

49. Austin Fisher, "Albuquerque DA Appoints Special Prosecutor in 2020
Monument Shooting," *Source NM*, January 23, 2023, https://sourcenm
.com/2023/01/23/albuquerque-da-appoints-special-prosecutor-in-2020
-monument-shooting/.

50. Mara Hvistendahl and Alleen Brown, "Armed Vigilantes Antagonizing
Protesters Have Received a Warm Reception from Police," *Intercept*,
June 19, 2020, https://theintercept.com/2020/06/19/militia-vigilantes
-police-brutality-protests/.

51. Ibid.

52. Ibid.

53. "Canadian County Sheriff's Office Looking for Volunteers to Join
'Sheriff's Posse,'" KOCO 5, June 10, 2020, https://www.koco.com
/article/canadian-county-sheriffs-office-looking-for-volunteers-to-join
-sheriffs-posse/32815620.

54. Ryan Boetel, "Man Enters Plea for Shooting During 2020 Statue Protest
in Old Town Albuquerque," *Albuquerque Journal*, June 5, 2023, https://
www.abqjournal.com/news/local/man-enters-plea-for-shooting
-during-2020-statue-protest-in-old-town-albuquerque/article
_a4702b44-50f0-5acd-87b0-ff0341cab2d6.html.

55. Spencer Schacht, "2020 Oñate Protest Shooter Walks Free with
Suspended Sentence," KOB4, November 1, 2023, https://www.kob
.com/new-mexico/2020-onate-protest-shooter-walks-free-with
-suspended-sentence/.

56. Chris King, "Kimberly Gardner Attacked for Charging McCloskeys,"
St. Louis American, July 22, 2022, https://www.stlamerican.com/news

/local_news/kimberly-gardner-attacked-for-charging-parkeys/article
_b74dd486-cc23-11ea-99ea-3f8d38368ef4.html.

57. "Missouri Governor's Comments on Coronavirus, McCloskeys Raise
Eyebrows," *St. Louis Post-Dispatch*, July 20, 2020, https://www.stltoday
.com/news/local/government-politics/missouri-governor-s-comments
-on-coronavirus-mccloskeys-raise-eyebrows/article_aeac1f42-9460
-5605-9fe5-73ca3ca72b2f.html.

58. Vanessa Romo, "The Couple Who Waved Guns at BLM Protesters
Plead Guilty to Misdemeanors," NPR, June 17, 2021, https://www.npr
.org/2021/06/17/1007984646/patricia-mark-mccloskey-waved-guns-blm
-protesters-plead-guilty-misdemeanors.

59. Ibid.

60. Joan E. Greve, "St Louis Couple Who Threatened Black Lives Matter
Protesters Speak at RNC," *Guardian*, August 25, 2020, https://www
.theguardian.com/us-news/2020/aug/24/st-louis-couple-rnc-mark
-patricia-mccloskey.

61. William Melhado, "U.S. Army Sergeant Found Guilty of Murder in
2020 Shooting of Austin Protester Garrett Foster," *Texas Tribune*, April 7,
2023, https://www.texastribune.org/2023/04/07/daniel-perry-austin
-protest-garrett-foster/.

62. Jolie McCullough and Meena Venkataramanan, "U.S. Army Sergeant
Who Shot Austin Protester Garrett Foster Posted Tweets About
Retaliating Against Demonstrators," *Texas Tribune*, July 31, 2020, https://
www.texastribune.org/2020/07/31/daniel-perry-austin-protest-garrett
-foster/; Jolie McCullough, "Daniel Perry Is Sentenced to 25 Years for
Killing an Austin Protester. Gov. Greg Abbott Has Pledged to Pardon
Him," *Texas Tribune*, May 10, 2023, https://www.texastribune.org/2023
/05/10/daniel-perry-murder-austin-protestor/.

63. Spencer Silva, "Fox News Defends Texas Man Convicted of
Murdering Black Lives Matter Protester and Attacks DA Who
Prosecuted the Case," Media Matters, April 12, 2023, https://www
.mediamatters.org/tucker-carlson/fox-news-defends-texas-man
-convicted-murdering-black-lives-matter-protester-and.

64. Ibid.

65. @GregAbbott_TX, Apr. 8, 2023, https://twitter.com/GregAbbott_TX
/status/1644778789493243907.

66. William Melhado, "Gov. Greg Abbott Pardons Daniel Perry, Veteran
who Killed Police Brutality Protester in 2020," *Texas Tribune*, May 16,

2024, https://www.texastribune.org/2024/05/16/daniel-perry-greg
-abbott-pardon.

67. Ibid.

68. Jess Bidgood, "The Car Becomes the Weapon," *Boston Globe*,
October 31, 2021, https://apps.bostonglobe.com/news/nation/2021/10
/vehicle-rammings-against-protesters/tulsa/.

69. Video of the incident is available at https://www.kjrh.com/news/local
-news/tulsa-co-da-no-charges-filed-in-horse-trailer-incident, https://
www.newson6.com/story/5ed5896c10eece0c35ad6cb8/ohp
-investigating-situation-involving-truck-trailer-on-i244-during
-protest, and https://tulsaworld.com/new-video-of-truck-incident-on
-the-i-244-bridge-during-protests/video_910cad4c-b45f-5dbc-a6e6
-16b00c5428c4.html.

70. Bidgood, "The Car Becomes the Weapon."

71. See ibid.

72. H.B. 1674, 2021 Reg. Sess. (Ok. 2021).

73. Jim Puzzanghera, "Putting the Law on the Driver's Side," *Boston Globe*,
November 2, 2021, https://apps.bostonglobe.com/news/nation/2021/10
/vehicle-rammings-against-protesters/legislation/.

74. Ibid.

75. Kavitha Surana, "A White Man Pulled a Gun at a Florida Protest. Black
Men Took the Blame," *Tampa Bay Times*, January 28, 2021, https://
www.tampabay.com/special-reports/2021/01/28/a-white-man-pulled-a
-gun-at-a-florida-protest-black-men-took-the-blame/.

76. Paige Williams, "Kyle Rittenhouse: American Vigilante," *New Yorker*,
June 28, 2021, https://www.newyorker.com/magazine/2021/07/05/kyle
-rittenhouse-american-vigilante.

77. Our account of Rittenhouse's killings draws principally on the
in-depth reporting of Paige Williams. See Paige Williams, "Kyle
Rittenhouse, American Vigilante," *New Yorker*, July 5, 2021, https://
www.newyorker.com/magazine/2021/07/05/kyle-rittenhouse
-american-vigilante; Paige Williams, "The Trial of Kyle Rittenhouse
Begins with Gruesome Videos and a Plea for Fact-Finding," *New
Yorker*, November 8, 2021; Paige Williams, "The Complex Task Facing
the Kyle Rittenhouse Jury," *New Yorker*, November 15, 2021, https://
www.newyorker.com/news/news-desk/the-complex-task-facing
-the-kyle-rittenhouse-jury. We also rely on widely disseminated videos
of the shootings; a Reuters report, "How Kyle Rittenhouse Went from

Cleaning Graffiti to Shooting 3 People," November 19, 2021, https://
www.reuters.com/world/us/how-kyle-rittenhouse-went-cleaning
-graffiti-shooting-3-people-2021-11-11/; and a *New York Times*
reconstruction of Rittenhouse's movements, Haley Willis et al.,
"Tracking the Suspect in the Fatal Kenosha Shootings," *New York
Times*, August 27, 2020, https://www.nytimes.com/2020/08/27/us
/kyle-rittenhouse-kenosha-shooting-video.html.

78. Neil MacFarquhar, "When Armed Vigilantes Are Summoned with
a Few Keystrokes," *New York Times*, October 16, 2020, https://www
.nytimes.com/2020/10/16/us/kenosha-guard-militia-kevin
-mathewson.html.

79. Reuters, "How Kyle Rittehouse."

80. Scott Bauer, "In Rittenhouse Case, Americans See What They Want to
See," Associated Press, October 30, 2021, https://apnews.com/article
/wisconsin-police-shootings-george-floyd-race-and-ethnicity-cd4aca9c
8ef4d3b18f727ca69a6d6af9.

81. Dennis Romero and Samira Puskar, "Men Shot by Rittenhouse Can't
Be Called 'Victims' During Trial, But 'Rioters,' 'Looters' Are OK,
Judge Rules," NBC News, October 26, 2021, https://www.nbcnews
.com/news/us-news/men-shot-rittenhouse-can-t-be-called-victims
-during-trial-n1282466.

82. Brian Stelter, "Fox's Tucker Carlson Gets Exclusive Access to Kyle
Rittenhouse and His Defense Team During Trial," CNN, November 21,
2021, https://www.cnn.com/2021/11/20/media/tucker-carlson-kyle
-rittenhouse/index.html.

83. Stephanie Mencimer, "Kyle Rittenhouse, the MAGA Star That Wasn't,"
Mother Jones, March 8, 2023, https://www.motherjones.com/politics
/2023/03/kyle-rittenhouse-maga-social-media-star-that-wasnt/.

84. Bauer, "In Rittenhouse Case"; Williams, "Kyle Rittenhouse."

85. Kelly Weill, "GOP Lawmakers Fall Over Each Other to Offer Jobs to
Kyle Rittenhouse," *Daily Beast*, November 19, 2021, https://www
.thedailybeast.com/kyle-rittenhouse-is-acquitted-republican-lawmakers
-fall-over-each-other-to-offer-him-a-job.

86. H.R. 6070, 117th Cong., 1st Sess. (2021).

87. Brian Niemietz, "Kenosha Gunman Kyle Rittenhouse Launches
YouTube Channel about Firearms," *New York Daily News*, October 17,
2022, https://www.nydailynews.com/2022/10/17/kenosha-gunman
-kyle-rittenhouse-launches-youtube-channel-about-firearms/.

88. Shannon Power, "Kyle Rittenhouse Using 'Therapy Dog' Sparks Fury," *Newsweek*, November 29, 2023, https://www.newsweek.com/kyle -rittenhouse-book-ptsd-therapy-dog-1847834.

89. Aliss Higham, "Kyle Rittenhouse Smiles at Shooting Joke During Book Promo," *Newsweek*, November 29, 2023, https://www.newsweek.com /kyle-rittenhouse-smiles-shooting-joke-book-promo-1847888.

90. Mencimer, "Kyle Rittenhouse."

91. DeNeen L. Brown, "Trump Rally in Tulsa, Site of a Race Massacre, on Juneteenth Was 'Almost Blasphemous,' Historian Says," *Washington Post*, June 13, 2020, https://www.washingtonpost.com/history/2020/06/11 /juneteenth-trump-rally-tulsa-race-massacre/.

92. "Remarks at a 'Make America Great Again' Rally in Tulsa, Oklahoma," American Presidency Project, June 20, 2020, https:// www.presidency.ucsb.edu/documents/remarks-make-america-great -again-rally-tulsa-oklahoma.

93. Ibid.

94. Video is available at https://www.youtube.com/watch?v=j_1lmw3IICg.

95. Robert Downen and William Melhado, "Trump Vows Retribution at Waco Rally: 'I Am Your Warrior, I Am Your Justice,'" *Texas Tribune*, March 25, 2023, https://www.texastribune.org/2023/03/25/donald -trump-waco-rally-retribution-justice/.

96. Jacob Ware, "The Violent Far-Right Terrorist Threat to American Law Enforcement," Council on Foreign Relations, January 24, 2023, https://www.cfr.org/blog/violent-far-right-terrorist-threat-american -law-enforcement.

97. Andrew Goudsward, "New York Judge Latest Target of Threats Aimed at US Officials," Reuters, January 11, 2024, https://www.reuters .com/legal/new-york-trump-judge-latest-target-threats-aimed-us -officials-2024-01-11/; Jesus Jimenez, "Man Indicted over Threats to D.A. and Sheriff in Trump's Georgia Case," *New York Times*, October 30, 2023, https://www.nytimes.com/2023/10/30/us/elections/fani-willis -patrick-labat-threats-indictment.html.

CHAPTER 8: "WE'RE GOING TO BE WATCHING"

1. Our account of Rusty Bowers's story is taken principally from his testimony before the House Select Committee on the January 6th Attack and deposition with the committee's staff. See Hearing Before the Select Committee to Investigate the January 6th Attack on the United States

Capitol, 117th Cong., 2d Sess., June 21, 2022; interview of Russell Bowers, June 19, 2022. See also Ed Pilkington, "Ousted Republican Reflects on Trump, Democracy and America: 'The Place Has Lost Its Mind,'" *Guardian*, August 21, 2022, https://www.theguardian.com/us -news/2022/aug/20/rusty-bowers-interview-trump-arizona-republicans. We use Bowers's first name to simplify our efforts to distinguish him from his daughter, Kacey Rae.

2. Yvonne Wingett Sanchez, "Alone in Washington, Rusty Bowers Tells World What Happened in Arizona," *Washington Post*, June 21, 2022, https://www.washingtonpost.com/national-security/2022/06/21/rusty -bowers-jan-6/.

3. "Gun Laws in Arizona," Everytown, https://everytownresearch.org /rankings/state/arizona/.

4. Pilkington, "Ousted Republican Reflects."

5. "GOP Election Rift Engulfs Mesa Lawmakers," *East Valley Tribune*, December 15, 2020, https://www.eastvalleytribune.com/news/gop -election-rift-engulfs-mesa-lawmakers/article_5b36c7e0-3e3b-11eb -9e91-232b09e884a4.html.

6. Jonathan J. Cooper, "Arizona GOP Censures Rusty Bowers After Jan. 6 Testimony," Associated Press, July 20, 2022, https://apnews.com/article /2022-midterm-elections-capitol-siege-donald-trump-presidential -censures-f8892631bd14e1b2266af4c9d00f6af8.

7. Samuel Perry, Andrew L. Whitehead, and Joshua B. Grubbs, "'I Don't Want Everybody to Vote': Christian Nationalism and Restricting Voter Access in the United States," *Sociological Forum* 37 (2022): 4.

8. For Weyrich's speech, see https://www.youtube.com/watch?v=8G BAsFwPglw.

9. Michael Waldman, "Voting Rights Are Expanding in Blue States, Contracting in Red," Brennan Center for Justice, March 1, 2023, https:// www.brennancenter.org/our-work/analysis-opinion/voting-rights-are -expanding-blue-states-contracting-red.

10. Richard L. Hasen, *Election Meltdown: Dirty Tricks, Distrust, and the Threat to American Democracy* (2020), Chapter 1.

11. As of January 2024, the Georgia governorship, Senate, and House had been under continuous Republican control since 2005. See "Party Control of Georgia State Government," Ballotpedia, https://ballotpedia .org/Party_control_of_Georgia_state_government.

12. S.B. 202 (Ga. 2021).

13. GA Code section 21-2-230 (2022).

14. Ibid.

15. Carlisa N. Johnson, "Early Voters in Georgia Face Obstacles Under State's New Election Law," *Guardian*, October 22, 2022, https://www .theguardian.com/us-news/2022/oct/22/georgia-early-voting -obstacles-new-election-law.

16. Ibid.

17. "Voter Challenge Statutes by State," Bazelon Center for Mental Health Law, https://www.bazelon.org/wp-content/uploads/2017/11/2016 _Voter-Challenge-Statutes-by-State.pdf.

18. "Citizens Guide to Building an Election Integrity Infrastructure," Election Integrity Network, November 2021, https://www .documentcloud.org/documents/21195360-citizens-guide-to -building-an-election-integrity-infrastructure-november-2021. For an overview of the laws these efforts seek to exploit, see Michael Morse, "Democracy's Bureaucracy: The Complicated Case of Voter Registration Lists," *Boston University Law Review* 103 (2023): 2123.

19. Alexandra Berzon, "Lawyer Who Plotted to Overturn Trump Loss Recruits Election Deniers to Watch Over the Vote," *New York Times*, May 30, 2022, https://www.nytimes.com/2022/05/30/us/politics /republican-poll-monitors-election-activists.html?action=click &module=RelatedLinks&pgtype=Article.

20. Nick Corasaniti and Alexandra Berzon, "Activists Flood Election Offices with Challenges," *New York Times*, September 28, 2022, https://www.nytimes .com/2022/09/28/us/politics/election-activists-voter-challenges.html.

21. Ibid.

22. Alexandra Berzon and Nick Corasaniti, "Trump's Allies Ramp Up Campaign Targeting Voter Rolls," *New York Times*, March 3, 3024, https://www.nytimes.com/2024/03/03/us/politics/trump-voter-rolls.html.

23. Ibid.

24. Tess Owen, "Armed Fringe Groups Are Gearing Up to 'Protect' Midterm Ballot Dropboxes," *Vice*, October 6, 2022, https://www .vice.com/en/article/dy7wvj/lions-of-liberty-oath-keepers-midterm -ballot-boxes.

25. Isaac Arnsdorf et al., "Heeding Steve Bannon's Call, Election Deniers Organize to Seize Control of the GOP—and Reshape America's

Elections," ProPublica, September 2, 2021, https://www.propublica.org /article/heeding-steve-bannons-call-election-deniers-organize-to-seize -control-of-the-gop-and-reshape-americas-elections.

26. Corasaniti and Berzon, "Activitsts Flood Election Offices."

27. Our account here relies principally on the testimony of Shaye Moss before the House Select Committee on the January 6th Attack and Moss's deposition with the committee's staff. See Hearing Before the Select Committee to Investigate the January 6th Attack on the United States Capitol, 117th Cong., 2d Sess., June 21, 2022; interview of Wandrea Arshaye Moss, June 1, 2022. See also Second Amended Petition, *Freeman v. Hoft*, No. 2122-CC09815-01 (Circuit Court St. Louis City, January 10, 2023).

28. The following paragraphs rely on Jason Szep and Linda So, "Trump Campaign Demonized Two Georgia Election Workers—and Death Threats Followed," Reuters, December 1, 2021, https://www .reuters.com/investigates/special-report/usa-election-threats-georgia/. Guiliani's testimony can be viewed at https://www.youtube.com /watch?v=hRCXUNOwOjw.

29. Szep and So, "Trump Campaign Demonized."

30. Jim Hoft, "What's Up, Ruby? . . . BREAKING: Crooked Operative Filmed Pulling Out Suitcases of Ballots in Georgia IS IDENTIFIED," Gateway Pundit, December 3, 2020, https://www.thegatewaypundit .com/2020/12/ruby-breaking-crooked-democrat-filmed-pulling -suitcases-ballots-georgia-identified/.

31. "Donald Trump Georgia Rally Transcript Before Senate Runoff Elections December 5," Rev, December 6, 2020, https://www.rev.com /blog/transcripts/donald-trump-georgia-rally-transcript-before-senate -runoff-elections-december-5.

32. Lorenzo Franceschi-Bicchierai, "Giuliani Says Democrats Used 'USB Ports' Passed Around Like 'Vials of Heroin' to Commit Election Fraud," *Vice*, December 11, 2020, https://www.vice.com/en/article/7k94kz /giuliani-says-democrats-used-usb-ports-passed-around-like-vials-of -heroin-to-commit-election-fraud.

33. Lucien Bruggeman and Marjorie McAfee, "Mother-Daughter Election Workers Describe How They Lived through Trump-Backed Accusations of Conspiracy," ABC News, November 3, 2022, https://abcnews .go.com/US/mother-daughter-election-workers-describe -lived-trump-backed/story?id=92500318; Johnny Kauffman, "'You

Better Run': After Trump's False Attacks, Election Workers Faced Threats," NPR, February 5, 2021, https://www.npr.org/2021/02/05/963828783/you-better-run-after-trumps-false-attacks-election-workers-faced-threats.

34. Tresa Baldas et al., " 'Get to TCF': What Really Happened Inside Detroit's Ballot Counting Center," *Detroit Free Press*, November 6, 2020, https://www.freep.com/story/news/local/michigan/detroit/2020/11/06/tcf-center-detroit-ballot-counting/6173577002/.

35. Ibid.

36. Ibid.

37. Ibid.

38. Ibid.

39. Mimi Dwyer and David Shepardson, "Faced with Defeat, Armed Protesters in Arizona Insist Election Stolen," Reuters, November 8, 2023, https://www.reuters.com/article/idUSKBN27O02H/.

40. Danika Fears, "Nevada Election Official: I'm 'Concerned for the Safety of My Staff,' " *Daily Beast*, November 5, 2020, https://www.thedailybeast.com/clark-county-nevada-registrar-joe-gloria-says-hes-concerned-for-the-safety-of-my-staff-amid-election-count.

41. Hearing Before the Select Committee to Investigate the January 6th Attack on the United States Capitol, 117th Cong., 2d Sess., June 21, 2022.

42. Interview of Wandrea Arshaye Moss, June 1, 2022.

43. Michael Waldman, "The Great Resignation . . . of Election Officials," Brennan Center for Justice, April 25, 2023, https://www.brennancenter.org/our-work/analysis-opinion/great-resignation-election-officials.

44. Fredreka Schouten, "A Tide of Election Worker Resignations Raises Alarms Ahead of 2024," CNN, November 5, 2023, https://www.cnn.com/2023/11/05/politics/election-worker-resignations-2024-elections/index.html.

45. See, e.g., Trevor Hunnicutt, "Biden Aims for North Carolina as 2024 Election Comes into Focus," Reuters, January 18, 2024, https://www.reuters.com/world/us/biden-aims-north-carolina-2024-election-comes-into-focus-2024-01-18/.

46. Michael Mitsanas, "Arizona County Elections Director Resigns, Citing Politicization and 'Intimidation,' " NBC News, June 28, 2023, https://www.nbcnews.com/politics/politics-news/local-arizona-elections-director-resigns-citing-intimidation-rcna91591.

47. Julia Shapero, "Arizona Election Officials Resign over Threats About 2020," *Axios*, July 3, 2022, https://www.axios.com/2022/07/03/arizona-election-officials-resign-threats.

48. Rachel Leingang, "Arizona: Elections Director in County That Refused to Certify Results Quits," January 26, 2023, https://www.theguardian.com/us-news/2023/jan/26/arizona-elections-director-conchise-county-lisa-marra.

49. Joey Palacios et al., "A Texas County's Election Administrators All Resigned, Leaving the State to Step In," NPR, August 23, 2022, https://www.houstonpublicmedia.org/articles/voting/2022/08/23/431451/a-texas-countys-election-administrators-all-resigned-leaving-the-state-to-step-in/.

50. Neil Vigdor, "After Threats and Clashes with Republicans, Another Texas Election Official Quits," *New York Times*, April 18, 2023, https://www.nytimes.com/2023/04/18/us/politics/trump-supporters-election-official-threats.html.

51. Jane C. Timm, "Hounded by Baseless Voter Fraud Allegations, an Entire County's Election Staff Quits in Virginia," NBC News, April 10, 2023, https://www.nbcnews.com/politics/elections/buckingham-county-virginia-election-staff-quits-baseless-voter-fraud-rcna76435.

52. Tristan Scott, "How Lincoln County's 'Big Lie' Upended an Election Department," *Flathead Beacon*, May 17, 2023, https://flatheadbeacon.com/2023/05/17/how-lincoln-countys-big-lie-upended-an-election-department-libby-zinke-trump-fraud-security-integrity-montana-gop/.

53. "Trump Zeroes In on a Key Target of His 'Retribution' Agenda: Government Workers," NBC News, April 26, 2023, https://www.nbcnews.com/politics/donald-trump/trump-retribution-agenda-government-workers-schedule-f-rcna78785.

54. Ibid.

55. Martin Pengelly, "Outrage After DeSantis Says He'd 'Start Slitting Throats' If Elected President," *Guardian*, August 4, 2023, https://www.theguardian.com/us-news/2023/aug/04/ron-desantis-slitting-throats-federal-jobs-president-campaign.

56. Lauren Aratani, "Trump Says Pardoning Capitol Attackers Will Be One of His First Acts if Elected Again," *Guardian*, March 12, 2024, https://www.theguardian.com/us-news/2024/mar/12/trump-january-6-pardons.

57. Lalee Ibssa and Soo Rin Kim, "Trump Claims Liz Cheney and Jan. 6 Committee Should Be Jailed," ABC News, March 18, 2024, https://abcnews.go.com/Politics/trump-liz-cheney-jan-6-committee-members-jailed/story?id=108257827.

58. Emma Barnett and Jillian Frankel, "Trump Says There Will Be a 'Bloodbath' if He Loses the Election," NBC News, March 16, 2024, https://www.nbcnews.com/politics/donald-trump/trump-bloodbath-loses-election-2024-rcna143746.

59. Charles P. Pierce, "Arizona Is Sticking Election Workers in 'Encampments' for Their Own Protection Now," *Esquire*, March 25, 2024, https://www.esquire.com/news-politics/politics/a60294412/maricopa-election-violence-voting-tabulation-center/.

60. Khaya Himmelman, "Maricopa Transforms Tabulation Center into 'Encampment' to Avoid Another 'Lollapalooza for the Alt-Right,'" *Talking Points Memo*, March 23, 2024, https://talkingpointsmemo.com/news/maricopa-transforms-tabulation-center-into-encampment-to-avoid-another-lollapalooza-for-the-alt-right.

61. Ibid.

62. Ibid.

63. This account relies on Sasha Abramsky, "The Takeover of Shasta County," *Nation*, June 12, 2023, https://www.thenation.com/article/politics/shasta-county/; a series of *Los Angeles Times* reports; reporting from local outlet *A News Cafe*, all cited below.

64. "2016 California Presidential Election Results," *Politico*, December 13, 2016, https://www.politico.com/2016-election/results/map/president/california/.

65. County of Shasta, Presidential General Election, November 3, 2020, Statement of Vote, https://assets01.aws.connect.clarityelections.com/Assets/Connect/RootPublish/shasta-ca.connect.clarityelections.com/Election%20Results%202000-Present/2020/1103/Full%20SOV.SHASTA.11.3.2020.pdf.

66. Robert C. Ellickson, "Of Coase and Cattle: Dispute Resolution Among Neighbors in Shasta County," *Stanford Law Review* 38 (1986): 623, 682. See also Robert C. Ellickson, *Order without Law: How Neighbors Settle Disputes* (2009).

67. Shawn Schwaller, "Straight Outta Cottonwood: The Story of Northern California's Outlaw MAGA Militia," *A News Cafe*, January 29, 2023, https://anewscafe.com/2023/01/29/redding/straight-outta-cottonwood

-the-story-of-northern-californias-maga-outlaw-militia/. For an incisive history of the white power movements that presaged the growth of the Northern California militias, see Kathleen Belew, *Bring the War Home: The White Power Movement and Paramilitary America* (2018).

68. Anita Chabria and Hailey Branson-Potts, "Threats, Videos and a Recall: A California Militia Fuels Civic Revolt in a Red County," *Los Angeles Times*, May 19, 2021, https://www.latimes.com/california/story/2021-05-19/covid-19-california-militia-fueling-civic-revolt.

69. Ibid.

70. Ibid.

71. For video, see https://www.youtube.com/watch?v=trmtpXGn2OE.

72. Hailey Branson-Potts, "A Day Before Capitol Attack, Pro-Trump Crowd Stormed Meeting, Threatened Officials in Rural California," *Los Angeles Times*, January 10, 2021, https://www.latimes.com/california/story/2021-01-10/shasta-county-conservative-anger-trump-covid.

73. Ibid.

74. Hailey Branson-Potts and Jessica Garrison, "One Far-Right Leader Ousted. Another Barely Hangs On. Is Shasta Rejecting MAGA Politics?," *Los Angeles Times*, March 16, 2024, https://www.latimes.com/california/story/2024-03-16/shasta-voters-oust-far-right-leader.

75. Ibid.

76. Abramsky, "The Takeover of Shasta County."

77. The series is available at https://www.youtube.com/c/redwhiteandblueprint.

78. Jessica Garrison, "Shasta County OKs Election Results That Turned Back a Far-Right Revolt," *Los Angeles Times*, July 12, 2022, https://www.latimes.com/california/story/2022-07-12/shasta-county-far-right-candidates-mostly-lose-uprising-continues.

79. Scott Wilson, "How Far-Right Militia Groups Found a Foothold in Deep-Blue California," *Washington Post*, March 7, 2022, https://www.washingtonpost.com/nation/2022/03/07/california-far-right-militia/; County of Shasta, Presidential General Election, November 3, 2020, Statement of Vote.

80. Ibid.

81. Mike Chapman and Damon Arthur, "Shasta Supervisors Fire Health Officer. Karen Ramstrom Says She Didn't Deserve It," *Record Searchlight*, May 3, 2022, https://www.redding.com/story/news/2022/05/03/shasta-supervisors-vote-fire-health-officer-ramstrom/9635663002/.

82. Kelli Saam, "Shasta County CEO Matt Pontes Resigns," *Action News Now*, May 19, 2022, https://www.actionnewsnow.com/news/shasta -county-ceo-matt-pontes-resigns/article_83e30bbc-d797-11ec-ae2d -3b11ce55996d.html.

83. Jessica Garrison, "A New Voting System Reality; Shasta County, Which Ditched Dominion, Learns Handcounting Will Come at a Cost," *Los Angeles Times*, April 28, 2023.

84. Shawn Hubler, "In MAGA-Led Shasta County, Election Apprehension Reigns," *New York Times*, October 27, 2022, https://www.nytimes.com /2022/10/27/us/shasta-county-election.html.

85. Ibid.

86. Jessica Garrison, "A New Voting System Reality; Shasta County, Which Ditched Dominion, Learns Handcounting Will Come at a Cost"; Branson-Potts and Garrison, "One Far-Right Leader Ousted."

87. Branson-Potts and Garrison, "One Far-Right Leader Ousted."

88. See, e.g., Patricia Mazzei and Alan Feuer, "How the Proud Boys Gripped the Miami-Dade Republican Party," *New York Times*, June 2, 2022, https://www.nytimes.com/2022/06/02/us/miami-republicans -proud-boys.html.

89. David Benda, "Shasta's Longtime Registrar of Voters Cathy Darling Allen to Retire, Cites Health Concerns," *Record Searchlight*, February 2, 2024, https://www.redding.com/story/news/2024/02/02/shasta-countys-top -election-officcathy-darling-allen-announces-plan-to-retire-as-registrar -of-voters/72457713007/.

CHAPTER 9: "THE VERY DEFINITION OF LAWLESSNESS"

1. T. H. Marshall, *Citizenship and Social Class, and Other Essays* (2021); Blake Emerson, *The Public's Law* (2019); Alexander Meiklejohn, *Free Speech and Its Relation to Self-Government* (1948).

2. We explore the dynamics of this process and its effects on American federalism in Michaels and Noll, "Vigilante Federalism," 1187.

3. The discussion here is adapted from Michaels and Noll, "Vigilante Federalism."

4. *Thomas E. Dobbs v. Jackson Women's Health Organization*, No. 19-1392, https://www.supremecourt.gov/DocketPDF/19/19-1392/185344 /20210729162610813_Dobbs%20Amicus%20FINAL%20PDFA.pdf.

5. Amelia Abraham, " 'It's Been a Total Witch-Hunt. It Takes Its Toll': The LGBTQ+ Families Fleeing Red States," *Guardian*, June 6, 2023,

https://www.theguardian.com/world/2023/jun/06/lgbtq-rights-trans
-gay-texas-florida-north-carolina; Michael Hiltzik, "As Professionals
Flee Antiabortion Policies, Red States Face a Brain Drain," *Los Angeles
Times*, July 19, 2022, https://www.latimes.com/business/story/2022-07
-19/as-professionals-flee-anti-abortion-policies-red-states-start-to-see
-a-brain-drain; Kali Holloway, "Florida's 'War on Woke' Is Spurring a
Brain Drain," *Nation*, September 20, 2023, https://www.thenation.com
/article/society/desantis-florida-education/; Shefali Luthra, " 'We're Not
Going to Win That Fight': Bans on Abortion and Gender-Affirming
Care Are Driving Doctors from Texas," *The 19th*, June 21, 2023,
https://19thnews.org/2023/06/abortion-gender-affirming-care-bans
-doctors-leaving-texas/.

6. Transcript of Oral Arg., 47, *Whole Woman's Health v. Jackson*, No. 21-463
(U.S., November 1, 2021).

7. Ibid., 48.

8. *Lujan v. Defenders of Wildlife*, 504 U.S. 555, 563–67 (1992).

9. See *Whole Woman's Health v. Jackson*, 595 U.S. 30, 52 (2021) (Thomas, J.,
concurring in part and dissenting in part).

10. See Transcript of Oral Argument at 57–59, *United States v. Texas*, 142
S. Ct. 522 (2021) (No. 21-588) ("Suppose a governor filed this, you
know, had this model law and said anyone who brings a black child to a
white school is subject to, you know, and then we copy the law").

11. Ibid.

12. See, e.g., Daisy Bates, *The Long Shadow of Little Rock: A Memoir*
(2007), 83.

13. This discussion follows Michaels and Noll, "Vigilante Federalism,"
1232. See generally, e.g., Avery Hartmans, "A Harvard Psychologist
Explains the Rise in Passengers Getting Violent on Airplanes and
Customers Abusing Retail Workers: People Have Reached 'a Boiling
Point,'" *Business Insider*, July 24, 2021, https://www.businessinsider
.com/violence-on-airplanes-in-stores-explained-harvard
-psychologist-2021-7; Nathaniel Meyersohn, "Stores Want Shoppers to
Wear Masks. But Some Customers Refuse," CNN.com, April 23, 2020,
https://www.cnn.com/2020/04/23/business/grocery-stores-masks-face
-coverings-customers/index.html.

14. See, e.g., Francis X. Rocca, "Churches Push Back Against Coronavirus
Restrictions," *Wall Street Journal*, November 20, 2020, https://www.wsj

.com/articles/churches-push-back-against-coronavirus-restrictions
-11605867870.

15. See, e.g., Grace Kay, "A Mask-Less Trader Joe's Customer in Texas Had a Meltdown After Being Denied Entry—and It Reveals How States' New Rules Endanger Workers," *Business Insider*, March 8, 2021, https://www.businessinsider.com/mask-less-trader-joes-meltdown-texas-rules-impact-workers-2021-3; Abha Bhattaral, "Retail Workers Are Being Pulled into the Latest Culture War: Getting Customers to Wear Masks," *Washington Post*, July 8, 2020, https://www.washingtonpost.com/business/2020/07/08/retail-workers-masks-coronavirus/.

16. See, e.g., Laura J. Nelson and Connor Sheets, "Online Pastors, Form Letters: The Cottage Industry Helping Workers Avoid Vaccine Mandates," *Los Angeles Times*, February 6, 2022, https://www.latimes.com/california/story/2022-02-06/requests-religious-exemptions-covid-19-vaccine-letters; Ruth Graham, "Vaccine Resisters Seek Religious Exemptions. But What Counts as Religious?," *New York Times*, September 11, 2021, https://www.nytimes.com/2021/09/11/us/covid-vaccine-religion-exemption.html.

17. See, e.g., Alexandra Berzon and Nick Corasaniti, "Right-Wing Leaders Mobilize Corps of Election Activists," *New York Times*, October 17, 2022, https://www.nytimes.com/2022/10/17/us/politics/midterm-elections-challenges.html; Tresa Baldas et al., "'Get to TCF': What Really Happened Inside Detroit's Ballot Counting Center," *Detroit Free Press*, November 6, 2020, https://www.freep.com/story/news/local/michigan/detroit/2020/11/06/tcf-center-detroit-ballot-counting/6173577002/.

18. See, e.g., *Shelley v. Kraemer*, 334 U.S. 1 (1948) (prohibiting enforcement of racially restrictive housing covenants); *Sweatt v. Painter*, 339 U.S. 629 (1950) (rejecting "separate but equal" doctrine in higher education).

19. Michael J. Klarman, *From Jim Crow to Civil Rights: The Supreme Court and the Struggle for Racial Equality* (2006); James T. Patterson, *Brown v. Board of Education: A Civil Rights Milestone and Its Troubled Legacy* (2001).

20. Kevin M. Kruse, *White Flight: Atlanta and the Making of Modern Conservatism* (2013); Richard Rothstein, *The Color of Law: A Forgotten History of How Our Government Segregated America* (2017).

21. Alexis de Tocqueville, *Democracy in America* (1835), Chapter XII.

22. Dr. Martin Luther King, Jr., "Letter from a Birmingham Jail," April 16,

1963, https://www.africa.upenn.edu/Articles_Gen/Letter_Birmingham.html.

23. See, e.g., Richard L. Hasen, *Plutocrats United: Campaign Money, The Supreme Court, and the Distortion of American Elections* (2016); Lawrence Lessig, *Republic, Lost: How Money Corrupts Congress—and a Plan to Stop It* (2015).

24. Ezra Klein, "A Conversation with J. D. Vance, the Reluctant Interpreter of Trumpism," *Vox*, February 2, 2017, https://www.vox.com/2017/2/2/14404770/jd-vance-trump-hillbilly-elegy-ezra-klein-show; Patricia Garcia, "J. D. Vance for President?," *Vogue*, February 8, 2017, https://www.vogue.com/article/hillbilly-elegy-author-jd-vance-on-trump.

25. Tweet by J. D. Vance, November 17, 2021, https://twitter.com/JDVance1/status/1461074105759932423.

26. Zach Cunning, "J. D. Vance Says Kyle Rittenhouse Exhibited 'Basic Manly Virtue' During Kenosha Shootings," *Heartland Signal*, November 24, 2021, https://heartlandsignal.com/2021/11/24/j-d-vance-says-kyle-rittenhouse-exhibited-basic-manly-virtue-during-kenosha-shootings/.

27. Donald P. Moynihan, "Trump Has a Master Plan for Destroying the 'Deep State,'" *New York Times*, November 27, 2023, https://www.nytimes.com/2023/11/27/opinion/trump-deep-state-schedule-f.html; Tolouse Olorunnipa et al., "Trump Embarks on Expansive Search for Disloyalty as Administration-Wide Purge Escalates," *Washington Post*, February 21, 2020, https://www.washingtonpost.com/politics/were-cleaning-it-out-trump-embarks-on-expansive-search-for-disloyalty-as-administration-wide-purge-escalates/2020/02/21/870e6c56-54c1-11ea-b119-4faabac6674f_story.html.

28. Jon D. Michaels, "The American Deep State," *Notre Dame Law Review* 93 (2018): 1653.

29. Jerry L. Mashaw, "Prodelegation: Why Administrators Should Make Political Decisions," *Journal of Law, Economics and Organization* 1 (1985): 81.

30. Jerry L. Mashaw, *Reasoned Administration and Democratic Legitimacy: How Administrative Law Supports Democratic Government* (2018).

31. Jon D. Michaels, "Privatization, Constitutional Conservatism, and the Fate of the American Administrative State," in *The Cambridge Handbook of Privatization* (Avihay Dorfman and Alon Harel, eds., 2021), 144.

32. Sarah Jones, "Trump's Base Isn't Housewives. It's Tradwives," *New York*,

October 28, 2020, https://nymag.com/intelligencer/2020/10/trumps
-base-isnt-housewives-its-tradwives.html.

33. Martin Pengelly, "Ohio Senate Candidate JD Vance Blames America's
Woes on 'the Childless Left,'" *Guardian*, July 26, 2021, https://www
.theguardian.com/us-news/2021/jul/26/ohio-senate-candidate-jd-vance;
Shane Goldmacher and Luke Broadwater, "Republicans Play on Fears of
'Great Replacement' in Bid for Base Voters," *New York Times*, May 16,
2022, https://www.nytimes.com/2022/05/16/us/politics/republicans
-great-replacement.html.

34. *Webster v. Reproductive Health Services*, 492 U.S. 490, 557 (1989)
(Blackman, J., concurring in part).

35. *Gonzales v. Carhart*, 550 U.S. 124, 172 (2007) (Ginsburg, J., dissenting).

36. *Planned Parenthood v. Casey*, 505 U.S. 833, 856 (1992) (plurality op.).

37. *Dobbs v. Jackson Women's Health Org.*, 142 S. Ct. 2228, 2343–47 (2022)
(Breyer, J., dissenting).

38. Brittni Frederiksen et al., "Abortion Bans May Limit Essential
Medications for Women with Chronic Conditions," KFF, November 17,
2022, https://www.kff.org/womens-health-policy/issue-brief/abortion
-bans-may-limit-essential-medications-for-women-with-chronic
-conditions/.

39. *Dobbs*, 142 S. Ct. 2265, 2277, 2305.

40. Bryan Hughes, "The Texas Abortion Law Is Unconventional Because It
Had to Be," *Wall Street Journal*, September 12, 2021, https://www.wsj
.com/articles/texas-abortion-law-unconventional-lawsuit-pro-life-roe
-v-wade-heartbeat-six-weeks-11631471508.

41. Brooke Migdon, "Number of LGBTQ+ Elected Officials in the US Hits
Record High," *The Hill*, August 18, 2022, https://thehill.com/changing
-america/respect/equality/3607320-number-of-lgbtq-elected-officials
-in-the-us-hits-record-high/.

42. Scott Neuman, "The Culture Wars Are Pushing Some Teachers to
Leave the Classroom," NPR, November 13, 2022, https://www.npr
.org/2022/11/13/1131872280/teacher-shortage-culture-wars-critical
-race-theory; Luca Goldmansour, "Who Wants to Teach in Florida?,"
American Prospect, February 23, 2023, https://prospect.org/education
/02-22-2023-desantis-education-teacher-vacancies/; Talia Richman,
"Inside Texas's Explosion of Uncertified New Teachers Filling
Shortages," *Dallas Morning News*, October 15, 2023, https://www
.dallasnews.com/news/education/2023/10/15/inside-texas-explosion

-of-uncertified-new-teachers-filling-shortages/; Samantha LaFrance, "The Topics Teachers Are Too Afraid to Teach," PEN America, November 20, 2023, https://pen.org/the-topics-teachers-are-too-afraid -to-teach/.

43. Danielle Abril and Gerrit De Vynck, "Texas Wanted to Be the Tech Haven of the U.S. Its New Abortion Bill and Other Measures Are Causing Workers to Rethink Their Moves," *Washington Post*, September 13, 2021, https://www.washingtonpost.com/technology /2021/09/12/texas-abortion-law-tech-workers-reconsidering-relocation/; Maggie McGrath, "Survey: Two Thirds of College-Educated Workers May Avoid Texas Because of Abortion Ban," *Forbes*, September 2, 2021, https://www.forbes.com/sites/maggiemcgrath/2021/09/02/survey-two -thirds-of-college-educated-workers--may-avoid-texas-because-of --abortion-ban/?sh=499f548f6e4c.

44. Christopher Rowland, "A Challenge for Antiabortion States: Doctors Reluctant to Work There," *Washington Post*, August 6, 2022, https:// www.washingtonpost.com/business/2022/08/06/abortion-maternity -health-obgyn/; Arielle Dreher and Oriana González, "New Doctors Avoid Residencies in States with Abortion Bans," *Axios*, April 18, 2023, https://www.axios.com/2023/04/18/abortion-ban-states-drop-student -residents; Erum Salam, "Texas Doctors Depart as Attorney General Investigates Hospital's Gender-Affirming Care," *Guardian*, May 18, 2023, https://www.theguardian.com/us-news/2023/may/18/texas-hospital -inquiry-doctor-exodus.

45. Ronald Brownstein, "Democrats Are Losing the Culture Wars," *Atlantic*, December 9, 2021, https://www.theatlantic.com /politics/archive/2021/12/democrats-lose-culture-war/620887 /?scrolla=5eb6d68b7fedc32c19ef33b4; Leah Hunt-Hendrix, "To Overcome the Republicans' Culture War, Democrats Need to Punch Up, Not Down," *Politico*, April 11, 2022, https://www.politico.com /news/magazine/2022/04/11/democrats-inclusive-populism-culture -war-00024409 (cataloging arguments that Democrats should steer clear of the culture wars).

46. Fabiola Cineas, "The Rising Republican Movement to Defund Public Libraries," *Vox*, May 8, 2023, https://www.vox.com/politics/2023/5 /5/23711417/republicans-want-to-defund-public-libraries-book-bans; Brynn Tannehill, "The Republican Plan to Devastate Public Education in America," *New Republic*, August 11, 2022, https://newrepublic.com

/article/167375/republican-plan-devastate-public-education-america;
Julie Rovner, "Republicans Once Championed Public Health. What
Happened?," KFF, December 13, 2023, https://kffhealthnews.org/news
/article/health-202-gop-targeting-public-health-pepfar-nih/.

47. The strategy not coincidentally parallels the deliberate hollowing out of
the federal administrative state. See Michaels, *Constitutional Coup*; David
L. Noll, "Administrative Sabotage," *Michigan Law Review* 120 (2022): 753.

48. Our argument here is anticipated by Elizabeth Anderson, *Private
Government* (2017).

49. Heather McGhee, *The Sum of Us: What Racism Costs Everyone and How
We Can Prosper Together* (2021); Kristen Green, *Something Must Be Done
About Prince Edward County* (2015).

CHAPTER 10: "NOT WITHOUT ELECTORAL OR POLITICAL POWER"

1. 597 U.S. 215, 289 (2022).

2. Remarks by President Biden on Protecting Access to Reproductive
Health Care Services, July 8, 2022, https://www.whitehouse.gov
/briefing-room/speeches-remarks/2022/07/08/remarks-by-president
-biden-on-protecting-access-to-reproductive-health-care-services/.

3. Remarks by President Biden in a Political Event with Reproductive
Rights Groups, June 23, 2023, https://www.whitehouse.gov/briefing
-room/speeches-remarks/2023/06/23/remarks-by-president-biden-in-a
-political-event-with-reproductive-rights-groups.

4. The White House, Remarks of President Joe Biden—State of the
Union Address as Prepared for Delivery, March 7, 2024, https://
www.whitehouse.gov/briefing-room/speeches-remarks/2024/03
/07/remarks-of-president-joe-biden-state-of-the-union-address-as
-prepared-for-delivery-2/.

5. Wendy Brown, "Alito's Dobbs Decision Will Further Degrade
Democracy," *Washington Post*, June 27, 2022, https://www
.washingtonpost.com/outlook/2022/06/27/alito-dobbs-decision-states
-rghts/.

6. Executive Order to Prohibit Indoctrination and Critical Race Theory in
Schools, January 10, 2023, https://governor.arkansas.gov/executive
_orders/executive-order-to-prohibit-indoctrination-and-critical-race
-theory-in-schools/.

7. Everton Bailey, "New Texas Law Limits How Cities Govern Themselves,"

Dallas Morning News, July 12, 2023, https://www.governing.com/policy
/new-texas-law-limits-how-cities-govern-themselves.

8. Hassan Kanu, "DeSantis' Suspension of Prosecutor Marks Perilous
Path," Reuters, September 12, 2022, https://www.reuters.com
/legal/government/desantis-suspension-prosecutor-marks-perilous
-path-2022-09-12/. As this book went to press, the conservative
Eleventh Circuit Court of Appeals ruled that Warren's ouster
potentially violated the First Amendment. *Warren v. DeSantis*, 90 F.4th
1115, 1118 (11th Cir. 2024).

9. "Ron DeSantis Suspends Second Elected Prosecutor as His 2024
Campaign Struggles," NBC News, August 9, 2023, https://www
.nbcnews.com/politics/2024-election/ron-desantis-suspends-second
-elected-prosecutor-monique-worrell-rcna98968.

10. H.B. 1010 (Miss. 2023).

11. Oliver Laughland et al., "Mississippi Bill Would Carve Out Separate
Judicial District for 80% of White Residents in Majority-Black City,"
Guardian, February 15, 2023, https://www.theguardian.com/us-news
/ng-interactive/2023/feb/15/mississippi-jackson-judicial-district
-unelected-judges-prosecutors.

12. Ibid.

13. Ibid.

14. "The Hostile Takeover of Blue Cities by Red States," *Businessweek*,
August 30, 2023.

15. Ibid.

16. 139 S. Ct. 2484 (2019).

17. The data we report here are from the 2022 Cooperative Election Study,
which surveyed more than fifty thousand adults about their political
opinions. For each state we mention, UCLA law librarian Caitlin
Hunter totaled the number of respondents who identified as Democrat
or Republican (field CC22_433a on the postelection survey) or did not
identify with either party but leaned Democrat or Republican (field
CC22_433b on the postelection survey). The partisan composition of
state legislative chambers is reported from the August 2023 National
Conference of State Legislatures survey, available at https://www
.ncsl.org/about-state-legislatures/state-partisan-composition. Several
states skew more Democratic than Gallup found in a 2018 poll, so we
have reported Gallup's findings in endnotes to the text. We prioritize

reported political alignment rather than voter registration because so many voters do not list their party affiliations; for instance, only 13 percent of registered voters in Arkansas list any party affiliation. To make matters more complicated, those who do register with a party at, say, age eighteen never bother to change their affiliation, even after their views and affinities might have changed dramatically over the years.

18. In Gallup's 2018 poll, Arkansas was 35 percent Democratic and 48 percent Republican.

19. In 2018, Gallup found Mississippi was 36 percent Democratic to 48 percent Republican.

20. In the Gallup poll, Florida was 42 percent Democratic to 41 percent Republican.

21. In Gallup, Texas was 39 percent Democratic to 42 percent Republican.

22. In Gallup, Ohio was 41 percent Democratic to 45 percent Republican.

23. As we've noted, the survey data we used may well overestimate the amount of enthusiasm for Democrats. If that's the case, then of course our claims of gerrymandering are less acute. But the hurdles faced in turning states that are truly supermajoritarian MAGA Republican blue, or even purple, remain just as high. (What's more, the prospects of capturing statewide offices—governor, attorney general, secretary of state—are even dimmer.)

24. See, e.g., Michelle Boorstein, " 'The Justins' Seem Like Civil Rights–Era Throwbacks. But 2023 Isn't 1968," *Washington Post*, August 5, 2023, https://www.washingtonpost.com/dc-md-va/2023/08/03/justin-pearson-justin-jones-tennessee-christianity-politics/.

25. See, e.g., "How a Tennessee Special Session on Gun Violence Ended in Chaos," *Time*, August 30, 2023.

26. In Gallup's 2018 poll, Montana was split 39 percent Democratic to 46 percent Republican.

27. "Montana Transgender Legislator Silenced after 'Blood on Your Hands' Comment," Reuters, April 28, 2023.

28. Robert A. Dahl, *How Democratic Is the American Constitution?* (2d ed., 2003), 48.

29. Ibid., 53 (noting that "between 1800 and 1860 eight anti-slavery measures passed the House, and all were killed in the Senate").

30. " 'The Senate Is Broken': System Empowers White Conservatives, Threatening US Democracy," *Guardian*, March 12, 2021, https://www

.theguardian.com/us-news/2021/mar/12/us-senate-system-white
-conservative-minority.

31. Michael Ettlinger and Jordan Hensley, "The 2023–2024 U.S. Senate Is
Exceedingly Unrepresentative in Many Ways," *Medium*, December 4,
2022, https://mettlinger.medium.com/the-2023-senate-will-be
-exceedingly-unrepresentative-72d39f83847a.

32. Ibid.

33. "What's Going On in This Graph? | Senate Representation by State,"
New York Times, October 27, 2022, https://www.nytimes.com/2022
/10/27/learning/whats-going-on-in-this-graph-nov-9-2022.html. Some
sources put the number even higher. See, e.g., Ronald Brownstein,
"Small States Are Getting a Much Bigger Say in Who Gets on Supreme
Court," CNN, July 10, 2018, https://www.cnn.com/2018/07/10/politics
/small-states-supreme-court/index.html.

34. See, e.g., Adam Jentleson, *Kill Switch: The Rise of the Modern Senate and
the Crippling of American Democracy* (2021).

35. "The Enormous Advantage That the Electoral College Gives
Republicans, in One Chart," *Vox*, January 11, 2021.

36. Ibid.

37. Matthew Yglesias, "Playing to Win Against the Attacks on LGBTQ
Progress," *Slow Boring*, March 23, 2022, https://www.slowboring.com/p
/winnable-lgbt?s=r.

38. Ruy Teixeira, "Democrats and the Abortion Issue," *Liberal Patriot*,
May 27, 2022, https://www.liberalpatriot.com/p/democrats-and-the
-abortion-issue.

39. Sean Illing, "Wokeness Is a Problem and We All Know It," *Vox*,
April 27, 2021, https://www.vox.com/22338417/james-carville
-democratic-party-biden-100-days.

40. "Conservatives May Control the Supreme Court Until the 2050s,"
Washington Post, December 14, 2021.

41. Adam Chilton et al., "The Endgame of Court-Packing," Social Science
Research Network, May 4, 2023, https://ssrn.com/abstract=3835502.

42. Data were compiled by UCLA law librarian Caitlin Hunter from
state supreme court websites as of August 2023. Party identification is
based on the party of the appointing governor, elected judges' declared
partisan affiliation, and, for states with nonpartisan judicial elections,
Ballotpedia's State Supreme Court Partisan Report (October 2022).

Arkansas justice Barbara Webb, who does not appear in the report, was coded as a Republican.

CHAPTER 11: "DIVIDE AND INFLAME"

1. Kim Philips-Fein, *Invisible Hands: The Making of the Conservative Movement from the New Deal to Reagan* (2009); Jacob S. Hacker and Paul Pierson, *American Amnesia* (2016).

2. See, e.g., Jacob S. Hacker and Paul Pierson, *Let Them Eat Tweets: How the Right Rules in an Age of Extreme Inequality* (2020), 22.

3. Brief for Major American Business Enterprises as Amici Curiae Supporting Respondents, *Students for Fair Admissions v. Harvard* (Nos. 20-1199 & 21-707), https://www.supremecourt.gov/DocketPDF/20/20 -1199/232357/20220801135424028_Nos.%2020-1199%2021-707%20-%20 Brief%20for%20Major%20American%20Business%20Enterprises%20 Supporting%20Respondents.pdf; Dieter Holger, "The Business Case for More Diversity," *Wall Street Journal*, October 26, 2019, https://www.wsj .com/articles/the-business-case-for-more-diversity-11572091200?st=tvf4 dxczc3kekek&reflink=desktopwebshare_permalink.

4. Eric Levenson et al., "Why Disney Has Its Own Government in Florida and How Control of It Could Change," CNN, February 7, 2023, https:// www.cnn.com/2022/04/21/us/reedy-creek-walt-disney-florida /index.html; Nicole Guadiano, "How Disney Became a Self-Governing Kingdom in Florida That Ron DeSantis and State Republicans Now Want to Unravel," *Business Insider*, April 19, 2022, https://www .businessinsider.com/disney-reedy-creek-improvement-district-self -governing-republicans-say-gay-2022-4.

5. Todd C. Frankel, "How Disney Fell Flat in Fight over LGBTQ Talk in Florida's Schools," *Washington Post*, April 1, 2022, https://www .washingtonpost.com/business/2022/04/01/disney-dont-say-gay-bill/.

6. Brett Heinz, "The Iron Grip of the Magic Kingdom," *American Prospect*, June 2, 2021, https://prospect.org/power/iron-grip-of-the-magic -kingdom-disney-florida-social-media-law/.

7. Hugo Martin, "Walt Disney Co. to Get $580-Million Tax Break for Moving California Jobs to Florida," *Los Angeles Times*, July 23, 2021, https://www.latimes.com/business/story/2021-07-23/walt-disney-co -gets-580-million-florida-tax-break-california-jobs.

8. See Chapter 5 in this book.

9. Frankel, "How Disney Fell Flat." The company did weigh in on the Stop WOKE Act, though that statute, unlike Don't Say Gay, exposed the firm to civil liability and harassment—and the House sponsor singled out Disney's DEI training program for promoting critical race theory.

10. Ibid.

11. David Kihara, "DeSantis Says Disney 'Crossed the Line' in Calling for 'Don't Say Gay' Repeal," *Politico*, March 29, 2023, https://www.politico.com/news/2022/03/29/desantis-disney-dont-say-gay-repeal-00021389.

12. "DeSantis Defends 'Don't Say Gay' Bill, Warns of Transgender Issues 'Injected' into Classroom Instruction," CBS Miami, March 4, 2022, https://www.cbsnews.com/miami/news/desantis-defends-dont-say-gay-bill-warns-of-transgender-issues-injected-into-classroom-instruction/.

13. David Moye, "Ted Cruz Skeeves Out Twitter Users with Lewd Joke about Mickey and Pluto Having Sex," *HuffPost*, April 19, 2022, https://www.yahoo.com/entertainment/ted-cruz-skeeves-twitter-users-210150963.html.

14. Aleks Phillips, "Lauren Boebert Joins Ron DeSantis' Fight Against Disney," *Newsweek*, May 12, 2023, https://www.newsweek.com/lauren-boebert-ron-desantis-disney-feud-no-fly-zone-1800005.

15. Arthur Delaney, "Josh Hawley Jumps on Anti-Disney Bandwagon with Copyright Bill," *HuffPost*, May 10, 2022, https://www.huffpost.com/entry/josh-hawley-disney-copyright_n_627ac821e4b046ad0d82c098.

16. Ariel Zilber, "Daily Wire Investing $100 Million in Kids Content to Battle 'Woke' Disney," *New York Post*, March 31, 2022, https://nypost.com/2022/03/31/daily-wire-investing-100m-in-kids-content-to-battle-disney/.

17. Steve Contorno and Kit Maher, "DeSantis Signs Bill That Gives Him More Control of Disney's Special District," CNN, February 27, 2023, https://www.cnn.com/2023/02/27/politics/desantis-disney-reedy-creek/index.html; Brooks Barnes, "DeSantis Declares Victory as Disney Is Stripped of Some 56-Year-Old Perks," *New York Times*, February 10, 2023, https://www.nytimes.com/2023/02/10/business/disney-world-florida-tax-board.html.

18. David D. Stewart and Benjamin Valdez, "Examining Florida's Removal of Disney's Special Tax District," *Forbes*, June 1, 2022, https://www.forbes.com/sites/taxnotes/2022/06/01/examining-floridas-removal-of-disneys-special-tax-district/?sh=3fd722944d29.

19. Dawn Chmielewski and Lisa Richwine, "Disney Cancels Plans for

$1 Billion Campus, 2,000 Jobs in Florida," Reuters, May 18, 2023, https://www.reuters.com/business/media-telecom/disney-cancels-plans -relocate-2000-jobs-florida-company-email-2023-05-18/.

20. Daniel Arkin, "Disney Sues Florida Gov. Ron DeSantis over Control of Self-Governing District," NBC News, April 26, 2023, https://www .nbcnews.com/business/business-news/disney-sues-ron-desantis-over -reedy-creek-control-rcna81587.

21. Again, Florida's MAGA leaders have been willing to lose real money on the project. The state is not only on the hook for all the tax revenue it has lost from Disney; the company also decided to jettison its plan to build a $1 billion corporate hub and, as noted above, is no longer moving thousands of high-skilled Imagineer jobs from Southern California to Central Florida. Chmielewski and Richwine, "Disney Cancels Plans."

22. Jacob D. Charles, "Securing Gun Rights by Statute: The Right to Keep and Bear Arms Outside the Constitution," *Michigan Law Review* 120 (2022): 581.

23. The requirements are published at the Texas State Law Library's website, https://guides.sll.texas.gov/gun-laws/businesses-private-property.

24. Fl. Stat. section 760.10(8)(a).

25. Maggie Q. Thompson, "Architect of 'Bounty-Hunter' Abortion Ban Wants List of Abortion Seekers," *Austin Chronicle*, September 29, 2023, https://www.austinchronicle.com/daily/news/2023-09-29/architect -of-bounty-hunter-abortion-ban-wants-list-of-abortion-seekers/; Amy Littlefield, "The Man Behind the Texas Abortion Ban Now Has an Even More Radical Plan to Reshape American Law," *Mother Jones*, April 5, 2022, https://www.motherjones.com/politics/2022/04 /jonathan-mitchell-the-mastermind-of-the-texas-heartbeat-statute -has-a-radical-mission-to-reshape-american-law/.

26. H.B. 787, 88th Leg. (Tex. 2022).

27. H.B. 20 (Tex. 2021); S.B. 7072 (Fl. 2021). Both laws have been stayed pending the resolution of legal challenges that contend they violate the First Amendment. The Supreme Court heard argument in the cases in February 2024.

28. Dominic Rushe, "Companies Scramble to Protect Abortion Access for Employees after Court Ruling," *Guardian*, June 25, 2022, https://www .theguardian.com/us-news/2022/jun/25/companies-abortion-access -employees-disney-levi-strauss-microsoft-jp-morgan.

29. "Lyft, Uber Will Pay Drivers' Legal Fees if They're Sued under Texas

Abortion Law," NPR, September 8, 2021, https://www.npr.org/2021
/09/08/1035045952/lyft-uber-will-pay-drivers-legal-fees-if-theyre-sued
-under-texas-abortion-law#:~:text=You%20know%2C%20one%20
of%20the,on%20women's%20right%20to%20choose.

30. Soo Youn, "Air Force Offers Help to LGBTQ Personnel, Families Hurt by
State Laws," *Washington Post*, April 16, 2022, https://www.washingtonpost
.com/politics/2022/04/16/air-force-lgbtq-laws-help-families/.

31. Michaels and Noll, "Vigilante Federalism," 1261.

32. Ibid., 1259–60.

33. Jesse Tarbert, *When Good Government Meant Big Government: The Quest to
Expand Federal Power, 1913–1933* (2022).

34. Neal E. Boudette, "Elon Musk Says He Has Moved to Texas, from
California," *New York Times*, December 8, 2020, https://www.nytimes
.com/2020/12/08/business/elon-musk-texas.html.

35. Isabelle Guis, "Tax Breaks Cushion Tesla's Texas Landing," *American
Prospect*, April 25, 2022, https://prospect.org/economy/tax-breaks
-cushion-teslas-texas-landing/; Hyunjoo Jin and Subrat Patnaik, "Tesla
Moving Headquarters to Texas from California," Reuters, April 8,
2021, https://www.reuters.com/business/autos-transportation/tesla
-moving-headquarters-austin-texas-says-ceo-musk-2021-10-07/; Kara
Wetzel et al., "Tesla's Texas Move Is Latest Sign of California Losing
Tech Grip," *Bloomberg*, October 8, 2021, https://www.bloomberg
.com/news/articles/2021-10-08/tesla-s-texas-move-is-latest-sign-of
-california-losing-tech-grip.

36. Kevin Stankiewicz, "Texas Governor Says Companies Moving
Headquarters to the State Has Turned into a 'Tidal Wave,'" CNBC,
December 11, 2020, https://www.cnbc.com/2020/12/11/gov-greg
-abbott-on-oracle-companies-moving-headquarters-to-texas.html.

37. Kara Frederick, "Combating Big Tech's Totalitarianism: A Road
Map," Heritage, February 7, 2022, https://www.heritage.org
/technology/report/combating-big-techs-totalitarianism-road-map;
Steven P. Bucci, "It's a Strategic Imperative to Manage Our National
Communications Spectrum Correctly," Heritage, October 2, 2023,
https://www.heritage.org/technology/commentary/its-strategic
-imperative-manage-our-national-communications-spectrum;
Christopher F. Rufo, "The DEI Regime," *City Journal*, July 13, 2022,
https://www.city-journal.org/article/the-dei-regime; Leor Sapir and
Joseph Figliolia, "Medicine with a 'Transgender Bias,'" *City Journal*,

November 8, 2023, https://www.city-journal.org/article/medicine
-with-a-transgender-bias.

38. Ed Pilkington, "Obamacare Faces New Threat at State Level from
Corporate Interest Group ALEC," *Guardian*, November 20, 2013,
https://www.theguardian.com/world/2013/nov/20/obamacare-alec
-republican-legislators.

39. Chris McGreal, "Rightwing Group Pushing US States for Law
Blocking 'Political Boycott' of Firms," *Guardian*, November 11,
2022, https://www.theguardian.com/us-news/2022/nov/11/alec
-anti-political-boycott-state-legislation; Sam Metz, "GOP Directs
Culture War Fury Toward Green Investing Trend," Associated
Press, May 19, 2022, https://apnews.com/article/technology
-cultures-climate-and-environment-government-politics-37bd9e48
94541275982a7ff99089cc7e.

40. David J. Lynch, "As DeSantis Takes Aim at Cruise Industry, Republicans
Step Up Attacks on Longtime Allies in Corporate America," *Washington
Post*, June 8, 2021, https://www.washingtonpost.com/us-policy/2021/06
/08/republicans-business-desantis-cruise/.

41. "Ron DeSantis Blocks Funds for Tampa Bay Rays after Team's
Gun Safety Tweets," *Guardian*, June 3, 2022, https://www
.theguardian.com/sport/2022/jun/03/ron-desantis-blocks-funds
-tampa-bay-rays-gun-safety.

42. Jessica Guynn, "'Woke Mind Virus'? 'Corporate Wokeness'? Why
Red America Has Declared War on Corporate America," *USA Today*,
January 4, 2023, https://www.usatoday.com/story/money/2023/01/04
/desantis-republicans-woke-big-business-war/10947073002/.

43. David Thomas, "Senate Republicans Warn U.S. Law Firms over ESG
Advice," Reuters, November 4, 2022, https://www.reuters.com
/legal/government/senate-republicans-warn-us-law-firms-over-esg
-advice-2022-11-04/.

44. *Sambrano v. United Airlines*, 45 F.4th 877, 883 (5th Cir. 2022) (Ho., J.,
concurring in denial of rehearing en banc) (quoting and seemingly
endorsing a claim made by 2024 GOP presidential candidate Vivek
Ramaswamy).

45. Stephanie Sly, "Children's Hospitals Become Targets of Anti-
Transgender Attacks and Harassment," PBS, August 31, 2022, https://
www.pbs.org/newshour/show/childrens-hospitals-become-targets-of
-anti-transgender-attacks-and-harassment.

46. On the phenomenon of "short-termism" and its tension with long-term value maximization, see Dennis Carey, "Why CEOs Should Push Back Against Short-Termism," *Harvard Business Review*, May 31, 2018, https://hbr.org/2018/05/why-ceos-should-push-back-against-short-termism.

47. Jon King, "Coordinated Hate Campaign Is Driving Anti-LGBTQ+ 'Backlash' Targeting Businesses, Experts Say," *Michigan Advance*, July 1, 2023, https://michiganadvance.com/2023/07/01/coordinated-hate-campaign-is-driving-anti-lgbtq-backlash-targeting-businesses-experts-say/.

48. Ibid.

49. Angela Li and Caitlin Moniz, "Corporations Have Given over $50 million to the Sedition Caucus," Citizens for Responsibility and Ethics in Washington, January 6, 2023, https://www.citizensforethics.org/reports-investigations/crew-reports/corporations-have-given-over-50-million-to-the-sedition-caucus/.

50. Jimmy Cloutier and Taylor Giorno, "Companies That Claim to Back the LGBTQ Community Send Political Contributions to State Lawmakers Who Advanced Anti-Transgender Bills," OpenSecrets, June 22, 2022, https://www.opensecrets.org/news/2022/06/companies-that-claim-to-back-the-lgbtq-community-send-political-contributions-to-state-lawmakers-who-advanced-anti-transgender-bills/.

CHAPTER 12: MORE LIKE 1850 THAN 1950

1. Mary L. Dudziak, *Cold War Civil Rights* (2000), 66. Unless otherwise noted, all quotations in this first section of the chapter are taken from Dudziak's invaluable volume.

2. Carolyn O'Hara, "Cold Warrior," *Foreign Policy*, March 2005, https://web.archive.org/web/20051101150423/http://www.foreignpolicy.com/story/cms.php?story_id=2817.

3. "The Charge in the Soviet Union (Kennan) to the Secretary of State," *Telegram*, February 22, 1946, https://nsarchive2.gwu.edu/coldwar/documents/episode-1/kennan.htm.

4. Dudziak, *Cold War Civil Rights*, 87.

5. Ibid., 91–92.

6. Ibid., 95.

7. Ibid., 107.

8. Ibid., 163–65.

9. Ibid., 180.

10. Derrick A. Bell, Jr., "Brown v. Board of Education and the Interest-Convergence Dilemma," *Harvard Law Review* 93 (1980): 518.
11. For an earlier survey of these trends, see Jason Stanley, *How Fascism Works* (2020).
12. Aurelien Breeden and Constant Meheut, "France's Far Right Surges into Parliament and Further into the Mainstream," *New York Times*, June 26, 2022, https://www.nytimes.com/2022/06/26/world/europe/france-far-right-parliament.html.
13. Tara John, "The 'Anti-Woke' Crusade Has Come to Europe. Its Effects Could Be Chilling," CNN, January 7, 2022, https://www.cnn.com/2022/01/07/europe/war-on-woke-europe-cmd-intl/index.html.
14. Clea Caulcutt, "France's Culture Wars Reignited after Macron Appoints 'Woke' Minister," *Politico*, May 30, 2022, https://www.politico.eu/article/france-culture-war-emmanuel-macron-government-woke-minister-pap-ndiaye-education-reform/.
15. Angelique Chrisafis, "France Passes Controversial Immigration Bill Amid Deep Divisions in Macron's Party," *Guardian*, December 20, 2023, https://www.theguardian.com/world/2023/dec/20/france-immigration-bill-passed-controversy-emmanuel-macron-marine-le-pen.
16. Roger Cohen, "Can Gabriel Attal Win Over France?," *New York Times*, February 23, 2023, https://www.nytimes.com/2024/02/23/world/europe/gabriel-attal-france-prime-minister.html.
17. Gordon Brown, "Brexiteers Want Us to Glory in Isolation," *Guardian*, May 12, 2019, https://www.theguardian.com/commentisfree/2019/may/12/brexiteers-britain-vision-introverted-selfish-brexit-gordon-brown.
18. David Theo Goldberg, "The War on Critical Race Theory," *Boston Review*, May 7, 2021.
19. Daniel Trilling, "Why Is the UK Government Suddenly Targeting 'Critical Race Theory'?," *Guardian*, October 23, 2020, https://www.theguardian.com/commentisfree/2020/oct/23/uk-critical-race-theory-trump-conservatives-structural-inequality.
20. Kelly Kasulis Cho, "U.K. Prime Minister on Gender: 'A Man Is a Man and a Woman Is a Woman,'" *Washington Post*, October 5, 2023, https://www.washingtonpost.com/world/2023/10/05/rishi-sunak-gender-identity-transgender/.
21. Pippa Crerar, "Teachers in England Will Have to Tell Parents if Children Question Their Gender," *Guardian*, July 17, 2023, https://

www.theguardian.com/society/2023/jul/17/teachers-in-england-will
-have-to-tell-parents-if-children-question-their-gender.

22. Aubrey Allegretti, "Millions in UK Face Disenfranchisement under
Voter ID Plans," *Guardian*, July 4, 2021, https://www.theguardian.com
/politics/2021/jul/04/millions-in-uk-face-disenfranchisement-under
-voter-id-plans.

23. Josiah Mortimer, "Voter ID: 'It's Far Worse than Any US State,'" *Byline
Times* (November 7, 2022).

24. Max Colchester and David Luhnow, "Former Brexit Champion and
Trump Supporter Shakes Up U.K. Election Race," *Wall Street Journal*,
June 5, 2024, https://www.wsj.com/world/uk/former-brexit-champion
-and-trump-supporter-shakes-up-u-k-election-race-742d0d50.

25. Paul Kirby, "Who Is Giorgia Meloni? The Rise to Power of Italy's
New Far-Right PM," BBC, October 21, 2022, https://www.bbc.com
/news/world-europe-63351655; *The Medhi Hasan Show*, MSNBC,
September 28, 2022, https://www.msnbc.com/the-mehdi-hasan-show
/watch/italy-s-giorgia-meloni-financial-speculators-149474373653.

26. Margherita Stancati, "Italy Strips Some Gay Couples of Parental
Recognition," *Wall Street Journal*, April 25, 2023, https://www.wsj.com
/articles/italy-strips-some-gay-couples-of-parental-recognition-4f3993c1.

27. Angelo Amante, "Italy's Meloni Ready to Risk Unpopularity over
Support for Ukraine," Reuters, March 21, 2023, https://www.reuters
.com/world/europe/italys-meloni-ready-risk-unpopularity-over
-support-ukraine-2023-03-21/.

28. Zach Beauchamp, "The Bizarre Far-Right Coup Attempt in Germany,
Explained by an Expert," *Vox*, December 9, 2022, https://www.vox
.com/2022/12/9/23500307/germany-coup-prince-heinrich-qanon.

29. James Angelos, "Germany's Far-Right AfD Is Soaring. Can a Ban Stop
It?," *Politico*, January 12, 2024, https://www.politico.eu/article/can-a
-ban-stop-the-rise-of-germanys-far-right/.

30. Eddy Wax, "This Time, the Far-Right Threat Is Real," *Politico*,
February 6, 2024, https://www.politico.eu/article/brussels-braces-for
-far-right-wave-as-eu-election-looms/.

31. Bruce Klingner et al., "Trump Shakedowns Are Threatening Two Key
US Alliances in Asia," Brookings, December 18, 2019, https://www
.brookings.edu/articles/trump-shakedowns-are-threatening-two-key-u
-s-alliances-in-asia/; Mark Esper, *A Sacred Oath: Memoirs of a Secretary of
Defense During Extraordinary Times* (2022); John Bolton, *The Room Where*

It Happened (2020); Jennifer Jacobs, "Trump Muses Privately About Ending Postwar Japan Defense Pact," *Bloomberg*, June 25, 2019, https://www.bloomberg.com/news/articles/2019-06-25/trump-muses-privately-about-ending-postwar-japan-defense-pact.

32. Stephanie Condon, "Donald Trump: Japan, South Korea Might Need Nuclear Weapons," CBS, March 29, 2016, https://www.cbsnews.com/news/donald-trump-japan-south-korea-might-need-nuclear-weapons/.

33. Josh Rogin, *Chaos Under Heaven: Trump, Xi, and the Battle for the Twenty-First Century* (2021).

34. Mark Esper, *A Sacred Oath* (2022).

35. Julian Ryall, "Japan Reportedly Wooing Donald Trump in a Preemptive Move to Stave Off Trade and North Korea 'Nightmare,'" *South China Morning Post*, January 18, 2024, https://www.scmp.com/week-asia/politics/article/3248914/japan-reportedly-wooing-donald-trump-pre-emptive-move-prevent-trade-and-north-korea-nightmare.

36. Shim Jae-Yun, "Prepare for Trump 2.0," *Korea Times*, December 13, 2023, https://www.koreatimes.co.kr/www/opinion/2024/02/137_365042.html.

37. Eric Brewer, "Why Trump's Retreat from US Allies Could Have Nuclear Consequences," *Defense One*, October 1, 2020, https://www.defenseone.com/ideas/2020/10/why-trumps-retreat-us-allies-could-have-nuclear-consequences/168896/; Hal Brands, "Why Japan Is Gearing Up for Possible War with China," *Bloomberg*, November 6, 2022, https://www.bloomberg.com/opinion/features/2022-11-06/why-japan-is-gearing-up-for-possible-war-with-china-over-taiwan.

38. Anthony Kuhn, "South Koreans Vote Political Conservative as New President," NPR, March 10, 2022, https://www.npr.org/2022/03/10/1085680648/south-koreans-vote-political-conservative-as-new-president; Gavan McCormack, "Japan's Peaceful Foreign Policy Is Under Siege from Right-Wing Militarism," *Jacobin*, May 2022, https://jacobin.com/2022/05/japan-peace-foreign-policy-right-wing-militarism-us-bases.

39. Rebecca Rommen, "Shutdown Funding Blocks Ukraine Aid as MAGA Moves GOP Toward Isolationism," *Business Insider*, October 1, 2023, https://www.businessinsider.com/shutdown-funding-blocks-ukraine-aid-maga-moves-gop-toward-isolationism-2023-10; Alex Shephard, "Republicans Are Ready to Abandon Ukraine," *New Republic*, February 23, 2023, https://newrepublic.com/article/170735/republican-primary-trump-abandon-ukraine.

40. Julian E. Barnes and Helene Cooper, "Trump Discussed Pulling U.S. from NATO, Aides Say Amid New Concerns over Russia," *New York Times*, January 14, 2019, https://www.nytimes.com/2019/01/14/us/politics/nato-president-trump.html; Jonathan Swan et al., "Fears of a NATO Withdrawal Rise as Trump Seeks a Return to Power," *New York Times*, December 9, 2023, https://www.nytimes.com/2023/12/09/us/politics/trump-2025-nato.html.

41. Barnes and Cooper, "Trump Discussed."

42. Philip Bump, " 'Genius,' 'Savvy': Trump Reacts to Putin's Moves on Ukraine Exactly as You'd Expect," *Washington Post*, February 22, 2022, https://www.washingtonpost.com/politics/2022/02/22/trump-reacts-putins-invasion-ukraine-exactly-youd-expect/.

43. Peter Baker and Susan Glasser, *The Divider: Trump in the White House* (2023).

44. Kate Sullivan, "Trump Says He Would Encourage Russia to 'Do Whatever the Hell They Want' to Any NATO Country That Doesn't Pay Enough," CNN, February 11, 2024, https://www.cnn.com/2024/02/10/politics/trump-russia-nato/index.html.

45. Brendan Cole, "Why Zelensky Is Right to Be Nervous about a Trump Return," *Newsweek*, April 15, 2023, https://www.newsweek.com/zelensky-ukraine-nervous-trump-return-2024-war-russia-putin-1794558.

46. Valerie Hopkins, "Belarus Is Fast Becoming a 'Vassal State' of Russia," *New York Times*, June 22, 2022, https://www.nytimes.com/2023/06/22/world/europe/belarus-russia-lukashenko.html.

47. Lee Drutman and Sean McFate, "The Real Winners of the 2024 Election Could Be China and Russia," *Time*, December 21, 2022, https://time.com/6242314/real-winners-of-the-2024-election-could-be-china-and-russia/.

48. Kevin Breuninger, "Russia Tried to Influence U.S. Elections in 2022 and Will Do So Again, Nation's Top Intel Agency Says," CNBC, March 8, 2023, https://www.cnbc.com/2023/03/08/russia-tried-to-influence-us-elections-in-2022-and-will-do-it-again-intel-agency-says.html.

49. Dustin Volz, "Russia Tried to Weaken Democrats Ahead of 2022 Midterm Vote, U.S. Spy Agencies Say," *Wall Street Journal*, December 18, 2023, https://www.wsj.com/politics/national-security/russia-tried-to-weaken-democrats-ahead-of-2022-midterm-vote-u-s-spy-agencies-say-f7978d09?st=fb1h274k2m5ixth&reflink=desktopwebshare_permalink.

50. "The Meticulous, Ruthless Preparations for a Second Trump Term," *Economist*, July 13, 2023, https://www.economist.com/briefing/2023/07 /13/the-meticulous-ruthless-preparations-for-a-second-trump-term.

51. William Pesek, "Xi Jinping Is Cheering for Trump to Win," *Nikkei Asia*, July 20, 2023, https://asia.nikkei.com/Opinion/Xi-Jinping-is-cheering -for-Trump-to-win; Michael Schuman, "Why Xi Wants Trump to Win," *Atlantic*, December 5, 2023, https://www.theatlantic.com /magazine/archive/2024/01/trump-reelection-china-xi-jinping/676129/.

52. Agathe Demarais, "Why China Is Rooting for Trump," *Foreign Policy*, February 7, 2024, https://foreignpolicy.com/2024/02/07/china-trump -biden-us-presidential-election-2024/.

53. Simone McCarthy, "Europe Is Nervous about a Potential Trump Win. China Sees an Opportunity," CNN, February 19, 2024 (quoting Noah Barkin of the German Marshall Fund), https://www.cnn.com/2024/02 /19/asia/europe-is-nervous-about-a-potential-trump-win-china-sees -an-opportunity/index.html.

54. Kevin Shalvey and Karson Yiu, "Putin Hosts China's President Xi in Moscow Amid Ukraine War," ABC News, March 20, 2023, https:// abcnews.go.com/International/chinas-president-xi-arrives-moscow -meeting-putin-amid/story?id=97980986.

CHAPTER 13: "A WORLD WHERE . . . TEXAS IS AT WAR WITH CALIFORNIA"

1. "Text of Proposed Laws (Including Proposition 12)," *California General Election Voter Information Guide*, Office of Secretary of State, November 6, 2018, https://vig.cdn.sos.ca.gov/2018/general/pdf/topl.pdf#prop12.

2. *National Pork Producers Council v. Ross*, 598 U.S. 356 (2023).

3. Ibid.

4. Mark Tushnet, "Constitutional Hardball," *John Marshall Law Review* 37 (2004): 523.

5. See, e.g., Danielle M. Ely and Anne K. Driscoll, "Infant Mortality in the United States, 2020: Data from the Period Linked Birth/Infant Death File," *National Vital Statistics System* 71 (September 29, 2022): 1, https://www.cdc.gov/nchs/data/nvsr/nvsr71/nvsr71-05.pdf; Megan Zahneis and Audrey Williams June, "In These Red States, Professors Are Eyeing the Exits," *Chronicle of Higher Education*, September 7, 2023, https://www.chronicle.com/article/in-these-red-states-professors-are -eyeing-the-exits.

6. Paul Krugman, "Kentucky on My Mind," *New York Times*, December 14, 2021, https://www.nytimes.com/2021/12/14/opinion/kentucky -tornado-federal-aid.html.

7. Andrew Van Dam and Linda Chong, "Do Blue-State Taxes Really Subsidize Red-State Benefits?," *Washington Post*, July 7, 2023, https:// www.washingtonpost.com/business/2023/07/07/states-federal-benefits/.

8. Ibid.

9. Sarah McCammon, "Some States Are Restricting Abortion. Others Are Spending Millions to Fund It," NPR, June 20, 2023, https://www.npr .org/2023/06/20/1182722556/abortion-funding-states-dobbs-supreme -court-restrictions-ban.

10. Shannon Young, "New York to Allocate $35M to Help Abortion Providers," *Politico*, May 10, 2022, https://www.politico.com/news/2022 /05/10/new-york-to-allocate-35m-to-help-abortion-providers-00031388.

11. Dani Anguiano, "California Abortion Clinics Braced for Out-of- State Surge as Bans Kick In," *Guardian*, June 27, 2022, https://www .theguardian.com/us-news/2022/jun/27/california-abortion-clinics-out -of-state-surge.

12. Cathren Cohen et al., "People Traveling to Illinois for Abortion Care after Roe v. Wade Was Overturned," UCLA School of Law Center on Reproductive Health, Law, and Policy, November 2022, https://law .ucla.edu/sites/default/files/PDFs/Center_on_Reproductive_Health /2211_Illinois_Abortion_Travel_FINAL.pdf.

13. Camilo Montoya-Galvez, "GOP Govs. Ron DeSantis, Greg Abbott Send Migrants to Martha's Vineyard and Vice President's Residence," CBS News, September 16, 2022, https://www.cbsnews.com/news /ron-de-santis-flies-texas-florida-migrants-marthas-vineyard-kamala -harris-residence/.

14. @realDonaldTrump, Twitter, April 17, 2020, https://twitter.com /realDonaldTrump/status/1251169217531056130.

15. David S. Cohen, Greer Donley, and Rachel Rebouche, "The New Abortion Battleground," *Columbia Law Review* 123 (2023): 1.

16. Christopher Rowland, "Groups That Aid Abortion Patients Pull Back, Fearing Legal Liability," *Washington Post*, July 15, 2022, https://www .washingtonpost.com/business/2022/07/15/abortion-aid-drying-up/. One of us was copied on an email penned by a prominent right-wing lawyer who cautioned a colleague of ours against encouraging donations

to abortion funds, lest those donors incur criminal and civil liabilities (email on file with authors).

17. Ibid.

18. *National Pork Producers Council v. Ross*, No. 21-468 (tr. oral argument).

19. Ibid.

20. *NYS Rifle & Pistol Assoc. v. Bruen*, 597 U.S. 1 (2022).

21. *Dobbs v. Jackson Women's Health Org.*, 597 U.S. 215 (2022).

22. *303 Creative LLC v. Elenis*, 600 U.S. 570 (2023).

23. Jon D. Michaels, "We the Shareholders: Government Market Participation in the Postliberal U.S. Political Economy," *Columbia Law Review* 120 (2020): 465.

24. We're of course not working off a blank slate. Some blue states have already taken steps in these directions. But quite a few have not. And even among those that have, it's important to remember that state-supported vigilantism works best where there are legal gaps that can be exploited. So at the risk of some redundancies, we urge consideration of additional, specific language that can be incorporated into state constitutions, statutes, regulations, and judicial opinions.

25. Penny Abernathy, "The State of Local News: The 2022 Report," Northwestern Medill Local News Initiative, June 29, 2022, https://localnewsinitiative.northwestern.edu/research/state-of-local-news/report/.

26. Ibid.

27. Students reporting from statehouses is far from novel, but in some critical states—including Mississippi, South Carolina, Iowa, and South Dakota—there were no student reporters at the statehouse in 2022. Carrie Blazina, "In Some States, Students Account for a Large and Growing Share of Statehouse Reporters," Pew Research Center, October 31, 2023, https://www.pewresearch.org/short-reads/2022/05/19/in-some-states-students-account-for-a-large-and-growing-share-of-statehouse-reporters/.

28. Grace Toohey, "Despite All the Critics, California Could Soon Rise to the World's 4th-Largest Economy," *Los Angeles Times*, November 2, 2022, https://www.latimes.com/california/story/2022-11-02/what-does-it-mean-if-california-becomes-worlds-4th-largest-economy.

29. Mark J. Perry, "Putting America's Enormous $21.5T Economy into Perspective by Comparing US State GDPs to Entire Countries," American Enterprise Institute, February 5, 2020, https://www.aei.org

/carpe-diem/putting-americas-huge-21-5t-economy-into-perspective
-by-comparing-us-state-gdps-to-entire-countries/.

30. "Real Per Capita Gross Domestic Product of the United States in 2022,
by State," Statista, March 2023, https://www.statista.com/statistics
/248063/per-capita-us-real-gross-domestic-product-gdp-by-state/.

31. "Trust Level Review," CalPERS Investment Office, September 30,
2023, https://www.calpers.ca.gov/docs/board-agendas/202311/invest
/item06a-01_a.pdf.

32. "DeNapoli: State Pension Fund Valued at $246.3 Billion at End of
Second Quarter," Office of the New York State Comptroller, November
17, 2023, https://www.osc.ny.gov/press/releases/2023/11/dinapoli-state
-pension-fund-valued-246-point-3-billion-end-second-quarter.

33. Investment Portfolio as of November 30, 2023, California State Teachers'
Retirement System, https://www.calstrs.com/investment-portfolio.

34. "Bill Analysis (Bill Number: SB 1173, as amended April 21, 2022),"
California State Teachers' Retirement System, https://www.calstrs
.com/files/54965536f/SB1173-amended-4-21-22.pdf; "Five-Year
Divestment Review," CalPERS Investment Committee, March 15,
2021, https://www.calpers.ca.gov/docs/board-agendas/202103/invest
/item09a-01_a.pdf.

35. Leah Malone et al., "ESG Battlegrounds: How the States Are Shaping
the Regulatory Landscape in the U.S.," Harvard Law School Forum
on Corporate Governance, March 11, 2023, https://corpgov.law
.harvard.edu/2023/03/11/esg-battlegrounds-how-the-states-are
-shaping-the-regulatory-landscape-in-the-u-s/.

36. 40 Illinois Compiled Statutes 5/1-110.16.

37. 5 Maine Revised Statutes sections 1957, 1958.

38. Resolution of the Minnesota State Board of Investment (May 29,
2020), https://mn.gov/sbi/documents/MSBI%20Resolution%20on%20
Thermal%20Coal%20Investments%20-%20May%2029,%202020.pdf.

39. Resolution of the Minnesota State Board of Investment
(September 2, 1998), https://msbi.us/sites/default/files/2022-06
/MSBI%20Tobacco%20Resolution%20September%202%201998.pdf.

40. Anne Barnard, "New York's $226 Billion Pension Fund Is Dropping
Fossil Fuel Stocks," New York Times, December 9, 2020, https://www
.nytimes.com/2020/12/09/nyregion/new-york-pension-fossil-fuels.
html?smid=fb-nytimes&smtyp=cur&fbclid=IwAR0JTlg2s8LX9ixw
Okyggm5C-zv5he8yMR0HqffzEXvPoDHbGHNqXZ83ofM.

41. "Comptroller Stringer and Trustees Announce Successful $3 Billion Divestment from Fossil Fuels," New York City Comptroller, December 22, 2021, https://comptroller.nyc.gov/newsroom /comptroller-stringer-and-trustees-announce-successful-3-billion -divestment-from-fossil-fuels/; "Comptroller Stringer and Trustees: New York City Pension Funds Complete First-in-the-Nation Divestment from Private Prison Companies," New York City Comptroller, June 8, 2017, https://comptroller.nyc.gov/newsroom /comptroller-stringer-and-trustees-new-york-city-pension-funds -complete-first-in-the-nation-divestment-from-private-prison -companies/; Liz Moyer, "New York City Pension Fund to Divest Itself of Gun Retailer Stock," *New York Times*, July 14, 2016, https:// www.nytimes.com/2016/07/15/business/dealbook/new-york-city -pension-fund-to-divest-itself-of-gun-retailer-stock.html.

42. Ron DeSantis et al., "Joint Governors' Statement on ESG," March 16, 2023, https://www.flgov.com/wp-content/uploads/2023 /03/Joint-Governors-Policy-Statement-on-ESG-3.16.2023.pdf.

43. Executive Order 8802: Prohibition of Discrimination in the Defense Industry (1941), https://www.archives.gov/milestone-documents /executive-order-8802; Executive Order 9346 (1943), https://www .presidency.ucsb.edu/documents/executive-order-9346-establishing -committee-fair-employment-practice.

44. Attorney General Ken Paxton, "Advisory on Texas Law Prohibiting Contracts and Investments with Entities That Discriminate Against Firearm Entities or Boycott Energy Companies or Israel," TexasAttorneyGeneral.gov, October 18, 2023, https://www .texasattorneygeneral.gov/sites/default/files/images/executive -management/OAG%20advisory%20on%20SB%2013%20and%20 19%2010.18.23.pdf.

45. Stephen Marche, "Secession Might Seem Like the Lesser of Two Evils. It's Also the Less Likely," *Washington Post*, December 31, 2021, https://www.washingtonpost.com/outlook/2021/12/31/secession -civil-war-stephen-marche/.

46. Steve Benen, "The Problem(s) with Rick Scott's 'Travel Advisory' for Florida," MSNBC, June 28, 2023, https://www.msnbc.com /rachel-maddow-show/maddowblog/problems-rick-scotts-travel -advisory-florida-rcna91583.

47. State Regulation of Foreign Ownership of U.S. Land: January to

June 2023, Congressional Research Service, July 28, 2023, https://crsreports.congress.gov/product/pdf/LSB/LSB11013.

48. Jenna Bednar and Mariano-Florentino Cuellar, "The Fractured Superpower," *Foreign Affairs*, September/October 2022, https://www.foreignaffairs.com/united-states/fractured-superpower-federalism-remaking-us-democracy-foreign-policy.

Index

Page numbers in *italics* refer to photographs.

Asia, 216–17
AT&T, 206–7
Atlanta, GA, 136–40
Atlantic, 2, 91
Attal, Gabriel, 213

Baca, Steven Ray, 115–17
Bannon, Steve, ix–xiv, 5, 12, 45, 52,
    76, 219
    "impose your will" directive of,
    x–xi
Barr, William, 110
Bartiromo, Maria, 45
Bassett, Burwell, Jr., 18–19, 23, 24
Beck, Glenn, 45
Bell, Derrick, 211
Bennett, Natalie, 215
Biden, Joe, 133, 185, 188, 217, 219
    in election of 2020, ix–xiv, 50,
        53, 109, 123–26, 129–32, 134,
        136–41, 185, 186, 206, 219
    in election of 2024, 143,
        219–20
    reproductive rights and, 173, 174
Biggs, Joe, 110
Black Lives Matter (BLM), 2, 10, 20,
    44, 53, 93, 109, 110, 114, 117,
    118, 120–21, 123, 124, 145
Blackmun, Harry, 165
Blake, Jacob, 121
Blow, Charles, 5
blue states, 12, 58, 177, 226–27
    counterstrikes against red states,
        223–50
    relocation to, 95, 98–100, 202,
        228, 236–37
    turning red states into, 180–82

Boebert, Lauren, 195
Boehner, John, 50
Bolton, John, 217
Bongino, Dan, 45
Bonner, Robert, 38, 39
Boston Globe, 120
Bouie, Jamelle, 68, 69
bounty hunters, 4, 9, 18, 20, 22, *24*,
    84–85, 87
Bowers, Kacey Rae, 129
Bowers, Russell "Rusty," 129–30,
    143
Brady Center, 112
Branch Davidians, 125
Brexit, 214
Breyer, Stephen, 158
Britain, 214–15
Brown, Gordon, 214
Brown, Jerry, 223
Brown, Wendy, 174
Buchanan, James, 212
Buchanan, Pat, 47–48
Bud Light, 205
Bush, George H. W., 47, 49, 104
Bush, George W., 38, 41, 104
Bush, Jeb, 57, 104, 105

California, 184, 193–94, 202, 223,
    227–31, 240, 244, 245
    pension holdings in, 241
    Proposition 12 in, 223–25, 230,
        233, 244
    Proposition 187 in, 37
    Shasta County, 144–49, 175
Carlson, Tucker, 45, 47, 76, 93, 118,
    122
Carlyle Group, 57

About the Authors

Jon D. Michaels is a professor of law at UCLA School of Law and is a graduate of Williams College, Oxford University, where he was a Marshall scholar. He also attended Yale Law School, where he served as an editor for the *Yale Law Journal*. Michaels clerked first for Judge Guido Calabresi of the U.S. Court of Appeals for the Second Circuit and then for Justice David Souter of the U.S. Supreme Court. A two-time winner of the American Constitution Society's Cudahy Award for scholarly excellence in administrative law, Michaels is a frequent legal affairs commentator for national and local media outlets.

David L. Noll is a professor of law at Rutgers University. His writing has appeared in the *New York Times*, *Slate*, the *New York Law Journal*, and many others. He clerked for Judges Pierre N. Leval and Raymond J. Lohier, Jr., on the U.S. Court of Appeals for the Second Circuit and Judge Richard J. Holwell on the U.S. District Court for the Southern District of New York.